Chaucer's Women

Nuns, Wives and Amazons

Priscilla Martin

First edition 1990
Reprinted (with alterations) 1996

Published by
MACMILLAN PRESS LTD
Houndmills, Basingstoke, Hampshire RG21 6XS
and London
Companies and representatives
throughout the world

ISBN 0–333–64141–8 hardcover
ISBN 0–333–64142–6 paperback

A catalogue record for this book is available
from the British Library.

10   9   8   7   6   5   4   3   2   1
05 04 03 02 01 00 99 98 97 96

Printed and bound in Great Britain by
Antony Rowe Ltd
Chippenham, Wiltshire

309494

*In memory
of two friends who talked and wrote about Chaucer*

*William Frost
and
Paula Neuss*

Contents

Acknowledgements

In writing this book I have been generally indebted to the Chaucerian scholarship of this century and to the theoretical debates and feminist criticism of recent years. I have been particularly helped and stimulated by my association with various universities and my discussions with individual friends. I should like to thank my colleagues and students at the University of California, Santa Barbara, and at the University of Washington, Seattle, for providing vital stimulation and support for the project. I am also grateful to the University of California at Riverside and at Irvine the University of Edinburgh, the Japanese Society for Medieval English Language and Literature, King's College London, the University of London Old and Middle English Research Seminar, the Medieval Association of the Pacific, the Medieval Colloquium of North-Western Universities at the University of Washington, the University of Puget Sound and Simon Fraser University for invitations to speak about Chaucer's women and for providing opportunities for discussion. Elizabeth Allen, Nola-Jean Bamberry, Peter Conradi, Janet Cowen, Elizabeth Simmons-O'Neill very nobly criticised parts of the book in manuscript and I owe much to their patience and perception. Carla Copenhaven, Brian Patrick McGuire and Leroy Perkins generously allowed me to read unpublished papers, which helped me greatly, and I found continuous enlightenment in Elizabeth Simmons-O'Neill's PhD dissertation. Debts to this material are acknowledged in the notes. Conversations with Derek Brewer, Sheila Delany, David Fowler, Martin Friedman, William Frost, Richard Helgerson, Anne Kernan, Leroy Perkins and Míceál Vaughan clarified my thoughts and cheered me up. Anna Baldwin, Malcolm Bradbury and Judith Peacock gave precious help and advice in the final stages.

List of Abbreviations

Works by Chaucer

AA	Anelida and Arcite
BD	Book of the Duchess
CT	Canterbury Tales
HF	House of Fame
LGW	Legend of Good Women
PF	Parliament of Fowls
RR	Romance of the Rose
TC	Troilus and Criseyde

Periodicals

AnM	Annuale Mediaevale
CE	College English
ChR	Chaucer Review
EIE	English Institute Essays
ELH	Journal of English Literary History
ES	English Studies
JEGP	Journal of English and Germanic Philology
JMRS	Journal of Medieval and Renaissance Studies
MA	Medium Aevum
MLN	Modern Language Notes
MLR	Modern Language Review
MP	Modern Philology
MS	Medieval Studies
N&Q	Notes and Queries
NM	Neuphilologische Mitteilungen
PMLA	Publications of the Modern Language Association of America
PQ	Philological Quarterly
RES	Review of English Studies

SAC   *Studies in the Age of Chaucer*
SP   *Studies in Philology*
TSE   *Tulane Studies in English*
TSL   *Tennessee Studies in Literature*
TSLL   *Texas Studies in Literature and Language*
UCSLL   *University of Colorado Studies in Language and Literature*

EETS   *Early English Text Society*
PL   *Patrologia Latina*

Preface to the 1996 Reprint

Several ages seem to have passed – in my own life and in Chaucer's — since I began the Introduction by observing that there were no books on the women in his poetry. There are now at least five more on the subject or, rather, in the area, since neither 'Chaucer' nor 'women' remains a very stable category. The area can certainly accomodate them. They are strikingly different from each other. They focus on various aspects of the work, ranging from the formal, such as the implications of genre and its metamorphoses, to the ethical, such as the Christian respect for virtues associated with the 'feminine'. Their findings range from affirmation of Chaucer's sympathy with his female characters and sense of their cultural oppression to scepticism about this possibility or commitment to its impossibility.* As I wrote my own book and read those of others, I became more and more convinced of the centrality of the issues for Chaucer, though I would now focus on the problem of gender rather than the subject of women. Despite our different approaches and conclusions we all concur in seeing gender as a locus of anxiety in Chaucer's work and in seeing the work as about gender. I intended *Chaucer's Women* as a feminist reading. It now looks equally like a general introduction to the major concerns of his poetry.

Priscilla Martin
1996

---

* Susan Crane, *Gender and Romance in Chaucer's Canterbury Tales* (Princeton, 1994)
Carolyn Dinshaw, *Chaucer's Sexual Poetics* (Madison and London, 1989)
Margaret Hallissy, *Clean Maids, True Wives, Steadfast Widows: Chaucer's Women and Medieval Codes of Conduct* (Westport, Connecticut, and London, 1993)
Elaine Tuttle Hansen, *Chaucer and the Fictions of Gender* (Berkeley and Los Angeles, 1991)
Jill Mann, *Geoffrey Chaucer* (London and New York, 1991)

Introduction

As I write this Introduction there are no full-length studies available of the women in Chaucer's poetry. There are a number of articles and chapters in recent books and I know of several works in preparation or in the press.[1] Chaucer's women have had to wait for the intense activity in feminist scholarship of the last two decades. Yet as early as 1915 Kittredge suggested that Chaucer's problems and preoccupations were analogous to those of the twentieth century: 'There is scarcely a political or social catchword of the present (even "feminism" . . .) which does not fit the fourteenth century.'[2] But 'feminism', softened by 'even' and segregated in a parenthesis, looks timidly provocative and in Chaucer studies Kittredge's suggestion was not taken up for about half a century.

It seems strange that such a major subject as Chaucer's representation of women should have been ignored, when so many other aspects of his work have received so much scholarly and critical attention. It makes one wonder if women have been, for all the emphasis on their appearance in medieval and later literature, invisible. Or if the Wife of Bath, despite her tendentious articulacy, is inaudible. Or if she, the lady White, Criseyde, Alceste, the heroines of the Legends, the Prioress and the Second Nun, Emily, Dorigen, constant Constance and patient Griselda and prudent Prudence, the almost indestructible Cecilia, the elastic wives of the fabliaux, all focal points in various discourses, are finally marginal.

Perhaps criticism has not seen Chaucer's women because it has been resistant to the problems they raise. If so, one might draw inferences from this gap about the power-structures of the critical establishment. Or perhaps the subject has seemed practically and theoretically too problematic. To one school of historical criticism it has presented no problem at all. D. W. Robertson influentially argued in the 1960s that medieval literature must be approached on its own terms and that it always teaches its own uniform orthodoxies. Among the 'quiet hierarchies' it assumes is the doctrine that the female is subordinate to the male. On this view a protofeminist Chaucer is unthinkable. To Robertson the Wife of Bath is merely an evil exemplar of 'rampant "femininity" and carnality', the Prioress a negative example of an aberrant nun and Amazons a whole society of 'up-so-doun'-ness, 'worthy precursors of the Wife of Bath ... figures for rampant sensuality or effeminacy'.[3] Critics who have not assumed that Chaucer's entire purpose must be to propagate one version of late medieval Christian conservatism as conceived by mid-twentieth-century nostalgia may still despair of his intentions being recoverable. To those who respect and wish to recover authorial intention, Chaucer's ironies, ambiguities and multiple narrators present a hall of distorting mirrors. One could construct a feminist or a sexist Chaucer using essentially the same evidence from his writings. But it is possible – and perhaps vital for our own demystification – to analyse images of women or constructions of masculine identity in literature independently of the author's intentions or opinions. A recently fashionable theory has also maintained that it is no more feasible to recover the author's context than the author, that neither original culture nor original individual exists to convey original meaning. Our interpretation of medieval texts is our interpretation, inevitably produced by our politics and prejudices and the more prejudiced if we deny our own historical circumstances and claim objectivity for our scholarship. The late medieval society that recent historical critics have recovered or constructed turns out to be not quietly hierarchical, uniform and static, but liminal, plural, mobile, divided, internally subverted and its literature, whether willingly or unwillingly, bears witness to its contradictions.

Amid such shifting indeterminacies there are two simple things that one can say with confidence. The first is that women and the relationships between the sexes are Chaucer's favourite subject. In poem after poem he presents women – virgins, wives and mistresses – and men intimate with women in sex, love affairs and marriage, and men and women interacting in the social processes of court and trade, city and country, war and peace, siege and pilgrimage. The second is that he treats their relationships as a problem area. He writes of the suffering caused to both sexes in their involvement with each other, of unrequited love, of unhappy marriages, of power struggles for 'maistrye'. He shows an unwillingness or inability to write of happy weddings. He even (and perhaps something of his 'intention' can be inferred from this) omits descriptions of joyful marriage ceremonies in his sources. When he explores the problems of pain and injustice, he uses women (Constance, Griselda) or men hopelessly in love with the same woman (Palamon and Arcite) as emblems of the suffering of humanity.

The problems generate famous questions: 'What do women want?' 'Who painted the lion?' To these celebrated enquiries I would wish to add the indirect question: 'God knows what she thought.' The first was later to be asked by Freud. The second is often quoted by feminist critics for whom it anticipates their awareness that gender is constructed in male-centred language, that the women in literature have mainly been created by male authors, and that female writers inherit a literary tradition largely transmitted by men. The third indicates female exclusion from oral as well as written discourse. I would find it hard to accept our recognition of these questions as only 'reader-created'. The questions take us straight into the subject of power. The answer to the first is that women desire power; the second identifies a particularly important source of power; the third is prompted by a symptom of powerlessness.

Chaucer lived in a time of growing access to and desire for the various forms of power — linguistic, economic, political and spiritual. The Peasants' Revolt was the most violent and visible example in his lifetime of the clash between those with and those wanting power. Other annexations of power were more stealthily successful. Literacy was growing among the laity; English was replacing French as the language of the upper classes in England; after the population decline caused by the Black Death labourers could command higher wages and enjoy more mobility; the secular and sacramental authority of the clergy was being questioned by theologians; the voice of the Commons was gaining in confidence. We do not know if Chaucer approved of all or any of these developments but he exemplifies some of the changes in English culture. He came from the merchant class and from a highly 'upwardly mobile' family, he was a member of the expanding category of literate laity, and he chose to write in English. His work, like that of many other medieval authors, contains expressions of respect for the ancient and traditional but also conveys a sense of the obsolescence of many values, forms and institutions. He uses traditional literary forms but is innovatory, experimental and frequently revisionary. His most celebrated poem takes the form of an institution that was increasingly under attack, the pilgrimage, which he treats as a kind of mobile obsolescence.[4] And the pilgrim who argues 'feminist' views explicitly is the Wife of Bath, a fictional character who represents the aspirations of marginal energy, female, bourgeois, newly rich, critical of the prejudices of the clergy and well aware that their literacy is a resource as powerful as weapons or wealth.[5]

Chaucer recognises the power of discourse and the implications of the traditional restriction of written discourse to a male clerical class. My first chapter deals with questions of role and textuality, male authorship and authority. Chaunticleer embodies in parodic form masculine pretensions to learning; Alison and Jankin confront each other over a book. Chaunticleer voices almost simultaneously the extreme idealisation and vilification of women, superficially opposed but profoundly connected. Alison protests the evil stereo-types and identifies their origins. The next two chapters continue the subject of role. In Chapter 2 I consider two medieval ideals, the Virgin Mary and the courtly lady, as they appear in Chaucer's earliest surviving poems. The Madonna is one of the most pervasive and persuasive images of womanhood in the late Middle Ages but in her impossible perfection and her virgin motherhood might function as a reproach rather than an inspiration to actual women. The courtly lady of medieval poetry has much in common with the images of the Virgin. Chaucer produces a particularly humane and intelligent version in White but she is absent from the poem in her honour: she is dead and she is recalled and recon-structed through the indirections of dream, literary convention and a conversation half-understood. In Chapter 3 I discuss two female pilgrims, the nun and the wife, who exemplify the two major roles available to women and who cannot fulfil these roles 'correctly'. In Chapter 4 I examine two examples of a dominant medieval literary form, the romance. It is a genre which commonly celebrates women as the object of desire without enquiring what they desire. But the question 'God knows what she thought', provoked by May's quietness in the *Merchant's Tale*, determines the structure of other poems by Chaucer: in the *Knight's Tale* the desires of the silent heroine are pointedly and belatedly revealed and the *Wife of Bath's Tale* pivots on the enigma of female desire. The next two chapters examine the relationships between sex and economics. In Chapter 5 I consider the changing valuations of sex and love in the First Fragment in terms of the medieval economic distinction between 'winners' and 'wasters'. Chapter 6 demonstrates the mercantile uses to which, in the absence of any other economic power, women put their sexuality. The wife in the *Shipman's Tale* is happy to sell herself, May in the *Merchant's Tale* sells herself and seeks happiness elsewhere. The Wife of Bath makes capital out of this resource but her desire for happiness is more complex: the *General Prologue* describes her as a clothmaker as well as defining her as a wife and it is made clear in the story of her five marriages that she needs money of her own. In 'Real Women in Imaginary Gardens' I return to the subject of genre and to a motif found in religious art and courtly poetry: the *hortus conclusus* is an emblem for the Madonna and the earthly paradise a setting for adoration of the courtly heroine. For all its beauty Chaucer is suspicious of the Garden of Love and the passions cultivated in it in lyric and romance: he analyses it critically in the *Parliament of Fowls*; he exposes it as a setting for fabliau intrigue in the *Merchant's Tale* and for fantasy in the *Franklin's*. In the chapter on saintly women I consider Constance, Griselda and Cecilia and the virtues they exemplify. The *Man of Law's Tale* treats the suffering of its heroine as the 'thraldom and penance' both of being a woman and being a Christian. The *Clerk's Tale* makes manifest the corresponding hierarchies of sexual politics as analogues of the class system and marriage as a microcosm of society. The problems of preaching patience and humility to the oppressed do not arise with Cecilia, whose active and celibate virtue is empowered by the marginality of the Church and the liminality of her time. The story of Criseyde demonstrates that women are part of the private life and politically expendable; despite Hector's denial, women are sold and exchanged in the civilised but beseiged Troy as much as in barbarous societies. Criseyde, neither a nun nor wife, is initially a heroine without a role; I consider how she becomes the stereotype of treacherous femininity. The last two chapters return to the problems of discourse. 'The Women in the Books' considers written discourse, the construction of women as the subjects of literature and the mediation of authority through patriarchal tradition. The last chapter deals with the power relationships between gender and speech and Chaucer's presentation of sex, discourse and silence.

My method in this study is to work from the particular to the general. Each section of each chapter begins with a specific passage from which I move to larger issues. This means that some poems are considered in more than one chapter. I have found it impossible to contain one character, the Wife of Bath, tidily in one section. She argues her way through several chapters, perhaps taking up a disproportionate amount of space. In this I am following my author.

1

The Man with the Book, or 'Who Painted the Lion?'

I

For al so siker as *In principio*,
Mulier est hominis confusio –
Madame, the sentence of this Latyn is,
'Womman is mannes joye and al his blis.'
CT vii 3163–6[1]

Chaunticleer the cock, hero of the *Nun's Priest's Tale*, is talking to Pertelote, his favourite of his hen wives. In these lines he encapsulates the most extreme medieval attitudes towards women when he quotes *'Mulier est hominis confusio'* ('Woman is the ruin of man') and translates it as 'Woman is man's joy and all his bliss'. Chaunticleer presents these generalisations as if they mean the same, though they actually say the opposite. Each proposes only one relationship (*'est'*, 'is') between the sexes. And that relationship is perceived from one point of view only, what 'Woman' means to 'Man' rather than what 'Man' means to 'Woman' or what a woman might mean to herself or to other women or to other men or to God. Seen, however, in their dramatic and cultural context, the lines are involved in a multiplicity of relationships. To name a few: the relationship between Man and Woman, between individual men and women, between Adam and Eve, between Adam and Eve and their descendents, between Eve and Mary, between the Old Testament and the New Testament, between the Bible and other texts, between Latin and English, between the sacred and the profane, between the clergy and the laity, between Chaunticleer and Pertelote, between his credulity and her scepticism, between the Nun's Priest and Chaucer, between the Nun's Priest and the Prioress, between the Nun's Priest and other members of the convent, between the Nun's Priest and other pilgrims, between the Nun's Priest's Tale and other Tales . . .

1

What does Chaunticleer mean by them? He has had an alarming dream about a murderous animal, yellow-red in colour, with black-tipped tail and ears, and glowing eyes. He takes this to be prophetic and he is proved right. Later that day he is seized by a fox. Pertelote, however, belittles his fears. Dreams, she says, are not significant: Cato advised against taking them seriously, they are produced by some physiological imbalance so that an excess of choler and melancholy accounts for the dream of a red and black animal, he ought to be more 'manly' or he will forfeit her love, and he had better take a laxative. Chaunticleer counters with a catalogue of *exempla* and authorities, as venerable as Cato, which support the theory that dreams are meaningful.[2] But finally he is overcome by desire for Pertelote with her scarlet eyes, throws prudence to the winds, and flies down from the beam to 'fethere' her and strut among his harem of hens.

It is at the end of his speech, as Chaunticleer is sliding from reason into sensuality, that the lines occur and the mistranslation is a signpost to his change of mood. Does he realise that he is mistranslating, that the Latin describes woman as the ruin, not the bliss, of man? Perhaps he does not understand the Latin himself and the Nun's Priest is alerting those of the audience who do to his pretensions. Or perhaps Chaunticleer mistranslates on purpose for fear of Pertelote or out of desire for her or to share a sneer with the masculine and learned among his audience at the expense of the (presumably) less-educated hen.[3]

And of course the absurdity of forming hypotheses about the educational background of the cock and hen alerts us to the absurdity of the humans they resemble. We lose either way. If they are absolutely different from us, our attempts to make sense of the world through allegory and analogy, fiction and fable, are entirely subjective. If they *are* like us, we look as foolish as they do. And among their resemblances to us, they are cast in the moulds of some favourite sexual stereotypes. Pertelote is seductive, practical, scolding, bossy, making her bid for *maistrye* by captivating her husband, cosseting him, and casting aspersions on his virility. Chaunticleer, however, has no dounts about his sexual prowess ('Of o thyng God hath sent me large grace' – vii 3159). He is henpecked but cocksure, vain, pompous, susceptible to flattery (a masculine secondary sexual characteristic which he shares with the fox), lecherous and uxorious. And some of these qualities – especially the last – are likely to remind us of the archetypal married couple. Chaucer coined the word 'archewyves' (*CT* IV 1195) to describe domineering women like the Wife of Bath. Pertelote is also perceived as standing in a line of descent from the archetypal archwife, Eve. Like Adam, as the narrator points out (VII 3254–9), Chaunticleer listens to his wife against his better judgement. Their Tale presents a comic latter-day version of the Fall, taking place in a garden where a treacherous adversary lies in wait. Their relationship alludes to that original model of marriage. Like so many other females, Pertelote is implicated in the sin of Eve and is a potential *confusio* to her husband. Like Eve, she gives bad advice, she fails to accept her inferior role in the sexual hierarchy, she excites her husband's lust and – if one were determined to blame Pertelote's counsel rather than Chaunticleer's conceit – she comes close to causing his abduction from the garden.[4]

But the Tale suggests this reading only to deride it. *In principio* are the opening words of the Bible, the beginning of Genesis, as well as of St John's Gospel, and they resound with all the authority of God's world revealed to humanity in Old and New Testaments. It is as certain ('siker') as *In principio*, the first words of this sacred text, that woman is the ruin of man. But this maxim is followed by a mistranslation which makes its meaning – or message – look far from 'siker'. Indeed, the more sacred the text the more commentaries and disputes and 'authorities' it attracts, a fact to be weighed against any facile commitment to its availability.[5] And the sacred text will be invoked to legitimise bastardisations of its meaning. *Mulier est hominis confusio* appears to follow *In principio* as if it too were the word of God. The *Nun's Priest's Tale* employs many echoes of the primal story but its rhetoric suggests that the analogy might be as false as Chaunticleer's mistranslation. In its mock-exegetic world, the fall is not fatal after all. Although Chaunticleer's dream was prophetic, its outcome was not predetermined. There was some leeway for common sense and evasive action. Perhaps Pertelote's rationalism has its place.

Finally, let us observe that the two generalisations are not only in different languages but in different traditions. Latin was, for western Christendom, the language of the Bible, the Church, the law, the educated. *Mulier est hominis confusio* stems from a Latin, biblical, official, clerical, learned, masculine, misogynistic tradition. Chaunticleer's mistranslation into English alludes to the unofficial courtly tradition, to – if you will – the counter-culture,[6] in which love between the sexes is the source of the deepest human happiness and in which women are revered rather than reviled. Courteous to ladies, as this tradition advocates, Chaunticleer addresses Pertelote as 'Madame' (though the honorific seems a little awry in the case of a hen). Here women are responsible not for the ruin of men but for their joy and bliss – perhaps an equally heavy burden to bear.

What the Latin and the English have in common is the medieval compulsion to polarise. Women are *'confusio'* or 'al his blis', Eves or Maries, Madonnas or whores, 'hooly seintes' or 'wikked wyves'. Women are all good or all bad – in Chaunticleer's confused account both all good *and* all bad. The two attitudes are more complementary than opposed and spring from the same needs, fears and frustrations. Mary balances Eve in the typology which traces relationships between the two Testaments. The heroine of romance provides a courtly analogue to the religious ideal and a purification of desire. Her purpose, according to Chaunticleer, is as man-centred as that of the temptress. She is less a guarantee that women can be good than that men can love them with impunity. When we consider the spirit rather than the letter, Chaunticleer's translation proves accurate after all.

II

He hadde a book that gladly, nyght and day,
For his desport he wolde rede alway;
He cleped it Valerie and Theofraste,
At which book he lough alwey ful faste.
And eek ther was somtyme a clerk at Rome,
A cardinal, that highte Seint Jerome,
That made a book agayn Jovinian;
In which book eek ther was Tertulan,
Crisippus, Trotula, and Helowys,
That was abbesse nat fer fro Parys;
And eek the Parables of Salomon,
Ovides Art, and bookes many on,
And alle thise were bounden in o volume.
And every nyght and day was his custume,
Whan he hadde leyser and vacacioun
From oother worldly occupacioun,
To reden on this book of wikked wyves.

He knew of hem mo legendes and lyves
Than been of goode wyves in the Bible.
For trusteth wel, it is an impossible
That any clerk wol speke good of wyves,
But if it be of hooly seintes lyves,
Ne of noon oother womman never the mo.
Who peyntede the leon, tel me who?
By God! if wommen hadde writen stories,
As clerkes han withinne hire oratories,
They wolde han writen of men moore wikkednesse
Than al the mark of Adam may redresse.

CT iii 669–96

There will be more – much more – to say about the Wife of Bath but let her speak for herself first. Let us begin not with the portrait of her in the *General Prologue* to the *Canterbury Tales* but with her own autobiographical prologue to her tale. This passage describes a strategy in the cold war between the Wife and Jankin, her fifth husband, which one night escalates into climactic violence. Like the extract from the *Nun's Priest's Tale* it shows a husband using the anti-feminine tradition against his wife and trying to score off her because of his greater knowledge of it. But it has none of the parodic elegance of the *Nun's Priest's Tale*. The cock and hen have considerably better manners than the human couple. Chaunticleer and Pertelote comport themselves with dignity, no matter how ruffled their feathers. Pertelote nags a little but makes her affection clear. Chaunticleer patronises his wife but flatters her too. But Jankin means to provoke and he succeeds. The Wife's boredom and resentment simmer until one evening they explode into a physical fight. The Wife tears three pages out of Jankin's book and fells him with a blow to the cheek.[7]

The passage contains a vignette and a question. The question, 'Who painted the lion?', derives from a fable in which a lion comments that the picture of a man winning a fight with a lion would look quite different if it had been painted by a lion. (What was Chaucer's lost 'Book of the Leoun' about?) Men have written the books, argues the Wife, they have been educated, their views have been heard. No wonder women have had a bad press. If the other sex had been authors and reported their experiences of men, the 'mark of Adam' (696) would never be able to make amends for their wickedness. 'Who painted the lion?' uncovers a central issue for feminism. It anticipates one of the most vexing questions in modern feminist criticism: women's inheritance of a predominantly masculine literary tradition. In *The Madwoman in the Attic*, for example, it is quoted to 'emphasise our culture's confusion of literary authorship with patriarchal authority'.[8] Milton is said to have made his daughters read to him in languages they did not understand: if apocryphal, this story presumably originated from the views on gender in *Paradise Lost*. Jankin's wife also suffers ordeal by literature, but she does understand and she does protest at her intellectual force-feeding. 'Stibourn I was as is a leonesse' (III 637), she recalls, and her stubborn opposition takes the form of snatching the book from the man and reducing him to a 'wood leoun' (794).

The vignette is of a man reading to a woman. This picture may itself suggest patriarchal authority in a society where even more women than men were illiterate. The fight breaks out one night when 'Jankyn, that was oure sire, / Redde on his book' (713–14). 'Sire' can mean 'husband', which is its obvious sense here, but the word carries inevitable associations of lordship and paternity. The spiritual fatherhood of the clergy is another aspect of Jankin's smug air of masculine authority. The book from which he reads is a collection of classics of anti-feminine material. The number of works 'bounden in o volume' (681) represents a hefty stockpile of psychological ammunition. Such miscellanies were compiled particularly for the purpose of dissuading young men from marriage and promoting ordination.[9] Jankin, who 'som tyme was a clerk of Oxenford / And hadde left scole' (527–8), a renegade cleric, is not one of the successes of this education. He has given up his clerical studies and any intentions of ordination, presumably in favour of worldly prospects such as marriage or money. He has, in fact, achieved both, in the form of a rich wife much older than himself. None the less, this gigolo is invested with the authority of the reading classes. He is a latter-day example of a venerable image: the man with the book. Behind him stretches a long tradition, in visual as well as literary art, of such figures as the Evangelists and the Doctors of the Church. For example, Jerome, whom he cites, is usually painted at work on the Vulgate, complete with cardinal's hat and tame lion. (Chaunticleer, the chicken with the book, is a surreal vision of the same figure.) And these masculine images carry the other clerical associations of teaching and preaching, of celebrating the sacraments, of hearing confessions, of providing spiritual guidance. Marriage is in Christian theology an analogue of the relationship between Christ and the Church. Jankin is treating his wife as a captive congregation of one.

The Wife is fully aware of the misogynistic succession, that behind Jankin are centuries of men vilifying women, that the anti-feminine tradition is 'man-made'. It is not objective, any more than the picture of the lion represents the lion's point of view. The literate have been men and in western Christendom they have increasingly tended to be members of an unmarried clergy. Jankin's favourite reading is propaganda for this cause. Not only have more books been written by men, but they have been written by men with a vocation for celibacy. Or worse, they have been written by clerics without a vocation for celibacy who are tormented by their own lapses and forbidden desires. The Wife, who is perhaps over-given to astrological determinism,[10] suggests that there is a natural hostility between the children of Venus and clerks, the children of Mercury. Since she describes herself as 'al Venerien' (609) this augurs ill for her marriage to the ex-clerk. But she also suggests that the sexual and the ideological are at war within the individual personality: when the clerk is old and can no longer perform the works of Venus, then he sits down and writes in his dotage that women are not to be trusted. Just the time to write a palinode. To adapt the moral of the *Physician's Tale*, he does not forsake sin before sin forsakes him.

The Wife herself has already made a backhanded use of anti-feminine satire in her Prologue. In her first three marriages to rich husbands much older than herself, the Wife relates how she would harass them by falsely accusing them of having made the stock accusations to her. She claimed that, after they had been drinking, they would 'preach' on the problems of marriage and the vices of women. The catalogue is familiar.[11] A poor wife will be expensive, a rich one will be proud. A beauty will be unfaithful, a plain woman hungry for lovers. These tirades are embellished by the usual rhetoric of anti-feminine satire. The lechery imputed to women is amplified with animal images. The ugly wife will leap on any man 'as a spanyel' (iii 267); there is no goose so grey that it cannot have a mate. Marriage is much more of a gamble than the purchase of domestic animals or consumer durables. 'Oxen, asses, hors and houndes' (285) can be bought on approval but not wives. Their faults cannot be discovered till it is too late. Obsession with female infidelity runs through these speeches: that is the only motive ascribed to a woman's wishing to dress well or even to go out of the house. A smart woman is like a sleek cat eager to go 'a-caterwawed' (354): better to singe the cat's skin so that it will stay at home. The defamations are well worn, some of them actually proverbial. Three things drive a man out of his house: a leaking roof, a smoking fire, a nagging wife. The jibes have the tiresome reductiveness of proverbs: no goose so grey that it cannot find a mate, like the modern 'all cats are grey in the dark', camouflages the variety of human feeling with its tedious monochrome. St Paul is inevitably quoted: a woman should be clothed in modesty rather than adorned with jewels, rich clothes and elaborate hair-styles. Finally, the husbands were accused of comparing the love of women to hell, to barren land, to wild fire, to destructive worms – and perhaps one could hardly blame them if they had. The Wife of Bath paints a dreadful picture of her first three marriages. Some of the grudges she attributes to her husbands seem justified, supposing an elderly man has the right to buy a young girl and expect her to prove a loyal affectionate wife. Instead, each marriage is a battlefield and the Wife presents herself as the mistress of the pre-emptive strike: 'Whoso that first to mille comth, first grynt; / I pleyned first, so was oure werre ystynt' (389–90). But whyever do her attacks on her husbands take this form? Her criticisms of them largely consist of a rehearsal of their imagined criticisms of her. Why not attack them for their own faults? Is Chaucer condemning her out of her own mouth, using his most articulate woman character to voice the case against women? Is it because there is no equivalent tradition of satire against men, so the Wife is forced to deploy the satire against women for her own ends? That attack, even with weapons like these, is the best form of defence? Perhaps, but I think that we should also take seriously the overt cause of this gargantuan resentment – and all the more if it hardly corresponds with her husbands' actual treatment of her. The worst thing men have done to women is create these images of them. The Wife's conflict is less with individual husbands than with the whole literary tradition of masculine satire – 'I ne owe hem nat a word that it nys quit' (425) – and masculine scripture: 'After thy text ne after thy rubriche, / I wol nat wirche as muchel as a gnat' (346–7).

Her fifth husband, the clerk, sees himself as the representative of this tradition and his use of it is vicious. Most of the accusations put into the mouths of the first three husbands seem relatively trivial compared with Jankin's. He wants to hurt. His relish in reading his book of wicked wives is underlined. He reads it 'gladly' (669), for entertainment ('for his desport' – 670) and obsessively ('nyght and day' –669; 'every nyght and day' – 682; 'alway' –670). It makes him roar with laughter ('At which book he lough alwey ful faste' – 672). We have heard a good deal about the idolatry of the courtly tradition, how it blasphemously exalts the beloved lady to quasi-divine status and sets up a rival good to the love of God.[12] But here we see that the misogynist tradition can be just as idolatrous, just as perversely distracting from the contemplation of the good and the divine. Jankin, the ex-clerk, seems to have substituted it for prayer and spiritual reading. He reads this book 'with ful good devocioun' (739) and turns to it whenever he has leisure 'from oother worldly occupacioun' (684). He knows more 'legendes' (686) – the usual term for the biography of a saint – and lives of wicked women than there are of good wives in the Bible. He uses the classical tradition to 'preche' (641) and 'teche' (642) of ancient Romans who divorced their wives. Jankin is a parody of a man reading a sacred or theological work. His wife's violent resistance to this travesty of spiritual guidance contrasts aptly with the silent attentiveness of the docile female pupil.

The nagging quality of his instruction makes it even harder to bear. The Wife, in her persecution of her first three husbands, pre-empted the insistent repetition of anti-female platitudes: 'Thou seist . . . thou seist . . .' (248, 251, 254, 257, 263, 270, 273, 278, 282, 285, 292, 293, 302, 337, 348, 362, 366, 376). The phrase that echoes through her account of Jankin's abuse of women is 'he read': 'he wolde rede alwey' (670), he 'redde on his book' (714), 'Tho redde he me' (721, 724), 'he redde it' (739), 'of wyves hath he red' (765), 'he wolde nevere fyne / To reden' (788–9). It is followed closely by the didactic-sounding 'He tolde me' (647, 740, 747, 757) and 'quod he' (775), 'quod he' (778), 'He seyde' (782) punctuate Jankin's monologue as he talks on into the night. His fireside lecture certainly sounds repetitive. 'Of . . . of . . . of . . .' resounds as he works through his agenda : 'Of Eva first' (715), 'Of Hercules and of his Dianyre' (725), 'Of Phasipha' (733), 'Of Clitermystra' (737), 'Of Lyvia . . . and of Lucye' (747), 'Of latter date, of wyves hath he red' (765). He intends to be exhaustive: 'No thyng forgat he' (727) of the marital sufferings of Socrates. This list of individual wicked wives expands into general denunciation: 'somme han . . . somme han . . . somme han' (766, 769, 771). And, to crown it all, he knew more proverbs on this subject than all the grass and herbs in the world.

Jankin's horrid tales of wicked wives could serve as *exempla* for
Chaunticleer's text *Mulier est hominis confusio*. But here we do not
have even a glimpse of the Eve/Mary typology which underlies
Chaunticleer's double-edged account. Women are *only* the destruc-
tion of men. Jankin begins, of course, 'Of Eva first, that for hir
wikkednesse / Was al mankynde broght to wrecchednesse, / For
which that Jhesu Crist hymself was slayn' (715–7). So women are the
root of all evil in the world and Eve's daughters have continued her
pernicious work. They appear, in Jankin's anthology of seduction
and betrayal by women, particularly malevolent in their love
relationships. Delilah betrayed Samson to be blinded by the
Philistines by cutting his hair and thus sapping his strength (721–
3). He becomes (like January in the *Merchant's Tale*) literally blind
because he has already been symbolically blinded by love. He
should have seen that sexual contact with women brings weakness
and mutilation. Hercules fell victim to a loving wife 'that caused
hym to sette hymself afyre' (726), literally acting out in his death the
symbolic burning of love's devotees. Stories of defilement follow.
Xantippe 'caste pisse' (729) on the head of Socrates, as if the body,
loathsome and female, rebels against the mind, reasonable and
male. The story of the bestiality of Pasiphae with the bull is too
horrible for the Wife to repeat, although Jankin enjoyed it ('Hym
thoughte the tale swete' – 733–4).[13] The adulterous Clytemnestra
murdered her husband 'for hire lecherye' (737). The avaricious
Eriphile delivered hers to his death for a bribe. The theme
adumbrated in the examples of Delilah and Deianira, that the love
and hate of women are equally destructive, continues in the stories
of Livia and Lucia. The first poisoned her husband deliberately, the
second accidentally with a love potion (747–56). Husbands want
their wives to die too: Arrius's neighbour asks him for a cutting
from the tree on which his three wives hanged themselves (757–64).
This anecdote is meant to illustrate female hatefulness rather
than male malevolence. The cautionary tales grow yet more
lurid as Jankin produces modern instances of lovers copulating all
night in the presence of the murdered husband's corpse (766–8). He
moves from learned tradition to common lore and concludes
with a salvo of proverbs. Better to live with a lion or a dragon than
with a nagging wife, a woman casts away her shame with her
smock, a fair woman without chastity is like a gold ring in a sow's
nose (782–5) . . . .

When it becomes clear that Jankin will read from 'this cursed book' (789) all night, his wife can bear it no longer. She tears three leaves from his book and hits him, he hits her back, she falls down and pretends to be dying, he bends over her to ask her forgiveness and she hits him again. The fight has its funny side, the knockabout humour of the Punch and Judy show, the comic capacity of the two actors to bounce. But Alison and Jankin are not puppets. Their blows hurt – Alison is left deaf in one ear – and their words hurt even more. Or rather, their words are weapons and their blows a kind of language. The Wife fights because she is wounded. 'Who wolde wene, or who wolde suppose, / The wo that in myn herte was, and pyne?' (786–7). She resorts to violence, an alternative language, because Jankin possesses all the conventional linguistic ammunition.

Whatever would the psychological effects of this satire be on women? There were, as the Wife points out, few women writers to give the 'lion's' point of view. One of Chaucer's female contemporaries, the poet Christine de Pizan, testifies both to the suffering caused by the misogynist tradition and to the difficulty of thinking critically about it:

Just the sight of this book, even though it was of no authority, made me wonder how it happened that so many different men – and learned men among them – have been and are so inclined to express both in speaking and in their treatises and writings so ᶜ many wicked insults about women and their behaviour. Not only one or two and not even just this Matheolus (for this book had a bad name anyway and was intended as a satire) but, more generally, judging from the treatises of all philosophers and poets and from all orators . . . it seems that they all speak from one and the same mouth. They all concur in one conclusion: that the behaviour of women is inclined to and full of every vice . . . .

I could hardly find a book on morals where, even before I had read it in its entirety, I did not find several chapters or certain sections attacking women, no matter who the author was. This reason alone, in short, made me conclude that although my intellect did not perceive my own great faults and, likewise, those of other women because of its simpleness and ignorance, it was, however, truly fitting that such was the case. *And so I relied more on the judgement of others than on what I myself felt and knew* [my italics]. I was so transfixed in this line of thinking for such a long time that it seemed as if I were in a stupor. Like a gushing fountain, a series of authorities, whom I recalled one after another, came to mind along with their opinions on this topic. And I finally decided that God formed a vile creature when He made woman, and I wondered how such a worthy artisan could have deigned to make such an abominable work which, from what they say, is the vessel as well as the refuge and abode of every evil and vice. As I was thinking this, a great unhappiness and sadness welled up in my heart, for I detested myself and the entire feminine sex as though we were monstrosities in nature.[14]

Christine's *persona* has internalised the material which Jankin uses against his wife.[15] Although she cannot see evidence of such evil in herself or in the women she knows well, she is unable to use her own judgement in the face of such indoctrination. The misogynist authorities pour their destructive messages into her mind until she hates herself and cannot see why God created women at all. Christine was an author herself and her solution was to write a book about virtuous ladies. But this option was open to only a very few well educated and highly intelligent women. The domestic brawl described by the Wife of Bath was within the means of more and, though finally counter-productive in its demonstration of female irrationality, could provide a little immediate satisfaction. And there were manoeuvres available besides violence and authorship. A sharp-witted competitor, such as the Wife of Bath, could adapt the doctrines of misogyny for use against the other sex, as in her citations of authority or the insidious backhanded logic of 'sith a man is moore resonable / Than womman is, ye mooste ben suffrable' (441–2). Or, then as now, there was the resource – exemplified by the Prioress rather than the Wife – of enjoying what fun there was to be had out of the more mindless aspects of femininity.

Modern feminism has opened our eyes to the sexist effects of 'man-made language'.[16] Chaucer is well aware of the influence of man-made literature. Throughout his life he was fascinated by the power of books. His own *persona* in his poems is a man who knows about life through reading. In his earliest surviving work the narrator dreams that he is in a room whose windows depict the story of Troy and whose walls are painted with the *Romance of the Rose*. In his valediction to his career, the Retractions to the *Canterbury Tales*, Chaucer asks forgiveness for 'thilke that sownen into synne'. The *House of Fame* culminates in a nightmare vision of an information explosion of truth and lies, unstoppable and inextricable. Many of his characters use books as their model for life. Even the hilarious sexual comedy of the *Miller's Tale* hinges on a re-enactment of the story of Noah. For Chaucer the most distinctively human attribute he can bestow on Chaunticleer and Pertelote in his beast fable is the habit of quotation. And Chaunticleer's quotation takes us deep into the heart of our culture and its masculine constructions of femininity.

Through Chaunticleer and Jankin Chaucer mocks the pompous and prejudiced uses men can make of books. Though himself a man with a book, his *persona* is not a teacher or preacher. A member of a growing class of literate laity, he presents himself as that familiar modern figure, the solitary reader. And he is puzzled by what he reads, 'daswed' (*HF* 658) by books, confused by conflicting messages, baffled by the caprices of Fame. Fame, in Chaucer's portrait, is unconcerned about the justice of the reports she authorises. But Chaucer draws attention to his responsibility in creating images of women. Criseyde fears that women will hate her for her infidelity and the narrator makes excuses to the ladies in his audience. In the Prologue to the *Legend* he is ordered to make amends by writing about good women. Such passages, whatever their ironies, foreground the problem. We have seen what Jankin can do with bad images. But the good images can be damaging in their own ways. The examples of the virtuous wronged women of antiquity seem to Dorigen to recommend suicide. Even the Clerk warns wives against trying to imitate the submission of patient Griselda. Let us look next at two of Chaucer's early versions of ideal women, one courtly and one religious.

2

Two Ideals: The *Dame* and the *Duchess*

Almighty and al merciable queene,
To whom that al this world fleeth for socour,
To have relees of sinne, of sorwe, and teene,
Glorious virgine, of alle floures flour,
To thee I flee, confounded in errour.
Help and releeve, thou mighti debonayre,
Have mercy on my perilous langour.
Venquisshed me hath my cruel adversaire.

ABC 1–8

The two earliest poems of Chaucer which we have are *An ABC* or *La Priere de Nostre Dame* and the *Book of the Duchess*, probably an elegy on the death of Blanche, Duchess of Lancaster, the first wife of John of Gaunt. She may have commissioned the former poem, as well as inspiring the latter. According to Speght's edition, it was produced 'as some say at the request of Blanche, Duchess of Lancaster, as praier for her privat use, being a woman in her religion very devout'.[1] The prayer and the elegy are linked in presenting ideals of women, the religious and the courtly. Despite Chaunticleer's ruin/ bliss antithesis and the Wife of Bath's rebellion against clerical misogyny, these ideals overlap and influence each other. They express similar emotional needs, they respect the same virtues. They often use identical language: courtly literature redeploys theological concepts of grace, penance and salvation in the service of romantic love; religious works accommodate the vocabulary of erotic poems. The fit can be so close that it is impossible to determine whether a short poem is pious or secular, addressed to the Virgin Mary or to an earthly mistress.

The *ABC* is not Chaucer's own original composition but his

14

translation of a passage in *La Pelerinage de la Vie Humaine* by Deguilleville, one of many expressions of devotion to the Virgin in late medieval Europe. Robinson's account, more judicious than warm, emphasises the centrality of its theme: 'The *ABC* being only a translation, reveals very little about Chaucer. If the tradition about the Duchesse Blanche is true, it is not possible even to credit him with the choice of the subject and to draw inferences therefrom. But the poem itself, if not an evidence of Chaucer's piety, is a characteristic expression of the piety of his age, and is by no means an unworthy specimen of the hymns and prayers evoked by the veneration of the Blessed Virgin'.[2] Chaucer himself, the '*grant translateur*', might not have dismissed the *ABC* as 'only a translation' or questioned the authenticity of the sentiments in a commissioned work or wished to distinguish between his own piety and that of his age.

But there is no need to defend the importance of the subject by an appeal to medieval aesthetics. If the poem is commonplace, it spoke for a large number of people. The veneration of Mary – together with the related emotional interest in the childhood and humanity of Christ – had been growing more zealous and widespread during the later medieval centuries. Churches and cathedrals were increasingly dedicated to her. During Chaucer's lifetime the Marian feasts of the Presentation and Visitation were established in western Europe. The Madonna was a constant figure in Chaucer's spiritual landscape, embodied in statues and stained glass, poems, plays and processions. Worship of the Virgin was part of the common Christian experience. It was expressed in countless hymns and prayers, a chorus of adoration in which we hear the voices of some of Chaucer's pilgrims and narrators. Both the nuns who tell Canterbury Tales preface their stories with invocations to the Virgin. *Troilus and Criseyde* ends with the prayer 'So make us, Jesus, for thi mercy digne, / For love of mayde and moder thyn benigne' (*TC* 1868–9). In his own voice in the Retractions to the *Canterbury Tales*, probably his last literary utterance, Chaucer thanks 'oure Lord Jhesu Crist and his blisful Mooder' for his virtuous compositions on holy subjects and prays to them for the salvation of his soul.

The *ABC* is in twenty-three stanzas, each beginning with a successive letter of the alphabet. The opening stanza states the main themes which will be elaborated with reverent variation throughout the work. The first line, 'Almighty and al merciable queene', announces some of the Virgin's major attributes in the later Middle

Ages: power, pity and courtliness. She is introduced – with doubtful orthodoxy – as 'almighty', her power almost equalling that of God. The poem is virtually an apotheosis of the Madonna. It is a symptom of the steady exaltation of the mother of Christ, a movement leading from the very minor character in the Gospels to the doctrine of the Immaculate Conception, her ascent – as this poem puts it – from 'ancille' to 'maistresse / Of hevene and erthe' (109–10).[3] In the New Testament Christ is the alpha and omega, the first and last letters of the Greek alphabet; here, analogously, Mary is the A to Z for the medieval Christian.

In this poem we see how Mary has popularly assumed the role of Christ in the theology of redemption. In the 'Xristus' stanza (the solution to the problem of the initial X) his Incarnation, Passion and Atonement are attributed to his mother: 'This thanke I yow, socour of al mankynde!' (168). Earlier, the Madonna is petitioned to remind God of these events – 'He vouched sauf, tel him, as was his wille, / Bicome a man' (57–8) – in a stanza which concludes in a statement of her power to placate God and to foil Satan. In the fourth stanza Mary, the 'queen of misericorde' (25), is defined as 'the cause of grace and merci heere' (26). Through her God 'vouched sauf , . . . with us to accorde' (27) and without her his justice would be totally punitive: 'The rightful God nolde of no mercy heere; / But thurgh thee han we grace' (31–2). The Virgin is the source of spiritual healing: 'thou art that same / To whom I seeche for my medicyne' . . . Myn hele into thin hand al I resygne . . . my soules leche' (77–8), 80, 134). In the first stanza all the world flees to her to be released from sin and sorrow. Both 'A*l*mighty' (1) and '*al* merciable' (1), she tempers absolute power with absolute compassion.

Mary is not only man's defence against the devil, the 'cruel adversaire' (8), but also his advocate against the justice of God the Father. The opposition between God's anger and Mary's pity is a central theme of the poem. The tendency to polarise the sexes substitutes Mary for her son in the justice/mercy debate. Legal imagery, balancing the claims of justice against the appeal to mercy, recurs throughout the poem. The speaker's 'sinne and confusioun' (18) have taken an action against him 'of verrey right' (21) and 'bi right' (22) would convict him as worthy of damnation, were it not for the Madonna. Later he implores for 'merci, ladi, at the gret assyse, / Whan we shule come bifore the hye justyse' (36–7). Mary is the best of defence counsels – 'We han . . . advocat noon that wole and dar so preye / For us, and that for litel hire as yee, / That helpen for an Ave-Marie or tweye' (100–5) – and, a traditional advantage of female labour, she gives her services for little or no payment. Finally, she is asked to adjourn his case to her own court, a court of mercy, 'unto that court . . . that clepid is thi bench . . . Ther as that merci evere shal sojourne' (158–60).

Some of the language used to heighten the contrast between God's justice and Mary's compassion suggests its source in child-hood terrors and dependencies:

> Help that my Fader be not wroth with me.
> Spek thou, for I ne dar not him ysee . . .
> Redresse me, mooder, and me chastise,
> For certeynly my Faderes chastisinge,
> That dar I nouht abiden in no wise,
> So hidous is his rightful rekenynge.
>
> 52–3, 129–32

Mary is the mother goddess to whom 'al this world fleeth for socour' (2), comfort and protection. She is 'Crystes blisful mooder deere' (28), the *mater dolorosa* who stood 'under the cros' (82) in indescrib-able grief, and, paradoxically, the 'Glorious mayde and mooder' (49) of the Virgin Birth. Chaucer adds to his source a traditional image, which he uses elsewhere, for Mary's 'unwemmed maidenhede' (91): the bush which Moses saw burning and not consumed.

The Christian paradoxes are prefigured in the burning bush, the symbol of the Madonna's motherhood and virginity. God's law and justice were revealed to Moses, redemption and mercy are enabled by Mary. Moses thought the bush 'a-fyr' (94); Mary is petitioned: 'from the fyr thou us defende / Which that in helle eternalli shal dure' (95–6). The story of the Virgin locates the truest strength in humility and obedience. Her magnificence has been won by her 'humblesse' (108). She occupies two positions paradoxically com-bined in her relationship to her divine son, that of submissive daughter or servant of God and that of omnipotent mother and protector of Man.

As striking as the contrast between the speaker's weakness and terror and the Madonna's power is the gulf between his personal unworthiness and her radiant purity. He is 'a beste in wil and deede' (45), 'worthi for to sinke' (123), wounded 'with thornes venymous' (149), 'in filthe and in errour' (157), 'fals and eek unkynde' (166). She is 'unwemmed' (91), the 'ladi bright' (16, 62, 181), the 'temple devout' (145), the dwelling place of God (145). He is 'confounded in errour' (5), prosecuted by 'my sinne and my confusioun' (18). Mary is the release from *confusio*, the other side of Chaunticleer's definition of woman.

The joy and bliss of romantic love is an element in the poem's adoration of the Madonna. It expresses a kind of chaste amorousness towards her. In the first stanza the language of love poetry adds to her celebration: she is 'of alle floures flour' (4), and, like the lady in the *Book of the Duchess*, she is 'debonayre' (6). 'Have mercy on my perilous langour' (7) is the cry of the Christian soul, sick unto death with its burden of mortal sin. It could equally be the plea of an Arcite or an Aurelius, men who feel desperately in need of their ladies' mercy and fear that the langour of love will be fatal to them. But this devotion has a great advantage over the earthly variety: 'Whoso thee loveth, he shal nat love in veyn' (71).

Like much of the love poetry, a prayer to the Virgin Mary spoken by a man inverts the usual power-structure of male/female relationships in medieval society. (The prayer could, of course, equally be spoken by a woman and may have been translated for one but the author and translator were men.) The Madonna is the mighty protector of the beleaguered soul. Her aid is sought in legal imagery, which casts her in a role improbable for a woman. Her support is also envisaged in military terms, which might imaginatively extend her valency into the masculine sphere: 'Fleeinge, I flee for socour to thi tente' (41). Yet the poem also dismantles such metaphors, emphasising that the spiritual force revealed at the Annunciation makes human heroism and traditional masculine formes of self-assertion redundant: 'He not to werre us swich a wonder wroughte, / But for to save us that he sithen boughte; / Thanne nedeth us no wepen us for to save' (116–18).

The Madonna is not only the mother and mistress of the soul but also its queen. The royal title used in the opening invocation re-echoes through the poem. Mary is 'hevene queene' (24), 'queen of misericorde' (25), 'queene of comfort' (77, 121). She is continually addressed as 'lady' (16, 36, 46, 47, 62, 81, 95, 158, 173, 181). She is also 'noble princesse' (97), 'maistresse / Of hevene and erthe' (109–10), 'vicaire and maistresse / Of al this world, and eek governouresse / Of hevene' (140–2), in witness of which God 'hath thee corowned in so rial wise' (144). Just as the Father/Mother/Son 'trinity' forms a heavenly analogue of a human family, so this vocabulary suggests that the Kingdom of Heaven is the celestial counterpart of a human court. The courtly virtues and graces can have a theological significance in the art of this period. Divinity manifests an exquisite courtesy towards humanity in the gift of the Incarnation. The courtly language both conveys the human appeal of the Madonna and assists in her elevation.

The role of queen probably seemed less 'unnatural' or miraculous than that of lawyer or soldier. A king needed a consort. And a woman could, in default of a male heir, become monarch in medieval England or France, a political fact with its relevance to the tradition of love poetry stemming from the troubadours and Marian poetry influenced by the love lyrics. 'Because a sovereign female was a familiar figure in medieval society, the Virgin was able to slip on the mantle of the poet's love object.'[4] But the coronation of the Virgin by her son, a highly popular subject in the visual arts, suggests both the sublimation and the subordination of Mary. It is a neat image of the mother's role in a patrilineal society, the channel of power rather than a power in her own right, subject first to father, then to husband, finally to son. The Virgin Mother, queen of heaven and handmaiden of the Lord, both mirrors and eludes the changing conditions of women in the centuries since Gabriel's visit.

Virgin and mother, intercessor, queen, courtly lady, healer of the soul, well of pity, burning bush, vicar of God, mistress of heaven and earth, temple of the Lord, light to the blind, ground of our substance . . . . The Madonna seems to have everything. But this image has significant omissions and ambiguities. She is all-powerful but lacks power in her own right: it is deputed to her by the Father and the Son. She lacks adult sexuality, except as the chaste object of sublimated devotion. She is *unfailingly* loving, gentle, compassionate and long-suffering. Does that not make her essentially different from all actual women and encourage the labelling of them as destructive Eves rather than redemptive Maries?

There is little evidence that the reverence and devotion lavished on the Virgin Mary had practical consequences for other women. But our subject is Chaucer's poems and in them we pervasively feel her influence. The *ABC* may be an early exercise but Chaucer continues to be moved by the virtues, sorrows and strengths that it extols. He will return to them in Griselda's rise from humbleness to majesty, in Cecilia's married chastity, in Constance persecuted with her child, in the grieving mother of the *Prioress's Tale*. He sees

the comedy of the gap between human behaviour and Christian
ideal. The Prioress's imitation of Mary seems more cosmetic than
contemplative. Nicholas, who seduces the carpenter's wife in the
bawdy *Miller's Tale*, sweetly sings '*Angelus ad virginem*', a hymn of
the Annunciation. Another parody of the Holy Family occurs in the
Merchant's Tale when a pregnant young wife with an old husband
swears by 'hir love that is of hevene queene!' (IV 2334) before
committing adultery. But Chaucer finds the virtues associated with
the Madonna in some women and considers these the highest
virtues. The value placed on female chastity may originally have
more to do with property than ˌpurity but Chaucer, like other
medieval Christians, thought virginity a source of spiritual power.
In so far as he polarises the virtues by gender, he suggests that men
should learn from and imitate such 'feminine' qualities as pity. The
justice/mercy male/female structure of the *ABC* is echoed in his
narrative works. The woman as intercessor, checking the vengeful-
ness of a harsh or impatient male authority, will change the course
of events in the Prologue to the *Legend of Good Women*, the *Knight's
Tale*, the *Wife of Bath's Tale* and the *Tale of Melibee*. Pity, for Chaucer,
is a proper use of power. Courtliness can be an image of divine
courtesy. And the allure of the Virgin's goodness and beauty finds
its earthly counterpart in the courtly lady.

II

I holde hit be a sicknesse
That I have suffred this eight yeer,
And yet my boote is never the ner;
For ther is phisicien but oon
That may me hele . . .

BD 36–40

The *Book of the Duchess* is a dream-vision, a form which Chaucer
was to use again in the *Parliament of Fowls*, the *House of Fame* and
the Prologue to the *Legend of Good Women*. If it is a consolation to the
bereaved John of Gaunt and a celebration of his Duchess Blanche, it
is tactful and indirect. The meeting with the knight in black and his
story of his dead lady White occur within the dream and the
characters are identified only punningly at the end of the poem.

The poem opens with an insomniac narrator, the earliest in Chaucer's series of self-mocking or self-disguising *personae*. One later version includes the incompetent versifier described by the Man of Law, defended by Alceste as too stupid to be responsible, and silenced impatiently by the Host in the middle of his own Canterbury Tale. Another is the poet of the *Parliament of Fowls* and *Troilus and Criseyde*, who writes of love but knows of it only from reading. This narrator, though equally bookish, is apparently in love but unsuccessfully. He is numb with misery and amazed that he can survive so long without sleep. This sickness that he has suffered for eight years is presumably love, since only one person could cure him, but it is useless to talk of that, so he drops the subject.

To pass the hours of a sleepless night, he decides to read and finds in a collection of stories (presumably Ovid's *Metamorphoses*) the tale of Ceyx and Alcyone. This story, like the one in the dream, is of bereavement. King Ceyx is lost at sea. After much anxiety and many enquiries his queen Alcyone prays to Juno that she may sleep and learn in a dream whether her husband is dead or alive. Juno tells Morpheus, the god of sleep, to assume the drowned body of Ceyx and appear to his widow in a dream. The apparition informs her of his death, bids her farewell, and advises her to give up her pointless sorrow. Alcyone, however, dies within three days.

For the depressed narrator the main interest in this story is the discovery of a god of sleep. He promises suitable votive offerings, such as a pillow and a feather bed, to Morpheus if the god will grant him sleep, and immediately he drops off and begins to dream. It is the dawn of a May morning and he is lying in bed, listening to the birdsong, in a richly decorated room. The stained-glass windows tell the story of Troy and the *Romance of the Rose* is painted on the walls. A hunt is leaving and the Dreamer joins it. After the hart eludes the hunters and the hounds, he wanders into the forest and comes upon a man in black who seems the picture of sorrow. The Dreamer overhears him recite a poem lamenting the death of his lady but, either incomprehending or providing him with an outlet for his grief, questions him. The knight explains that he has played a game of chess with Fortune and lost his queen. When the Dreamer says that his sorrow for a chess-piece seems excessive, he goes on to recount the story of how he fell in love with White (Blanche?), and won her love, and finally reveals that she is dead. 'Is that youre los? Be God, hyt ys routhe!' (1310) exclaims the Dreamer. The hunt returns to a 'long castel' (1318) (Lancaster?) on a 'ryche hil' (1319) (Richmond?) and the Dreamer awakes.

He wakes and finds himself lying in bed with the book 'Of Alcione and Seys the kyng / And of the goddes of slepyng' (1327–8). He thinks the dream so 'queynt' (1330) that he resolves in the course of time to put it into verse as best he can. It is a laconic ending. We do not know what, if anything, the narrator has made of his dream, whether the Man in Black has been helped by their conversation, or what lessons the audience might draw from the poem. In the absence of comment from the Dreamer, readers have supplied their own interpretations. The Dreamer might come to see his own distress as self-indulgent and self-inflicted, compared with the pain of the knight who has really lost a real love. The Man in Black might work out during their dialogue – or the reader might vicariously be instructed through him – that one should be indifferent to the wiles of Fortune and regard earthly losses and death in a Christian spirit. His devotion to his lady itself may be criticised. In ordinary human terms perhaps his grief is eased by expressing it to the Dreamer and his mood lightened by the memory of past happiness. He may be seen as more fortunate than the Dreamer in that he has won his love and experienced the height of human happiness. Or we might analyse the characters in terms of dream psychology as a 'splitting' of the narrator, the Man in Black a displacement of his own sorrow, the Dreamer an attempt to come to terms with it.[5]

Already in this early poem we find themes and structures which will remain among Chaucer's favourites: the love-vision form, the juxtaposing of analogous stories, the relation of the book to experience, the dialogue, the dream which verges on allegory but eludes interpretation, the narrator who does not participate in the action. The Dreamer and the Man in Black dramatise Chaucer's recurrent debate between authority and experience. The Dreamer suffers the first and the black knight both of the double sorrows which will be the subject of *Troilus*: love unrequited and love lost. Although these two main characters are men, the poem is haunted by women and goddesses whose problems and power are constant themes in Chaucer's work. Juno presides over one tale of bereavement, Fortune – with her instability, her ambiguous gifts, her capricious play with human beings – over the other. Alcyone, the wife left at home to worry and to grieve, anticipates the plight of Dorigen and heroines of the *Legend*. And there are the two absent women, present in imagination: the only one who could cure the narrator's sickness, presumably the distant mistress of the courtly tradition, and the dead White, more lively in the poem than her bereaved husband, who is also courtly, also adored from afar, but finally susceptible to pity.

Chaucer's favourite authors contribute to the *Book of the Duchess*. The two main characters, despite their despairing self-involvement, repeat constant patterns of joy and grief in human experience and re-echo the words of other poems on these themes. Chaucer was the pioneer of French models and meters in English. The main source for this poem is Guillaume Machaut's *Roy de Behaingne*. The description of Blanche owes much to the equivalent passage in Machaut: this ideal courtly lady is no more an individual private creation than the Virgin of the *ABC*. The story of Ceyx and Alcyone also occurs in Machaut but Chaucer's main source here is the *Metamorphoses*, and Ovidian themes – love, the remedies for love, urbane sexuality, the suffering of noble heroines – will recur in his work.

There are more general debts. The counsel that one should remain immune to the vicissitudes of Fortune by not caring for her gifts is that of Boethius in the *Consolation of Philosophy*, a book which Chaucer translated himself and which was one of the most profound influences on his thought.[6] The interior decoration of the Dreamer's dream waking – the story of Troy, the *Romance of the Rose* – symbolises his poetic environment. The fall of Troy and the return of the heroes – known directly from Latin rather than Greek sources, with many later accretions, romantic as well as heroic – are the epic background to European literature. White 'was as good . . . As ever was Penelopee of Grece' (1080–1), says the Man in Black and he would still have loved her best, had he been as 'hardy . . . as was Ector' (1064–5). The *Romance of the Rose*, which Chaucer translated from the French, was one of the most influential medieval poems on love. It was the work of two very different thirteenth-century poets. The first four thousand lines, by Guillaume de Lorris, describe how the narrator dreams that he enters a beautiful garden, is shot by the God of Love and falls in love with a rose. The rest of the fragment describes his dealings with the attributes that encourage him, such as Bialacoil, Pite and Fraunchise, the lady's good manners, sympathy and generosity, and the forces suspicious of love, Resoun, Shame and Daunger. The vast encyclopaedic continuation of the poem by Jean de Meun culminates in a spirited defloration. But it is a very delayed climax. *En route* Jean discusses, among other things, science, philosophy, sexuality, propagation, the failings of women, the corruption of the clergy. Jean's satire on women is one of the sources for the Wife of Bath's self-portrait in her Prologue. From Guillaume Chaucer inherited the dream-vision form, the paradisal garden and its inhabitants, the ambivalent and all-powerful God of Love, the analysis of inner conflict in the heroine.

More than half the *Book of the Duchess* consists of the conversation between the Dreamer and the Man in Black, in which the knight describes White and how he loved and won her. His love follows the conventional courtly pattern. In his youth he vowed himself to Love as to a religion. Out of all the branches of learning he chose it as his 'firste craft' (791). His time of life and his high place in society made him an apt devotee: like the lover in the *Romance of the Rose*, Youth governed him in Idleness. But he was not yet in love. He served the God of Love for many a year before his heart was set upon a lady and he prayed to the god to bestow it fittingly. At last he came one day into the fairest company of ladies that had ever been seen. One surpassed all the rest, like the sun the planets. He 'was ykaught / So sodenly, that I ne tok / No maner counseyl but at hir lok / And at myn herte' (838–41). He thought that it was better to serve her in vain than to succeed with anybody else.

The knight's description of White is lengthy, even prolix, and it includes most of the conventional attributes. She is tall and slim, with fair shoulders, white hands, round breasts, her hair like gold, her throat like a tower of ivory. She is Nature's best example of her work. But there is even more emphasis on her goodness than on her beauty. In the knight's first song, she 'was so fair, so fresh, so fre, / So good, that men may wel se / Of al goodnesse she had no mete!' (484–6). Her face is not only beautiful but 'stedfast' (833), 'sad, symple, and benygne' (918). Her speech is not only 'softe' (919) but 'frendly' (921), reasonable, eloquent, free of scorn, slander and chiding, and so truthful that her word is good as any bond or signature. She exemplifies the classical ideal of moderation: 'She nas to sobre ne to glad; / In alle thynges more mesure / Had never, I trowe, creature' (880–2).[7]

White maintains a perfect poise between gravity and joyfulness. Her eyes are both 'glade, and sadde' (860), both words which are repeated later in the description. 'Sad' had a larger range of meaning in Middle English than in Modern. Here it means 'steadfast', rather than 'sorrowful'. It does not contradict 'glad' but stabilises it. White is likewise praised for her 'stedfast countenaunce' (833) and her 'stedefast perseveraunce' (1007). She shares with Griselda of the *Clerk's Tale* the quality of 'sadness', but here it does not seem a deadly virtue. It coexists with a radiant happiness which is equally virtuous. White sings, dances, laughs and plays 'so womanly' (850) that 'so blysful a tresor' (854) was never seen. She is associated with images of light: the sun (821), a torch (963). Like the Madonna in the *ABC*, she is described as 'bright' (477. 821, 950, 963, 1180) and her lover comments that her name, White, suited her: 'she hadde not hir name wrong' (951). In his lover's memory she seems to generate her own light: 'Be hyt never so derk, / Me thynketh I se hir ever moo' (912–3). He, by contrast, is sunk in darkness: 'To derke ys turned al my lyght' (609). White's name contrasts with the Man in Black, her happiness with his mourning and with the grief of other characters, the bereaved Ceyx and the suffering narrator. There are different time-frames in the poem, dream and waking, reading and books, the present, the near past and the remote past, death and life. Paradoxically, the dead White seems more alive than the lover who survives her.

White is not flirtatious, a quality Chaucer does not admire in men or women, though her beauty and goodness involuntarily attract. They could also involuntarily mislead: 'Hir eyen semed anoon she wolde / Have mercy – fooles wenden soo – / But hyt was never the rather doo' (866–9). White shows no interest in her own power, indifferent or unconscious when 'many oon' (883) falls in love with her. A man at home was no closer to gaining her love than one in India. She does, however, feel a general Christian affection for many people: 'But goode folk, over al other, / She loved as man may do hys brother; / Of which love she was wonder large' (891–3). (This too can cause problems for the beholder. Othello does not stop to appreciate Desdemona's distinction that she 'never loved Cassio . . . but with such general warranty of heaven / As I might love'.) The knight describes her as a torch, giving light to everyone without diminution of herself. She is free from the teasing pride of some of the courtly ladies of fiction, with no desire to impose ordeals on admirers, the romantic version of the pilgrimage and the military career, as the price of her favour:

> Hyr lust to holde no wyght in honde,
> Ne, be thou siker, she wolde not fonde
> To holde no wyght in balaunce

By half word ne by countenaunce –
But if men wolde upon hir lye –
Ne sende men into Walakye,
To Pruyse, and into Tartarye,
To Alysaundre, ne into Turkye,
And byd hym faste anoon that he
Goo hoodles into the Drye Se
And come hom by the Carrenar,
And seye 'Sir, be now ryght war
That I may of yow here seyn
Worshyp, or that ye come ageyn!'
She ne used no suche knakkes smale.

1019–33

At first the knight's love for White seemed hopeless. For a long time, indeed, she knew nothing of it. Meanwhile, he languished in the proper ways. He composed love songs but was too terrified to reveal his feelings to her. But, if he did not tell her, he thought he would die. Finally he reflected that Nature never endowed a creature with such beauty without adding mercy as well. (He was following a tradition which holds that physical beauty embodies spiritual nobility. If true, this would justify falling in love at first sight.) So, almost too nervous to speak, he told her. At first he was too overcome to say more than 'mercy' (1219) but, when his heart returned to him, he begged her to be his lady and promised eternal fidelity. But White, it seemed, did not give a straw for this. Her answer was a firm 'Nay' (1243). The knight did not dare say another word but stole away in despair. His sorrow, he says, outdid Cassandra's when she lamented the destruction of Troy. But much later ('another yere' – 1258), he decided to approach White again and try to make her understand the depth of his suffering and the purity of his love. At this White relented. She gave him 'the noble yifte of hir mercy' (1270) and a ring. The knight was like one raised from death to life. They lived for many years in perfect accord:

Oure hertes wern so evene a payre,
That never nas that oon contrayre
To that other, for no woo.
For sothe, ylyche they suffred thoo
Oo blysse, and eke oo sorwe bothe;
Ylyche they were bothe glad and wrothe;

Al was us oon, without were.
And thus we lyved ful many a yere . . .
1289–96

Although the poem is probably (among other things) an elegy for John of Gaunt's wife, the relationship described does not seem to be marriage. One cannot be certain, as the matter is treated with delicacy. The lady bestows a ring on her suitor as a sign of favour, rather than exchanging rings with him. A sexual relationship seems to be excluded, at least initially: 'My lady yaf me al hooly / The noble yifte of hir mercy, / Savynge hir worship, by al weyes, – / Dredles, I mene noon other weyes' (1269–72). In both his approaches to the lady the lover emphasises his concern for her 'worship' and good name: 'al hir worship for to save / As I best koude, I swor hir this –' (1230–1); 'I ne wilned thyng but god, / And worship, and to kepe hir name / Over alle thynges, and drede hir shame' (1262–4). The lady continues to have the dominant position that she held during the knight's wooing: 'She took me in hir governaunce' (1286) and was always ready to forgive him when he was in the wrong.

The knight is granted his desire but the *Book of the Duchess* does not end happily ever after. No earthly story can. White and her lover live in harmony for many a year, until death takes her from him. In this early love poem, as in *Troilus*, his most mature, Chaucer presents even the deepest human affections in the perspective of transience. Troy and the Rose, tragedy and romance, are interwoven in both stories. In the *Book of the Duchess* Chaucer scarcely uses one of the most lovely features of the *Romance of the Rose*, the garden, with its earthly version of the eternal spring of Paradise. Chaucer's narrator wakes to a beautiful May morning, the traditional setting of romance, but the knight's story of love is related in the forest, green background to the black and white figures of human grief and goodness. The forest has natural powers of renewal:

Hyt had forgete the povertee
That wynter, thorgh hys colde morwes,
Had mad hyt suffre, and his sorwes,
Al was forgeten, and that was sene.
For al the woode was waxen grene . . .
410–14

But within it meet human beings whose losses are, in human terms final. Paths lead into the forest and disappear. The dog who briefly joins the Dreamer soon flees into its depths. The hart eludes the hunters in its recesses. The hart/heart sound echoes through the poem. The Man in Black tells the story of his heart: how he entrusted it to the God of Love, how it was captivated by the lady's glance, how he feared it would break at her first refusal of him, how at last their hearts were 'so evene a payre' (1289) that they felt all woe and joy equally. 'Where is she now?' (1298) asks the Dreamer. The knight has forgotten his sorrow in reliving the past. Now he seems to turn to stone. 'She ys ded!' (1309). The hunters return, 'al was doon, / For that tyme, the hert-hunting' (1312–13) and the Dreamer wakes.

For poet and patron there must have been advantages in the fictive quality of the story. Chaucer does not intrude upon John of Gaunt's actual grief or lack of grief. And he need not himself be embarrassed by factual particulars in his exploration of devotion and bereavement. He paints absolutes of love, beauty, goodness and sorrow. Like other medieval love poets, he focuses here on courtship rather than on marriage. The realities of marriage in medieval society may well account for this idealisation of desire. The lady of romance, like the Madonna she so often resembles, has little to do with the exhausted housewives at one end of the social scale and the political pawns at the other. The arranged marriages of the rich encouraged the reaction that love could occur only outside marriage. In his later poetry Chaucer will be as interested in marriage as in falling in love. In romance, fabliau and saint's life he will discuss the marital relationship. Here he focuses on courtship and courtliness, on chaste devotion and the virtues of its object.

The courtesy of the court poet is one reason for the delicacy and indirection of the narrative. But through the obliquities of the fiction Chaucer not only diverts our gaze from the private history of the great lord but makes us aware of the literary convention and personal bias which shape our perceptions. A dream inspired by a book misunderstood, a view through windows painted with a poem, a conversation at cross-purposes. These are the media in which the radiance of the lovely, absent, dead White is reflected and survives. White shares and reflects the beauty and goodness, the power, pity and courtliness of the Madonna but she is both more and less real. The perfection of the Virgin is a kind of ontological proof of itself. The perfection of the courtly lady is an ideal precariously sustained in the imperfect conditions of life. In the *ABC* the Madonna is trusted to lead us 'into the hye tour / Of Paradys' (153–4): the experience of the poem is to close in the felicity of heaven. The dream of the duchess leads back into itself, into the castle on the hill, and back to 'the book that I hadde red' (1326). In later dream poems Chaucer gestures towards others' visions of heaven but defines his own arena as this world; in his later heroines he investigates how experience resists authority and authority shapes experience.

3

Two Misfits: The Nun and the Wife

Ther was also a Nonne . . .
          CT ɪ 118

A good Wif was ther . . .
          CT ɪ 445

Of the 'nyne and twenty' pilgrims whom Chaucer joins for the journey to Canterbury, only three are women: the Prioress, the Second Nun and the Wife of Bath. All three tell a story, but in the *General Prologue* there are portraits only of the Prioress and the Wife. Whereas the men are defined in terms of a large number of professions – knight, innkeeper, parson, ploughman, merchant, lawyer, etc. – we see women in only two roles; the nun and the married woman. Each is defined in terms of sexuality or its renunciation, each defined, in a sense, in relation to men.

Any modern feminist would be likely to notice this contrast and to find it unjust. But how far are modern and feminist ideas about justice, equality, cultural conditioning, personal growth and self-realisation appropriate in discussing medieval literature? Are not our ideas of character and self-expression anachronistic and irrelevant, the products of Romantic individualism and Victorian liberalism? Perhaps Chaucer regarded his characters primarily as performers of God-appointed roles and saw very few roles for women. Perhaps the pilgrims, men and women, are defined entirely in terms of vocation, not appreciated for unique personal qualities but assessed according to how well they fit their stations in life. The appropriate question may be not 'What sort of person is this?' but 'How well does this creature fulfil his/her obligations as monk, knight, wife, nun, etc.?' And, even within these terms, men may be permitted more variety than women. Medieval society was considered by some political theorists to consist of three estates –

those who work, those who fight and those who pray – and women were sometimes lumped together as a fourth estate.[1]

The two portraits in the General Prologue exemplify the two major roles for women in fourteenth-century England.[2] Neither woman fits her role perfectly. This may suggest that women are depraved or that the roles are constricting and deforming. The Prioress is described as 'nat undergrowe' (I 156). Perhaps she would feel it cramping to compress herself within her role. The Wife of Bath knows much about 'wandrynge by the weye' (467), as if she were straying beyond the outlines of hers. Behind the nun and the wife stand the archetypal figures of Mary and Eve, model and reproach. Between them many contrasts are implied. The two women are as different as they could be – one of many reasons why only two portraits can say so much – but the differences are not between poverty, chastity and obedience in the nun and contented marital love, family life and motherhood in the wife. We do not see the nun in private prayer or the wife caring for a husband and children.

Contrasts and criticisms are implied, not stated. Chaucer does not overtly judge the characters he describes in the General Prologue. Or, in as far as he judges, his verdicts are nearly always ostensibly favourable. Most of the pilgrims are described as 'gentil', 'worthy' or the best examples of their kind that you could meet. It is left to the audience to evaluate the character from the apparently haphazard collection of attributes reported by the narrator. The narrator, indeed, seems so naive that critics sometimes treat 'Chaucer the pilgrim' as another fictional character on the pilgrimage and quite distinct from 'Chaucer the poet'.[3]

The portrait of the Prioress is a study in role-playing and a joke against it. The standard accounts analyse how she falls short as a nun, though the pilgrims, including the narrator, find her attractive as a woman. She breaks the rules of her order by indulging in personal adornment, by keeping pets, and, indeed, by going on the pilgrimage. But before we consider the conflicting roles of nun and lady, let me suggest that Chaucer has deftly exposed something more fundamental: the Prioress is playing the role of being a woman. It seems obvious now that 'masculinity' and 'femininity' are largely socially constructed. Chaucer almost certainly believed thay were innate. But he does not depict them as natural, in the sense of being spontaneous or taken for granted. Masculinity and femininity carry great charges of anxiety and power in his poems. They are not merely maleness and femaleness but are attributes that men and women can cultivate and parade. The Prioress is a virtuoso performer. She is one of those women who seem to be engaged in a continuous act of female impersonation.[4]

The first point made in the description is that her smile is 'symple and coy'. 'Symple', here, is an example of the first set of definitions of the word in the *OED*: 'Free from duplicity, dissimulation or guile, innocent and harmless; undesigning, honest, open, straight-forward . . . Free from . . . ostentation or display; unpretentious . . . Free from elaboration or artificiality; artless; unaffected; plain; unadorned.' But if a smile is described as unaffected, its naturalness comes into question. Later details in the portrait ('peyned hire to counterfete cheere / Of court, and to been estatliche of manere / And to ben holden digne of reverence') suggest that Madame Eglantyne is striving for effect.

'Coy' is another double-edged word. Derived ultimately from the Latin *quietus*, it may mean only 'quiet, still', but it may be beginning its slide into implications of affectation and flirtatiousness. Here is the *OED* definition: 'Of a person: displaying modest backwardness or shyness (sometimes with emphasis on the displaying); not responding readily to familiar advances; now *esp.* of a girl or young woman'. The Host seems to think the adjective proper only for women. He tells the Clerk, 'Ye ryde as coy and stille as dooth a mayde' (iv 2) when he wants to spur him into some manly self-assertion. Soon it will suggest not only femininity but contrivance. There is also an idiom, 'to make it coy', which the *OED* first cites in 1529 and defines: 'to affect reserve, shyness or disdain'. The combined connotations of 'symple and coy' range from suggesting a silent, self-denying, celibate withdrawal from the world and a self-conscious, consciously feminine, almost flirtatious concern with it. John Livingstone Lowes has investigated the occurrences of the phrase in other medieval poetry and finds 'simple et coie' particularly common in French pastoral.[5] The genre, like the Prioress, is dedicated to the artifice of innocence. She seems like the religious equivalent of a china shepherdess.

The portrait continues to suggest coyness in the modern sense with its praise of the Prioress's ladylike oath, 'St Loy', and the details of her fastidious table manners. Consideration for others can hardly be wrong and the medieval imagination (as we saw in the *ABC*) had found a place for courtesy in Christianity. Yet it seems incongruous to single out neatness at table as a salient character-istic of one who has renounced the world and to give it more space in the description than any other feature. It contributes to an air of 'gentility' (also in the modern sense) about the portrait of the bourgeois lady, with her East London French 'after the scole of Stratford atte Bowe' (I 125), who tries 'to countrefete cheere of court' (139–40) and follow the most fashionable models. I described her mild expletive as 'ladylike' but, if Hotspur's sense of social nuance two centuries later is relevant here ('Swear me, Kate, like a lady, as thou art, / A good mouth-filling oath' – 1 Henry V III 251–2), it also places her as genteel, fitting to neither court nor convent. The encomium on her table manners may have had amorous, as well as worldly, associations for its audience. Its source is a passage in the Romance of the Rose where a young lady is advised on how to behave fetchingly in order to attract a suitor.[6]

The Prioress certainly attracts the narrator. She is pretty, polite, friendly and sweet-natured. But is she not altogether too charming? Adjectives and adverbs used in the portrait include 'symple and coy' (119), 'ful semely' (123, 136), 'faire and fetisly' (124), 'ful plesaunt, and amyable of port' (138), 'charitable' (143), 'pitous' (143). The words have worldly connotations or are ambiguous or are applied in unexpected ways. Continually the suggestion is of a daintiness, a preoccupation with effect, a fondness for worldly objects unbecoming to a religious. She has a flair for dress which can make even her nun's habit stylish. Her rosary, of fine coral with a gold pendant, doubles as a bracelet. Her wimple, 'ful semely . . . pynched' (151), becomes more decorative than decorous: contrary to the rules, it reveals her high forehead, a particularly admired feature in this period. Her looks are described in the stock vocabulary of romantic poetry: 'hir nose tretys, hir eyen greye as glas' (152). Her mouth is small, like that of a heroine of romance, and her lips are not only red but (a moment of quite inappropriate fantasy!) 'softe' (153). Her fragrant name might come from a love poem. The entry to the new life of the religious is symbolised by the assumption of a new name. We should expect a saint's name, not 'Madame Eglantyne', for a nun who has renounced her worldly identity. Details such as these are commonplace in medieval satire against nuns but Chaucer does not include the slur of unchastity which usually accompanies them. The Prioress is compromising rather than committing major sin. She herself seems hardly conscious of her deviations from the austere path of perfection. The ambiguities of the description dramatise her self-deception. Her singing of the divine service is 'semely': appropriate for the worship of God or becoming in the eyes of men? Her sensitivity to the sufferings of animals is her version of Christian qualities of

'conscience' and 'tendre herte'. The ambiguities culminate in the
emblem on her rosary: *Amor Vincit Omnia* (Love conquers all) –
human love or divine?

In an excellent essay on the images of women in Chaucer, Hope
Phyllis Weissman argues that the Prioress has made the wrong
choice of the two approved role models available, the courtly lady
and the Madonna.[7] I think that the portrait is yet more complex. The
Prioress is her own work of art and, like greater artists in the later
Middle Ages, she produces a synthesis of human and divine. She
does model herself on the Madonna and her comic confusions are
nourished by the contemporary emphasis on the humanity of
Mary. Madame Eglantyne is described in terms used in lyrics which
might be secular or religious, since the same vocabulary expresses
the adoration of mistress or of Madonna. The visual arts contribute
to the effect. Her 'symple' (artless?) smile is fashionable in the
spiritual sphere: the tender smile on the face of the Madonna
develops in the sculpture of the fourteenth century. Jill Mann has
demonstrated that nuns were positively recommended to view
their vocation in a romantic light, that there was a 'tradition of
translating the role of the courtly heroine into a religious sphere'.
This translation occurs in sermons as well as in satires. 'In the
serious ideal . . . Christ, in his role as the nun's heavenly Bride-
groom . . . is discussed in terms appropriate to a courtly lover.'[8]

The Prioress manifests the loving-kindness and ready emotions
of late medieval piety,[9] though her objects are not the conventional
ones. She has a prized spiritual talent, the gift of tears, but she
weeps if her dogs are beaten or killed, rather than over the
scourging and passion of Christ.[10] She should not have had pets at
all, much less weep over them or spoil them with expensive food
when people were starving. But we can understand why she did.
Pets were forbidden in religious houses and the authorities waged
war against them for centuries in vain. The dogs and cats always got
back. They must have met some emotional needs for a large number
of people who were in religious orders but had no religious
vocation. The Prioress is clearly one of these. On the sternest view,
her dogs arouse idolatrous devotion which should be offered to
God.[11] A more humane response is that they are a godsend to her
affectionate nature. They are surrogates for the children she cannot
have. This aspect of the Prioress, her yearnings and the limitations
in her experience, finds expression in her Tale.

The *Prioress's Tale* is the only Canterbury Tale whose central
character is a child. It begins with a prayer. The first stanza is

addressed to the Lord, whose glory is exalted not only by great men but by babes and sucklings, as it will be by the boy in her Tale, living and dead. The rest of the Invocation extols the Virgin, 'the white lylye flour / Which that the bar and is a mayde alway' (VII 461–2). In the last lines the speaker casts herself as an infant, 'as a child of twelf month oold, or lesse, / That can unnethes any word expresse' (484–5), too weak to bear the weight of praising the Virgin and needing her guidance in telling the story.

The Tale is about the murder of a Christian child by a community of Jews in Asia. The boy is seven years old and the son of a widow. He is taught the hymn '*Alma Redemptoris*' by an older schoolboy, who cannot explain the Latin words but knows that it is sung in honour of the Virgin. The younger child memorises the hymn and sings it as he walks through the Jews' street on his way to and from school. Satan inspires the Jews to kill him and throw his body into a cesspit. His mother, distracted with grief, searches for him and asks the Jews in vain if they have seen him. But the child's body, with its throat cut, miraculously continues to sing the '*Alma Redemptoris*' from the pit. The crime is thus discovered and the Jews are tortured and executed. The boy's body continues to sing, until a grain placed on his tongue by the Virgin Mary at the moment of death is removed and she releases his soul and takes it to her.

This story evidently has considerable sentimental appeal for the Prioress. Just as in the Invocation she could regard the Virgin Mary as model and mother, so in the Tale she can identify with both the anguished widow and the innocent child. She is entranced by the pathos of the murder and the vulnerable charm of the young boy, whom she repeatedly describes as 'litel'. His ignorance makes him even sweeter, a kind of holy fool, singing a sacred hymn of which he does not understand the words. Childishness and sanctity merge in his song, unstoppable in the street of the Jews, unquenchable by death. He exemplifies the Christian promise that the humble shall be exalted by his triumph over death. The heavenly Mother takes him to her and he follows the Lamb in the New Jerusalem with the white procession of virgin martyrs. He makes vivid the meaning of the Christian command to become as little children. His legend has the power of simplicity with its absolutes of black and white, its wicked Jews inspired by Satan and its pure little hero supported by the Virgin Mother, its total poetic justice. The pilgrims are silent with emotion when it ends.

It is obviously a highly dangerous story. The *Canterbury Tales* are full of sex and violence but the gentle Prioress tells the only story that could seriously corrupt anybody. Beside her Tale the cynical Pardoner's account of his avaricious sharp practices seems harmless. My reaction is inevitable for a late twentieth-century reader and it may be anachronistic. But it probably is not. The Church had prohibited dissemination of rumours of ritual murders of Christian children by Jews. This Tale not only relates an event which took place once upon a time far away in Asia but brings it up to the moment with its final prayer to 'yonge Hugh of Lincoln, slayn also / With cursed Jewes, as it is notable, / For it is but a litel while ago' (VII 684–6).

The Prioress's allusions to Jewish tradition seem to emphasise her inability to grasp the implications of her narrative. Her comparison of the Virgin Mary to the 'bussh unbrent, brennynge in Moyses sight' (468) is a traditional piece of typology, which Chaucer also uses in the *ABC*, but the reminder of God's revelation to Moses seems at odds with her description of the Jewish heart as the wasp's nest of Satan (558–9). The grieving mother is also presented in an Old Testament figure: She is a 'newe Rachel'. The story of Rachel prefigures, the *Prioress's Tale* recalls Herod's Slaughter of the Innocents. But that massacre was of *Jewish* children, though they were to be co-opted as the first Christian martyrs, and re-enactments of it were fomented by stories such as these. Ironically, the story advocates the 'eye for an eye, tooth for a tooth' ethic that Jesus wanted to amend. The provost remarks 'Yvele shal have that yvele wol deserve' (632) before putting the Jews to death.

I am presenting an interpretation which is, in more than one sense, partial. I am emphasising the negative aspect of the Tale, its cruelty and prejudice. Other critics have been moved, like the pilgrims, by its pathos and devotion.[12] It belongs to the spiritual tradition of 'affective piety', playing on profound emotions for the purposes of awe and prayer. It could be argued that the other purposes to which these emotions have been roused are irrelevant to Chaucer's poem. I am also dwelling on the dramatic aspect of the Tale, viewing it as an expression of the Prioress's charm and limitation. The relationship of story to narrator is certainly variable throughout the *Canterbury Tales*: sometimes it is obviously close and significant, sometimes apparently perfunctory.[13] All readers would agree that this miracle of Our Lady is a generally apt Tale for the Prioress; not all would wish to analyse its details for what they yield about her psychology. Some critics have used the dramatic approach in defence of the Tale. It has been described as a kind of fairy-story, appropriate to the childlike nature of its teller.[14] This, of course, is precisely what is wrong with it.[15] If we are tempted to think of it as taking place in a Never-never-land remote from actual life, the closing reference to Hugh of Lincoln jolts us back into the horrors of the actual world. And this is what the Prioress knows little about. She is in some ways not 'worldly' enough. She lives at a level of moral theory to which no adult is entitled. This emotional immaturity is not necessarily due to the convent or to the Christian ideal of virginity. It is inseparable from the cultivation of ignorance as delectably intrinsic to femininity.

The *Prioress's Tale* may be wicked but the Prioress is not. Like the child in her story, who sings a song which he does not understand, she is not exactly conscious of what she is expressing: affection and affectation, religious grace and social graces, love human, divine and animal. These are certainly different aspects of *Amor* but the lesser versions are imperfect rather than evil. The Prioress is, probably through no fault of her own, in the wrong kind of life. She has adapted her role until she can play it prettily and even be applauded for it.

One moral we can draw from the contrast between the Prioress and the Wife of Bath will be more unpalatable to the feminist than to the sexist. Gentle sabotage will get you further than open rebellion. This, though not a very moral moral, has some psychological truth. As the narrator of the *Franklin's Tale* suggests, the distinction between self-sacrifice and self-interest may not be absolute: 'Pacience is a heigh vertue . . . For it venquysseth . . . Thynges that rigor sholde nevere atteyne' (v 773–5). So perhaps patience, rather than honesty, is the best policy. The Prioress quietly bends all the rules and no one even notices. The pilgrims, including apparently the narrator, think she is lovely. She inspires even the bossy Host to courtesy; her story, so horrific to modern sensibilities and probably also to informed contemporary opinion, unites the noisy bickering pilgrims in awed silence. The Wife of Bath questions the rules and assorted clerics in her audience – Friar, Pardoner, Clerk and Parson – close ranks against her.

The Prioress is indeed extremely 'feminine'. She emanates an excess of misplaced femininity, though in a very sexist society no one is likely to complain of that. Ironically, she is considerably more seductive than the much-married Wife of Bath. The Wife seems, like many feminists, not very 'feminine'. In her own Prologue she gives the astrological explanation: she was born under the contradictory influences of Venus and Mars. Venus contributed her 'likerousnesse', Mars her 'hardynesse' (iii 609–12).[16] In the portrait in the *General Prologue* her martial qualities are very evident and compromise her conventional feminine attributes: spinning, dressing smartly and husband-hunting. Like the Virtuous Woman of the Book of Proverbs, she spins and makes fine linen, but this traditional female skill is presented in terms of capitalism and competition, not service and self-abnegation.[17] She is a successful businesswoman, surpassing even the renowned clothmakers of the Low Countries, and so proud of herself that she is out of all charity if anyone takes precedence over her in church. She has evidently taken a lot of trouble and spent a lot of money on her outfit – a traditional female vanity, according to the satirists – but the general effect is more strident than seductive. Despite her nun's habit, there is something gauzy about the Prioress. The Wife's attire seems loud ('Hir hosen weren of fyn scarlet reed' – 1456), heavy ('Hir coverchiefs . . . weyden ten pound' – 454), and abrasive ('spores sharpe' – 473). Unlike the Prioress with her 'coy' smile, the Wife talks and laughs freely. Whereas the Prioress strains ('peyned hire' – 139) to comport herself correctly, the Wife is vulgarly relaxed and sits 'esily' (469) on her ambler. The effect of masculinity is reinforced by her hat, 'As brood as is a bokeler or a targe' (471), and her vast experience in 'wandrynge by the weye' (467). She is a parody of a knight-errant. The narrator exclaims over the *weight* of her headdress as one might over a soldier's armour or equipment.

'Wandrynge by the weye' has further implications. Has the Wife been on too many pilgrimages, married too many times, done too much, seen too much, thought too much? The Prioress, by contrast, despite the blurring of her Rule, is inexperienced: she knows the French of Stratford-at-Bow but has never been to Paris. At the beginning of her Prologue the Wife backs experience against authority. She is a latter-day Eve, repeating the original sin of intellectual curiosity when she should comply in obedience.[18] She *deviates* rather than following a straight and narrow path. And her intellectual presumption leads her into direct conflict with the masculine exponents of orthodoxy, the clerks. We are told in the *General Prologue* that she is 'somdel deef' (446) and learn in her own Prologue that it is the result of a blow from her fifth husband, an ex-clerk. She is also partly deaf – not absolutely – to the voice of authority.

The five marriages suggest more than intellectual desires. She is 'gat-tothed' (468), a physiognomic sign of a lecherous nature, and there is the suggestion, in her 'wandrynge by the weye' (467) and knowledge of 'the olde daunce' (476) that she has also been adulterous. The narrator does not commit himself on this point. 'Withouten oother compaignye in youthe' (461) is ambiguous. It may mean that she did have lovers in youth or that she did not. The next line, 'But therof nedeth nat to speke as nowthe' (462), is usually taken to be incriminating. I think that the second line may compound, rather than dissolve, the ambiguity of the couplet. We learn at the opening of the Wife's own Prologue that she was first married at twelve, the earliest age according to canon law. She was sold off to a rich husband at the first opportunity. Was she therefore cheated out of a normal romantic life at the proper stage? Does the narrator drop the subject because the poet is to complicate it further in the Wife's own Prologue?

The two portraits of women in the *General Prologue* say a great deal. But there is one major female experience which is absent. Neither woman is a mother. The Prioress, a celibate, has an imaginary child while she tells her Tale. The Wife of Bath, though she has been married five times, seems to be childless. If she has had children, surely she would say so. She says almost everything else. She knows about 'remedies of love' (I 475), which may suggest contraceptive practices. The frank enjoyment of sex described in her Prologue shows that her intentions are by orthodox standards perverse, that, like Chaunticleer, she makes love 'moore for delit than world to multiplye' (VII 3345). In her Prologue she quotes God's command to increase and multiply as a literal justification for sex and marriage (III 28) without clinching her argument by adducing the evidence of children. There could be a natural explanation: her first three marriages were to old men and by the time she was free to marry the younger husbands of her choice she was middle-aged herself. The abuse she puts into the mouths of her first three husbands suggests literal as well as metaphorical barrenness:

> Thou liknest eek wommenes love to helle,
> To bareyne lond, ther water may nat dwelle.
> Thou liknest it also to wilde fyr;
> The moor it brenneth, the moore it hath desir
> To consume every thyng that brent wole be.
>
> III 371–5

In contrast to the Madonna's virgin motherhood, which the Prioress likens to the bush that burned and was not consumed (VII 468), the Wife fears that her barren sexuality resembles wild fire, destructive and insatiable. Both women, the nun and the wife, seem in their totally different ways, to be doing what they can with roles which have proved unfulfilling.

The oldest profession – prostitution – is not represented on the pilgrimage. We may note, however, in passing, that the Shipman's boat is called the 'Maudelayne'. An ambiguity to rank with *Amor Vincit Omnia.*

4

The Amazon and the Wise Woman, or 'God Knows What She Thought'

> Whilom, as olde stories tellen us,
> Ther was a duk that highte Theseus;
> Of Atthenes he was lord and governour,
> And in his tyme swich a conquerour,
> That gretter was ther noon under the sonne.
> Ful many a riche contree hadde he wonne;
> What with his wysdom and his chivalrie,
> He conquered al the regne of Femenye,
> That whilom was ycleped Scithia,
> And weddede the queene Ypolita,
> And broght hire hoom with hym in his contree
> With muchel glorie and greet solempnytee,
> And eek hir yonge suster Emelye.
>
> *CT* I 859–71

The *Iliad* ends with the line, 'Such were the funeral rites of Hector tamer of horses'.[1] In antiquity some continuations of the epic went on to describe the arrival of Queen Penthesilea and adapted the line to 'Such were the funeral rites of Hector. And now there came an Amazon'.[2] In view of the later development of the epic tradition it is a suggestive mutation. In the stark world of the *Iliad*, our earliest work of European literature, women are primarily slaves, chattels, spoils of war. The poem opens with the quarrel of Agamemnon and Achilles over a female captive. This is the background to even the most tender of personal relationships. Hector foretells that after his death Andromache will be sold into slavery to sleep with her master and work for his wife. At the funeral of Patroclus the voices of his comrades are joined by a chorus of women slaves who lament for the dead warrior but are really grieving for themselves.[3] But the female characters of the *Odyssey* are not pathetic. Odysseus is supported by the powerful goddess Athene, seduced by the enchanting Circe and Calypso, impressed by the courageous young princess Nausicaa and inspired throughout his journeyings by the thought of his loyal wife Penelope waiting for him in Ithaca. Domestic happiness replaces military glory as the mainspring of the hero's actions.

During the medieval period the epic was succeeded as the dominant narrative form by the romance. The story of Troy generated new episodes and new characters. Love stories were devised for the heroes. The tragic passion of Troilus and Criseyde evolves from characters who were little more than•names in antiquity.

Chaucer wrote two long narratives set in the classical past, *Troilus and Criseyde* and the *Knight's Tale*. The *Knight's Tale* is a romance which has descended from the epic. It is a latter-day variation on the other great tragic saga of antiquity, the story of Thebes. It is ultimately derived from Statius's *Thebaid* but its immediate source is Boccaccio's *Teseida*, a story of love and war. Chaucer adapts Boccaccio's poem, not departing from the main outline but making excisions and additions of his own. The *Knight's Tale* is much shorter than the *Teseida*. Chaucer cuts most of the military narrative, emphasising the cost of war rather than its glory. In the world of the *Knight's Tale* we are never allowed to forget that, in love and war, one person's gain is another's loss. And more of his poem deals with love than with war.

The *Knight's Tale* begins with the victory of Theseus over the Amazons, the 'regne of Femenye' (1 866) and his dynastic marriage to their queen Hippolyta. On a simple iconographic level Theseus, in conquering the Amazons, asserts male supremacy over the unnatural race of warrior women.[4] In marrying him Hippolyta abandons her monstrous regiment in favour of the conventional role of wife. These mighty rulers from the mythical past are symbols of opposing ways of life now reconciled. The founder of Athens, source of western civilisation and philosophy, tames the 'barbarous Scythian', from classical times to *King Lear* the emblem of savagery. He rides back to Athens with due pomp, taking with him his wife 'And eek hir yonge suster Emelye' (871). Emily is an object and an appendage in this opening paragraph – does she feel honoured or exiled by her transportation to Athens? – and she remains passive throughout the Tale, though she is the cause of its main action. In her helplessness she is an ironic inversion of the Unmoved Mover of the grand cosmic scheme which Theseus expounds at the end.

Throughout the poem Emily tends to be relegated to the second half of a line or the end of a sentence, as if she were tacked on as an afterthought. She is often, as at her first appearance, a syntactical adjunct to her sister the queen. Theseus is deflected on his journey home 'And sente anon Ypolita the queene / And Emelye hir yonge suster sheene, / Unto the toun of Atthenes' (971–3). In the second part of the poem Theseus goes hunting 'with his Ypolita, the faire queene, / And Emelye, clothed al in grene' (1685–6). When he condemns to death Palamon and Arcite, the two young Thebans who have disobeyed his orders for love of Emily, 'the queene anon, for verray wommanhede, / Gan for to wepe, and so dide Emelye' (1748–9). He decides to show mercy 'At the request of the queene that kneleth heere, / And eek of Emelye' (1819–20). In Part IV strict protocol is observed as the nobles ride to the tournament which will decide Emily's future, Theseus, then Palamon and Arcite, 'And after rode the queene and Emelye' (2571) and are seated, 'Theseus ful riche and hye, / Ypolita the queene, and Emelye' (2578). When the victor Arcite dies, there is more grief than at the death of Hector and for Arcite, as for Patroclus, women weep who have their own priorities: ' "Why woldestow be deed,' thise wommen crye, / 'And haddest gold ynough, and Emelye?" ' (2835–6). To Arcite's funeral 'com this woful Theban Palamoun ... And passynge othere of wepynge, Emelye' (2882, 2885). In the funeral procession walk Egeus, the old father of Theseus, Theseus, 'Palamon, with ful greet compaignye; / And after that cam woful Emelye' (2910–11). After several years Theseus, who wishes to make an alliance between Athens and Thebes, decides that Palamon and Emily should marry; 'For which this noble Theseus anon / Leet senden after gentil Palamon ... Tho sente Theseus for Emelye' (2975–6, 2980).

In all these passages Emily appears as addition or object or both. She is a very passive heroine, more passive than the lady Chaucer found in the *Teseida*. I shall discuss the implications of three changes Chaucer made to this character, all of which serve to detach her from the romantic interest she inspires. The first is simply the omission of a detail from Book I of the *Teseida*, most of which Chaucer passes over as 'to long to heere' (875). In Boccaccio's poem the wedding of Teseo and Ipolita is described, other Athenians marry other Amazons and Teseo plans a marriage between Emilia and his cousin Acate. Chaucer mentions only the marriage of Theseus and Hippolyta and cuts all the description of the festivities. The *Knight's Tale* is not a world hospitable to celebration: human suffering has a tendency, as Theseus soon discovers, to 'perturben' the 'feste with criynge' (906). The Tale begins with a wedding and a funeral, it ends with a funeral and a wedding, but the funerals are given far more space. And Chaucer's heroine is from the outset less nubile than Boccaccio's. There is no marriage lined up for her as she rides towards Athens.

Theseus's triumphal journey is interrupted by the supplications of some weeping ladies dressed in black, the first of several sharp contrasts made in the Tale between joy and grief, Fortune's favourites and Fortune's victims. These mourners were all once queens or duchesses but their husbands have fallen in battle at Thebes and King Creon refuses to bury their bodies. Theseus takes pity on the women and rides to Thebes to redress their wrongs. He sacks the city and buries the bodies of their husbands. In the ecological system of the *Knight's Tale* this act of mercy produces further suffering and more bodies. The pillagers, the vultures of the medieval battlefield, get to work and discover in a heap of corpses two young men, half-dead, half-alive. They are Palamon and Arcite, cousins and blood-brothers, of the Theban royal house, and Theseus condemns them to perpetual imprisonment in Athens.

II

This passeth yeer by yeer and day by day,
Til it fil ones, in a morwe of May,
That Emelye, that fairer was to sene
Than is the lylie upon his stalke grene,
And fressher than the May with floures newe –
For with the rose colour stroof hire hewe,
I noot which was the fyner of hem two –
Er it were day, as was hir wone to do,
She was arisen and al redy dight,
For May wole have no slogardie anyght.
The sesoun priketh every gentil herte,
And maketh it out of his slep to sterte,

And seith 'Arys, and do thyn observaunce.'
This maked Emyele have remembraunce
To doon honour to May, and for to ryse.
Yclothed was she fressh, for to devyse:
Hir yellow heer was broyded in a tresse
Bihynde hir bak, a yerde long, I gesse.
And in the gardyn, at the sonne upriste,
She walketh up and down, and as hire liste
She gadereth floures, party white and rede,
To make a subtil gerland for hire hede;
And as an aungel hevenysshly she soong.

CT i 1033–55

Some years later, Palamon and Arcite see Emily from the window of
their prison in the tower and fall in love with her. Here again,
Chaucer's radiant description of Emily presents a rather different
girl from the equivalent passage in the *Teseida*.[5] As Emily walks in
the garden, she sings and gathers flowers. Boccaccio tells us twice
that Emilia sings songs of love, 'beautiful love songs with an angelic
voice'.[6] Chaucer omits the love songs and emphasises the angelic
quality. His Emily sounds celestial, other-worldly, perhaps even
asexual: 'as an aungel hevenysshly she soong' (1055). Boccaccio's
heroine plucks 'the fresh rose', the symbol of love, 'weaving many
other flowers with it into a garland for her golden hair'.[7] Emilia, a
girl with a rose in a garden, becomes an erotic miniature of that
great backdrop of love and sex, the *Romance of the Rose*. Chaucer
makes this association less specific, not mentioning the rose by
name and not giving it pride of place in the garland: 'She gadereth
floures, party white and rede, / To make a subtil gerland for hire
hede' (1053–4). In case we are tempted to identify and decode the
flowers, the roses of love are mingled with the lilies of purity.

There is also a crucial difference in her response to the young
prisoners – or rather, there is no response at all. Chaucer's Emily is
unaware of their presence and their admiration. They adore her for
years with no hope of reciprocation, not only because of their
sentences of life imprisonment and Arcite's later exile on pain of
death, but because she knows nothing at all of their feelings. As
Theseus deflatingly puts it in the forest scene, 'She woot namoore of
al this hoote fare, / By God, than woot a cokkow or an hare!' (1809–
10). Boccaccio's Emilia, however, hears and sees the young men,
feels flattered by their attention, and takes care to look even better

the next time she walks in the garden: 'At the sound of that "alas" the young girl quickly turned to her left and her eyes flew straight away nowhere else but to the little window . . . as she went away she was not unmindful of that "alas", and although she was as yet a maiden unready for love's fulfilment, she was nonetheless aware of what it implied. And thinking that she knew the truth of the matter, she rejoiced in being found attractive and thought herself lovelier and made herself look fairer the next time she went into that garden.'[8]

Palamon and Arcite fall in love instantly, hopelessly and irrevocably with this girl glimpsed from their prison window. The convention of love at first sight is stretched to its extreme. The young men disown all their previous affection and loyalty to each other, become deadly rivals for this unattainable lady, and dispute over which of them has the stronger claim to her. It is preposterous but it is also intensely convincing. The prison and the adjacent garden are further emblems of grief and joy. Emily is more visionary than erotic and she is a vision of freedom. The May morning stirs her from sleep and she rises in harmony with nature, 'as was hir wone to do' (1040) before dawn. Palamon cannot respond spontaneously to such impulses. He rises 'as was his wone, by leve of his gayler' (1064). We are told several times that he roams up and down in his chamber. It sounds like the pacing of the caged tiger. Emily roams up and down, wherever she wishes, in the garden. Her angelic song suggests that she is hardly subject to the confines of a mortal body. Palamon wonders aloud whether she is a woman or a goddess.[9]

Emily also has a kind of inner freedom. The *Knight's Tale* is deeply influenced by one of Chaucer's favourite books, the *Consolation of Philosophy*. Both are examples of a philosophical prison literature which derives ultimately from Plato.[10] Boethius wrote the *Consolation* when he was in exile and on a capital charge. He was later put to death. The *Consolation* takes the form of a dialogue between Boethius and the allegorical figure of Philosophy, who insists to him that much of his suffering is self-inflicted. True happiness springs from inner sources. The Emperor could not imprison him or exile him from home or deprive him of his possessions in any important sense. Only he could imprison himself in grief and exile himself from his true nature and overvalue the transient gifts of Fortune. The *Knight's Tale* investigates freedom in these Boethian terms. Palamon and Arcite imprison themselves a second time, and perhaps more seriously, when they are captivated by Emily. The physical imprisonment means little to them by comparison. When Arcite is released from the tower but forbidden ever to return to Athens, he regards his freedom as a worse form of imprisonment:

> He seyde, 'Allas that day that I was born!
> Now is my prisoun worse than biforn;
> Now is me shape eternally to dwelle,
> Noght in purgatorie but in helle . . .
> 1223–6

> O deere cosyn Palamon,' quod he,
> 'Thyn is the victorie of this aventure.
> Ful blisfully in prison maistow dure –
> In prison? Certes nay, but in paradys!'
> 1234–7

The prison from whch he can look at Emily is now defined as paradise; freedom away from her is hell. The *Knight's Tale* is the source for *A Midsummer Night's Dream* and surely this speech influenced Hermia's account of the 'blessings' of being in love:

> Before the time I did Lysander see,
> Seem'd Athens as a paradise to me.
> O then what graces in my love do dwell,
> That it hath turn'd a heaven into a hell.
> ɪ i 204–7

For both Arcite and Hermia love reverses all previous values and destroys earlier loyalties and friendships. Arcite presents a peculiar variation on the Boethian idea of the true happiness that a prisoner can enjoy in his cell. Hermia worships love for its power to make her life a misery. Emily, by contrast, is serene. She can enjoy the beauty of the May morning because she is not in a prison of the psyche. She walks 'in maiden meditation, fancy-free' (ɪɪ i 164); perhaps she inspired this Shakespearian description of the freedom of chastity.

Yet Emily is not free. No one in the *Knight's Tale* is. The Tale investigates the question of human freedom and its answer is mainly negative. Gods, Fortune and Destiny dominate the events in the Tale. The weeping queens who appeal to Theseus are the first emblem of human helplessness. Arcite advises Palamon to 'taak al in pacience / Oure prisoun, for it may noon oother be' (1084–5) – until he too sees Emily. The contrasts between Theseus and the widows, Theseus and the prisoners, the prisoners and Emily, the prison and the garden make vivid the vicissitudes of Fortune. But the powerful and the fortunate are not free either. The world which Theseus rules and tries to order is at the mercy of supernatural powers which seem largely indifferent to human feeling. He finally describes life itself as a 'foul prisoun' (3061) from which Arcite has escaped. Emily is not free because the conditions of human life permit little or no freedom. But she is less free even than the other characters in the Tale because she is a woman.

This begins to emerge in the scene in the forest. Both lovers are now at large. Arcite has secretly returned from exile, Palamon escapes from prison and the two meet unexpectedly 'at unset stevene' (1524) in a wood. They agree to battle to the death for Emily and the next day they fight like wild animals until they are interrupted by Theseus and his hunting party. Theseus's first reaction is that the disguised exile and the escaped prisoner deserve death. But the queen, Emily and all the ladies burst into tears, fall to their knees and beg him to have mercy. Their sympathy is contagious. Theseus is moved to pity, especially when he reflects on the absurd extremes to which the young are driven by love. He points out to Palamon and Arcite that Emily has been quite ignorant of their passion and that, even if they were to fight for ever, she cannot marry both of them. He devises a tournament, to be held a year later, as a way of deciding the issue. Emily is not consulted. 'I speke as for my suster Emelye' (1833), says Theseus unblushingly and promises to 'yeve Emelya to wyve' (1860) to the winner. Everyone – or almost everyone – is delighted:

> Who looketh lightly now but Palamoun?
> Who spryngeth up for joye but Arcite?
> Who kouthe telle, or who kouthe it endite,
> The joye that is maked in the place
> Whan Theseus hath doon so fair a grace?
> But down on knees wente every maner wight,
> And thonked hym with all hir herte and myght,
> And namely the Thebans . . .
>
> 1870–7

Not a word is spoken of Emily's feelings. Does she share in this general rejoicing? In Part III we learn what she wants and it is not marriage.

III

> Chaste goddesse, wel wostow that I
> Desire to ben a mayden al my lyf.
> Ne nevere wol I be no love ne wyf.
> I am, thow woost, yet of thy compaignye,
> A mayde, and love huntynge and venerye,
> And for to walken in the wodes wilde,
> And noght to ben a wyf and be with childe.
> Noght wol I knowe compaignye of man.
>
> *CT* ɪ 2304–11

During the next year Palamon and Arcite each collect a hundred knights to fight on their behalf in the tournament. Meanwhile, Theseus builds a magnificent circular arena for the spectacle. On east, west and north of this theatre he places three temples, to Venus, Mars and Diana. On the morning of the tournament Palamon, Arcite and Emily go to pray at the shrines of their presiding deities. Palamon begs Venus, goddess of love, to bestow Emily upon him and her statue signifies that his prayer will eventually be granted. Arcite petitions to Mars, the god of war, to grant him victory in the tournament and his prayer likewise seems to be approved. Only Emily's wish is denied. The pantheon mirrors human society in this.

Emily prays to Diana, goddess of chastity. It is the first and only time that we hear her speak in the poem. It seems to me that this gives her words particular force. The consensus of critical opinion is that Emily is a very dull heroine, a nonentity, because she says so little and complies so quietly.[11] But her silence itself is an eloquent sign of her predicament.[12] Are we to take more seriously the compulsive talkers of literature? On a mere numerical count of lines spoken, Polonius's opinion would outweigh Horatio's. Emily's one speech is the more vibrant for being unexpected and for saying something unexpected, like the one line of Pylades – whom the audience had perhaps supposed mute – in the *Choephoroi*.

Chaucer several times employs a narrative structure which can be summed up by the adaptation of a line from the *Merchant's Tale*: 'God knows what she thought'. A female character is viewed exclusively from the outside for a long time. Her thoughts, when we learn them, are very different from the thoughts projected on to her. May is another girl who has little say in her marriage. She is the purchase and victim of January, a rich old man of loathsome character. He talks on and on about the happiness he expects from marriage and the kind of girl he should choose. His wedding to May is described with ironic eloquence and finally 'the bryde was broght abedde as stille as stoon' (IV 1818). January's love-making sounds repulsive. At dawn he sits up in bed, with the slack skin shaking on his neck, and the narrator remarks: 'God woot what that May thoughte in hir herte' (1851). May is very quiet but her silence proves to be stealth. When we do learn her thoughts, she is thinking of a lover. At the end of the story she is magically granted the gift of a ready excuse for any wrongdoing, so that what she thinks in her heart will always be opaque to her husband.

During the first book of *Troilus and Criseyde* the heroine is seen entirely in public contexts. She does not speak at all. She is first the faithless Criseyde whose guilt is reported by the poets. As the daughter of a traitor, she attracts the suspicion and indignation of the populace. She appeals to Hector for protection, then goes home and 'held hir stille' (I 126). Troilus falls in love with her from a distance and suffers agonies of longing and despair without her knowledge. In Book II Pandarus visits Criseyde at home to plead on his behalf and in this private domestic setting we begin to learn what she is like.

The closest analogue to Emily's prayer comes in the *Parliament of Fowls*. This dream-vision contains a debate, which takes place on St Valentine's Day and is presided over by Nature, to decide the contest between three noble eagles who are rival suitors for the same female. They produce arguments and avowals very like those of Palamon and Arcite. One contends, like Palamon, that he has loved her for longer than the previous speaker. Each claims to love her more than the others and to be absolutely faithful to her for ever. All the lesser birds have their views on the matter and many have little patience with this romantic idealism. Finally Nature determines that the lady eagle should make her own choice. She replies that she does not wish to serve Venus or Cupid yet and asks for a year's respite in which to make up her mind between the lovers. Nature grants her request. The lesser birds, untroubled by such

problems of choice, joyfully take their mates and sing an exuberant
song to welcome summer and praise St Valentine for the gift of
fertility.

The lady eagle asks only for a year's grace. Sex is natural, Nature
rules the animal world and the poem ends with a chorus of mating
songs. Emily's reluctance to serve Venus and Cupid is more far-
reaching. Here again she contrasts with Boccaccio's Emilia who,
like the eagle heroine, feels unready for marriage rather than
absolutely opposed to it. Emilia prays to Diana to quench the
desires of the young men 'if it is best for me as a young maiden still
to remain among your fellowship'.[13] Emily, however, reminds the
'chaste goddesse' that 'I / Desire to ben a mayden al my lyf' (ι 2304–
5). If she must marry, Emilia asks Diana to decide between her
suitors 'for they both seem so pleasant to me that I cannot choose for
myself'.[14] Chaucer's Emily is less susceptible: this remark is
omitted.[15]

Chaucer also adds a motive which does not appear in Boccaccio:

> I am, thow woost, yet of thy compaignye,
> A mayde, and love huntynge and venerye,
> And for to walken in the wodes wilde,
> And noght to ben a wyf and be with childe.
>
> ι 2307–10

As far as I know, Emily is the only woman in English literature until
the twentieth century to express the desire not to have children,
though it seems a reasonable enough choice at a time when
childbearing was so dangerous. We have just been reminded of this
fact. Although a virgin goddess, Diana presides over childbirth. In
her temple is a grim picture of the process:

> A woman travaillynge was hir biforn;
> But for hir child so longe was unborn,
> Ful pitously Lucyna gan she calle . . .
>
> 2083–5

Diana is also the huntress, the 'chaste goddess of the wodes grene'
(2297). Hunting and chastity are juxtaposed in her temple:
'Depeynted been the walles up and doun / Of huntynge and of
shamefast chastitee' (2054–5). Her statue is clothed 'in gaude grene
. . . With bowe in hond and arwes in a cas' (2079–80). Emily is
associated with the goddess of the green woods. She loves

'huntynge and venerye / And for to walken in the wodes wilde' (2308–9). When Theseus and his hunting party come upon Palamon in the forest, Emily is 'clothed al in grene' (1686). Emily's reluctance to marry has been interpreted as conventional, the well-bred shyness of the aristocratic girl, a Madonna-like absence of sensuality.[16] But this view ignores the fact that she is an Amazon, a votary of the goddess who presides over the natural and the wild. Diana's chastity has its savage aspect. One of the paintings in her temple shows how the hunter Actaeon was transformed into a stag and eaten by his own hounds as a punishment for seeing the naked goddess bathing. (Venus, by contrast, is depicted naked in her temple.) Perhaps this myth is behind the rather distasteful lines in which the narrator emphasises that he cannot describe how Emily washed herself before the sacrifice (2282–8). He may be anxious to avoid the fate of Actaeon.

Shakespeare's Theseus has hounds so well-ordered that they bark in harmony. Like the *Knight's Tale*, *A Midsummer Night's Dream* contains a scene in which Theseus with his hunting party comes upon the errant lovers asleep in a forest. He finds a positively Chaucerian excuse for them, 'No doubt they rose up early to observe / The rite of May' (iv i 132–3), tactfully ignoring the fact that they have been out all night. He wakes them with words that remind us of the power of Nature in the *Parliament of Fowls*: 'Good morrow, friends. St Valentine is past. / Begin these woodbirds but to couple now?' (iv i 139–40). I used to think that Shakespeare had far more respect for the green world than Chaucer. Three of the five acts of *A Midsummer Night's Dream* take place in the forest and the lovers emerge from it with their problems solved. Chaotic though these three acts are, Oberon, the lord of the forest, whose personal life is so selfish and disordered, produces more harmony than Theseus with his laws, his self-control, his dynastic marriage and his musical hounds. The Theseus of the *Knight's Tale* brings the quarrel back to Athens for solution within the bounds of society. He imposes laws and restraints upon the anarchic private passion of the lovers. They must wait a year before they fight for Emily, they compete with groups of a hundred rather than in single combat, they provide a great public spectacle and entertainment and they battle – perfect image of pattern – in a circular arena. But Chaucer's Theseus, like Shakespeare's, does not have absolute control. His attempts to create order are also sabotaged, first by individual desire and then by supernatural intervention. The divine beings in the *Knight's Tale* are less benevolent than Oberon. Arcite wins the tournament, as Mars had promised, but – so that the undertakings of Venus to Palamon may also be honoured – Saturn strikes him down at the moment of his triumph. And his body is returned for its funeral to the forest. Like Shakespeare, Chaucer honours the green woods and what they represent in human nature. But unlike Shakespeare, Chaucer considers chastity as natural a power as sexuality.

Neither Theseus nor Diana grants Emily's wishes. It does not even occur to Theseus to listen to them. Like Nature in the *Parliament of Fowls*, he makes the lovers wait a year. Unlike Nature, he does not bestow the final choice on the heroine. Emily must marry but not, as in the *Parliament*, because natural sexual desire will prevail. Emily must marry because princesses are too valuable not to. Some years after Arcite's death Theseus wishes to make an alliance with Thebes. This can be cemented by a marriage between Palamon and Emily and he reconciles them to Arcite's death with his long speech about the design of the First Mover. The Creator has bound the world in a chain of love and established a duration for all creatures. The corruptible is part of a 'parfit' and 'stable' (3009) whole. It is philosophical not to rebel but to make a virtue of necessity. It is also politically expedient for Theseus. It is the kind-hearted and hard-headed solution. Emily does have a kind heart. She is moved to pity by the scene in the forest and, even in her prayer to remain unmarried, she shows compunction for the pain she is causing: she prays to Diana for her suitors as well as for herself, that they may stop loving her or fall in love with someone else. She begins to warm to Arcite during the tournament, which draws from the narrator the cynical comment: 'For wommen, as to speken in commune, / Thei folwen alle the favour of Fortune' (2681–2). It is difficult to see what else they can do when, in the *Knight's Tale*, as in the *Iliad*, they are still the victor's prize.

IV

'I grante thee lyf, if thou kanst tellen me
What thyng it is that wommen moost desiren.'
CT III 904–5

The contrast in feeling between the Wife of Bath's Prologue and

Tale is very sharp. On a first reading of the *Canterbury Tales* students usually expect her to relate some coarse witty fabliau and Chaucer may originally have intended the *Shipman's Tale*, a story of this kind, for her. Instead her racy account of her five marriages is followed by an Arthurian romance. Yet her Prologue and Tale have some common ground. Both deal with the question of sovereignty in marriage, both culminate in a victory for the wife but both conclude with a relationship more mutual, equal and contented than seemed possible. However, the endings are reached by quite different routes. The Wife in the Prologue wins by force and deceit, the Wife in the Tale by reason and *gentillesse*. The realism of autobiography is complemented by the idealism of romance. Yet it is a romance with a difference. The genre belongs to the chivalrous Knight more than to the bourgeois Alison. She appropriates it to question the assumptions of his class and sex. She prepares for the happy ending with a pillow-lecture to prove that *gentillesse* is not hereditary. And her story hinges on the question which romance despite its celebration of women so often ignores: what do women want?

The Tale takes place 'In th'olde dayes' (857) of rewards and fairies, where problems can be solved by magic and people can be transformed into the heart's desire.

> In th'olde dayes of the Kyng Arthour,
> Of which that Britons speken gret honour,
> Al was this land fulfild of fayerye.
> The elf-queene, with hir joly compaignye,
> Daunced ful ofte in many a grene mede.
> This was the old opinion, as I rede;
> I speke of manye hundred yeres ago.
> But now kan no man se none elves mo.
> For now the grete charitee and prayeres
> Of lymytours and othere hooly freres,
> That serchen every lond and every streem,
> As thikke as motes in the sonne-beem,
> Blessynge halles, chambres, kichens, boures,
> Citees, burghes, castels, hye toures,
> Thropes, bernes, shipnes, dayeryes –
> This maketh that ther ben no fayeryes.
> For ther as wont to walken was an elf,
> Ther walketh now the lymytour hymself

> In undermeles and in morwenynges,
> And seyth his matyns and his hooly thynges
> As he gooth in his lymytacioun.
> Wommen may go saufly up and doun.
> In every bussh or under every tree
> Ther is noon other incubus but he
> And he ne wol doon hem but dishonour.
>
> 857–80

Once upon a time there were fairies here. The elf-queen and her company danced in the meadows. The central character in this poem will see such a dance. But now, in these modern times, the fairies have disappeared, scattered by the ministrations of the ubiquitous friar. The friars are everywhere, busily blessing every kind of human habitation, including the 'kichenes, boures . . . dayeryes' where they will encounter women. There is now no danger of meeting an elf lover. Women may walk anywhere safely without fear of being seduced by an incubus. The friar has exorcised the demon lover and taken his place. Everywhere there is a friar saying his prayers, in every bush, under every tree, and he won't do anything to women – but dishonour them. The Church preaches a view of sex which is heavily compromised by the behaviour of the preachers themselves. There may be an element of 'quitting' here between the Wife of Bath and the Friar, who has interrupted her to exclaim on the 'long preambel' of her Prologue and who will tell the next tale. But a serious point is being made too, one which extends the argument of the Prologue: it is not only the rebellious laity who find experience at odds with authority.

The poem opens in the far-off time of chivalry, with King Arthur's court and its 'greet honour', with Britain as Fairyland, and then turns to the wife's own unromantic surroundings and the seductive insinuation of the friars. It seems as though the squalid hypocrisy of the present is being contrasted with the magical splendour of the past. But when the Wife returns to her narrative of Arthur's days, she draws the curtain on another vignette of *dishonour*:

> And so bifel that this kyng Arthur
> Hadde in his hous a lusty bacheler,
> That on a day cam ridynge fro ryver;
> And happed that, allone as he was born,

> He saugh a mayde walkynge hym biforn,
> Of which mayde anon, maugree hir heed,
> By verray force he rafte hire maydenhed.
>
> 882–8

'And so', the Wife continues, in one of those suave and baffling Chaucerian transitions. 'And so' let's go back to our main story? Or 'and *so*'? in just the same way as the glosing friar, the 'lusty bacheler', the vigorous young knight of Arthur's court, saw a maid and raped her. This is hardly the sort of behaviour we expect of Arthurian knights. The opening to the Wife's Tale questions both the major literary areas for discussion of sexual relationships, the Christian and the courtly, suggesting that the chaste ideal of the one and the romantic ideal of the other are equally fictitious.

The knight is condemned to death by the king. The queen and her ladies intercede for him. It has been suggested that the ladies, headed by the adulterous Guinevere, are soft on the rapist.[17] The queen, however, is not named in the Tale, perhaps because Chaucer wished his audience not to make that inference. And the connection between rape and a passionate, long-term extramarital affair is tenuous indeed. The queen does not, in fact, ask that the crime be pardoned. She proposes re-education as a possible alternative to the death sentence. The knight is given a year to find the answer to the question which Freud was later to ask: 'What thyng is it that wommen moost desiren?' (905). If he cannot produce the answer, he will die.

The punishment fits the crime. The knight has acted in brutal disregard of a woman's wishes; now he is obliged, on pain of death, to find out what women do desire But the knight is not the only person who needs to know the answer. He searches for it for a year, asking everyone he can find. But no two people can agree. The queen has set him to investigate a genuine mystery. The various replies he is given provide an opportunity for a quick review of the main charges made against women by satirists: that they like money, smart clothes, sexual pleasure, flattery, honour, reputation. The reasonable suggestion that 'we loven best / For to be free, and do right as us lest' (935–6) blends smoothly into 'And that no man repreve us of oure vice' (937), as if the desire for freedom were merely the wish to sin without criticism. The Wife, good-humoured about incriminating herself, concurs with this and with some of the other answers. Women, she agrees, are won with flattery and 'ylymed' (934) (a revealing metaphor) with constant care and attendance. She does not point out that a list of men's desires would be almost identical: sex, money, flattery, etc. Some of the same words, such as 'honour', would occur in both lists but with a different range of meanings. These answers expose some of women's faults – or some of the prejudices against women – but none is *the* answer. Why should there be only *one* answer? According to the Tale there is and almost nobody knows it.

The Wife disagrees with one of the reports about women, that they wish to be considered steadfast and discreet. One of her admissions about herself in her Prologue was that she could never be trusted to keep her husband's secrets. As evidence, she tells the story of how Midas's wife revealed to the reeds the secret that her husband had asses' ears. In the source, Ovid's *Metamorphoses*, the disclosure is made by his indiscreet barber rather than his indiscreet wife, which has led to the speculation that Jankin tailored this story for Alison's benefit. In Ovid's version the tell-tale barber is only a minor character in the narrative of the follies of Midas. The asses' ears were imposed on him by Apollo, god of music, as a punishment for preferring the pipes of Pan to his own playing. His taste is asinine, so the god makes him literally asinine.[18] Yet here Chaucer changes the emphasis of the story from the deafness of the husband to the loquacity of the wife, from his ears to her mouth. In the Wife of Bath's Prologue we observed a wife deafened (in both senses) by her husband's words and blows. This adaptation of the Midas story employs the same motifs, garbles authority so that a tale becomes anti-feminist in the transmission and provides an ironic *exemplum* in the context of the full narrative. Women are unable to keep secrets – yet the knight has to wander despairingly for a year trying to find out what it is they want.

On the very last day, when the knight is bound for home without the answer, he happens to ride 'under a forest syde' (990), where he sees four-and-twenty ladies dancing. As the knight approaches they vanish, and he sees only a hideous old woman sitting on the grass. It does not occur to the knight that he has just witnessed the dance of the elf-queen and that there is something very mysterious about the hag who seems to have materialised in its place. He takes her at face value. 'Thise olde folk kan muchel thyng' (1004), she says, and he asks if she can solve his problem. She agrees, provided he will plight his troth to do the next thing she requests. The knight makes his pledge to her and (like Midas's wife?) she whispers the answer in his ear.

The knight returns to the court and gives the answer:

> Wommen desiren to have sovereynetee
> As well over hir housband as hir love,
> And for to been in maistrie hym above.
>
> 1038–40

What women most want is not sex or esteem or material goods but a change in their position. None of the ladies can contradict it. He has saved his skin. But he is not allowed to stop at merely mouthing the words. He has to learn what they mean. The hag exacts marriage as her reward, the knight protests in horror but is obliged to keep his troth, and his re-education continues on the wedding night. As well as parroting the answer from his wife, the knight is forced to enact a woman's experience. No wonder he feels 'disparaged' (1069): in addition to marrying someone who seems to be of a lower class, he is trapped in a reversal of sex roles. The narrator of the story, the Wife of Bath, is, as we have seen, described in significantly masculine terms in the *General Prologue* and she usurps two of the roles almost exclusively occupied by men, the soldier and the preacher. She presents the converse experience in her hero. At the beginning of the Tale he is introduced as a very masculine man. He is a young blade, a 'lusty bacheler', a description which seems to cast an indulgent light upon the rape. He is manly, vigorous, aristocratic, a hunter, a knight. Ignoble though his action is, his caste is invested with glamour. Even after he has been condemned and set his alternative task by the queen, he falls into a conventional and honourable role, the knight on a quest.

But the balance shifts during the Tale. The narrator is a woman and she tells of a woman's world. It is inhabited by female characters, the raped maiden, the queen and her ladies, the four-and-twenty dancers and the hag. The only other man in the story is the king, who promptly hands over his authority to the queen. The knight's predicament is an ironic variation on the plight of Emily or Criseyde, heroines of male narrators in worlds governed by men. The other characters in the *Canterbury Tales* who make pledges with unforeseen results are women, Dorigen and Griselda. When the knight gives the answer to the court, he speaks 'with manly voys' (1036). But his position changes as soon as the hag demands him in marriage. In romance and folk-tale a princess or a beautiful lady is the goal of the knight's quest or the reward for his answer to the riddle or his success in battle. Suddenly this knight finds that *he* is

the prize. 'Taak al my good, and lat my body go' (1061), he wails, as
if someone were trying to rape *him*. The sexual anxieties with which
the Tale opened have found a new home.

The knight joins a particular category of Chaucerian heroine, the
reluctant bride. The wedding is the conventional happy ending to a
story, particularly to a romance. But Chaucer's presentation of
weddings and wedding nights is almost consistently negative or
ironic. He uses the conventions of the epithalamium primarily for
satiric purposes. He even seems somewhat reluctant himself to
write of weddings: he actually omits some of the joyful nuptials in
his sources. At the opening of the *Knight's Tale* the multiple
weddings of Athenians and Amazons are deleted and only the
essential dynastic union of their rulers is briefly summarised. Emily,
when we belatedly overhear her wishes, proves to want celibacy,
although she is finally content to comply with the arrangements
and rearrangements of Theseus. Chaucer, however, is not willing
to elaborate on the ceremony as does his source: he reduces
Boccaccio's description of the wedding to the phrase 'with alle
blisse and melodye' (I 3097). In the *Man of Law's Tale* Constance first
appears invested with pathos, pale and tearful, though patient and
courageous, at the prospect of sailing from home, family and
Christendom to marry the Sultan. The narrator intervenes to
express his pity for a girl embarking on an arranged marriage to an
unknown husband. Her fears are justified: her wedding feast is a
literal shambles when her husband and all her Christian entourage
are slaughtered at the table on the orders of her mother-in-law. In
the *Second Nun's Tale* Cecilia wears a hair shirt to her wedding and
sternly ignores the music (this qualifies her to be the patron saint of
the art): she is resolved on celibacy and has a guardian angel to
protect her from the advances of her husband. May, in the
Merchant's Tale, has no power to refuse her elderly bridegroom.
Their wedding is one of Chaucer's virtuoso passages of sustained
irony, glittering with a panoply of rhetorical weapons, purporting
to celebrate the union, actually making it look twice as squalid as it
did before, culminating in the double-edged assertion that 'Whan
tendre youthe hath wedded stoupyng age, / Ther is swich myrthe
that it may nat be writen' (IV 1738–39). May is 'broght abedde as
stille as stoon' (1818). One assumes she is numb with horror,
powerless to resist, but she does not reveal her feelings to husband,
reader or narrator: 'God woot what that May thoughte in hir herte'
(1851). In the last poem of the *Legend of Good Women* the marriage of
Lyno and Hypermnestra is attended with all the proper ceremonial

– burning torches, bright lamps, sacrifices, incense, garlands, 'the soun of minstralcye, / Of songes amorous of maryage' (*LGW* 2615–6) – but the bride is as pale as an ash and shakes like a leaf when she is privately commanded to murder her husband on their wedding night. These heroines have very different reasons to fear marriage but the grim junketings have common features which form a Chaucerian configuration: a reluctant bride, a wedding undesired by one partner, a gap between outward ceremony and inward reality, a silent compliance.

Unlike Chaucer's women who are trapped in unwelcome marriages, however, the knight does feel free to complain about it. He marries the hag as furtively as possible and goes into hiding for a day. On his wedding night he can do nothing but 'walwe and wynde' (1102). His wife asks why he is so 'daungerous' (1090), a word more often applied to a woman's sexual aloofness, though the Wife of Bath has already used it of Jankin ('I trow I loved hym best, for that he / Was of his love daungerous to me', 513–4). The knight does not conceal his horror at being married to someone old, ugly and of low birth:

> Thou art so loothly, and so oold also,
> And therto comen of so lough a kynde,
> That litel wonder is thogh I walwe and wynde.
> 1100–2

His wife replies with a long speech of more than a hundred lines, in which she tries to demonstrate that these disadvantages are trivial or imaginary. Most of the speech is concerned with the subject of *gentillesse* or nobility. Following arguments in Boethius and Dante, which Chaucer uses elsewhere, the hag argues that *gentillesse* belongs to one of noble character rather than of noble birth. A virtuous disposition is not necessarily inherited from an ancient family. True *gentillesse* comes from God rather than from social status. 'He is gentil that doth gentil dedis' (1170) and, although the wife does not argue *ad hominem*, the knight should realise that he has debased himself more effectively by raping the maiden than by marrying a hag. She is poor but, she points out, Christ himself chose to lead his human life in poverty and she quotes Seneca, Juvenal and 'othere clerkes' (1184) on the positive aspects of having little. She closes with the 'problem' of her old age and her ugliness. The old should be honoured, as we know even before we turn to

'auctoritee' (1208) and 'auctours' (1212). And at least he need have
no fear of being cuckolded by a hideous elderly partner. Finally, she
offers him a choice. Does he want her to stay old and ugly and be
true and humble? Or would he prefer her to be young and beautiful
and run the risk of infidelity? When the knight puts himself into her
power and leaves the choice to her, he gains in both ways: she is
transformed into a young and beautiful woman who is also a true
and faithful wife.

This transformation has not, however, been seen by all readers as
an unambiguously happy ending. It has been objected that, after
the apparent seriousness with which the Tale takes the question of
female needs, the conclusion is a surrender to masculine fantasy
and stereotypes of the perfect woman: young, beautiful, faithful
and obedient.[19] The fairy-tale motif also gratifies feminine fantasy:
perhaps it is a kind of rueful wish-fulfilment on the part of the
middle-aged narrator who falls in love with a man half her age and
is now looking for her sixth husband. Some critics have argued that
the whole inspiring lecture on *gentillesse* is beside the point: the hag
addresses herself to the problems of low birth and poverty, when
the knight is really repelled by her age and ugliness.[20]

But the lecture is as enchanting as its outcome and the two are
connected. The transformation takes place in the knight's mind
before he draws the curtain and actually sees his beautiful young
wife. He has evidently been persuaded by her explication of
gentillesse to love her for her virtue and her wisdom. Before her
speech he is full of ungallant complaints: immediately after it he
addresses her as his 'lady', his 'love', his 'wyf so deere' (1230) and
entrusts himself to her 'wise governance' (1231). Both the answer
and the reward have now been given in spirit as well as in letter.
The knight had to realise women's experience before he could
understand their need for sovereignty. His wife wanted love from
him as well as marriage. 'I am youre owne love and youre wyf'
(1091), she insists to her unwilling partner. She seems to have no
qualifications to be either. Old and ugly, she does not look like a
mistress. Poor and low-born, she does not rank as a wife. The
second factor is an even worse blow to the proud knight than the
first: 'Alas! that any of my nacioun / Should evere so foule
disparaged be!' (1068–9). But now she has demonstrated to him the
beauty of *gentillesse* and its independence from superficial
advantages. It may reside in the old, the poor, the ugly, in those
low-born as well as those of gentle birth. And should we infer –

though the wife does not spell this out to her husband – in women as well as men?

The element of wish-fulfilment also has profounder implications than can be dismissed in a sneer at the middle-aged woman's quest for a husband. The wife of the Prologue and the wife of the Tale present an idea of fractured femininity which the transformation attempts to restore to a wholeness of person. The first line of the knight's answer – 'Wommen desiren to have sovereynetee' (1038) – is often quoted in isolation, but it continues 'As wel over hir housbond as hir love', emphasising the disjunction between the romantic and the marital relationship. His own wife wants to be loved as well as married. The women in the Tale polarise: the helpless rustic maiden, the powerful queen; the attractive young victim, the repulsive old hag. The magical ending to the Tale is balanced by the speeded-up progression from youth to age as the lovely dancers dissolve into the lonely old woman. In some respects the wife in the Tale is a mirror-image of the Wife of Bath, like but opposite. She achieves a similar end by very different means. Fantastic though her power proves, her arguments are orthodox. She has the proper respect for the Bible and the classics and the great authors of the past and she cites them correctly. Whereas the Wife of Bath cheerfully perverts the scriptural advice to lay up treasure in heaven, not on earth where rust and moth may corrupt, by wearing her best clothes as often as possible –

> [I] wered upon my gaye scarlet gytes.
> This wormes, ne thise motthes, ne thise mytes,
> Upon my peril, frete hem never a deel;
> And wostow why? for they were used weel.
>
> 559–62

– the wife of the Tale makes the correct distinction between the gifts of God and the gifts of Fortune:

> 'God, of his goodnesse,
> Wole that of hym we clayme our gentillesse';
> For of oure eldres may we no thyng clayme
> But temporel thyng, that man may hurte and mayme.
>
> 1129–32

Gilbert and Gubar have explored the relationship between the Madwoman in the Attic and the Angel in the House, the price paid for the domestic hypocrisies of the parlour and the bedroom.[21] But

the Wife of Bath does not shelter behind domestic hypocrisy or an
angelic *persona*. So the Wise Woman of the Forest is her ideal self:
calm, reasonable, right, supported by authorities, a force for
reconciliation in the confusing world in which an exemplar of
chivalry can so easily become the Madman in the Meadow.

The Prologue and the Tale have similar and paradoxical endings.
Both end with reconciliation. Throughout the Prologue and
throughout her five marriages, Alison fights for mastery. Finally, on
that fateful evening, she and Jankin actually come to blows. She
wins. He gives her control over house and land and over his own
words and deeds and, best of all, he burns his book! But when his
wife has

> geten unto me
> By maistrie, al the soveraynetee,
> And that he seyde, 'Myn owene trewe wyf
> Do as thee lust the terme of al thy lif;
> Keep thyn honour, and keep eek myn estaat' –
> After that day we hadden never debaat.
> God helpe me so, I was to hym as kynde
> As any wyf from Denmark unto Ynde,
> And also trewe, and so was he to me.
>
> 817–25

Once the struggle for supremacy has ceased to be an issue,
supremacy itself seems not to matter. Alison and Jankin 'fille
acorded' (812), never quarrel again, and are true and kind to each
other. The inequality of one partner leads to domestic revolution
but, once she has won her victory, she is able to surrender it again.
The Tale hinges on the discovery that women desire sovereignty
and mastery and, when the husband makes the crucial choice, his
wife echoes Alison's words: 'Thanne have I gete of yow maistrie?'
(1236), she asks. But like her narrator, she then proves to be good,
true and compliant and bestows herself upon him in words that
might come from a Griselda: 'Dooth with my lyf and deth right as
yow lest' (1248). It is a romantic ending but it has its own
psychological realism. Both partners in a loving relationship are
interdependent, no matter who might be the nominal leader.[22]

The transformation is also a form of reconciliation, an attempt to
deal with the fourteenth-century versions of our platitudes that
'brains and beauty don't go together' or 'you can't be clever and

popular'. Chaucer seems to have adapted the question to express this kind of prejudice. The dilemma in the analogues is: should the wife be fair by night and foul by day or vice versa? Her husband is offered a choice between sex object and status symbol. This certainly has its grisly appeal: it is neat and symmetrical and encapsulates some of the classic problems between men and women. Why did Chaucer try to improve on it? The choice in his version presupposes some of the favourite either/or stereotypes of women found in anti-feminine satire. In the propaganda against marriage there are arguments such as these, which the Wife of Bath plays back to her first three husbands: if you marry a poor woman, she will be a financial drain on you; a rich wife will be intolerably proud; a beautiful woman will be so courted that she will be unfaithful; an ugly wife will desperately pursue lovers herself. In other words, you can't win. Any marriage with any kind of woman will predictably result in misery. It is a mechanical view of human and female behaviour. One way of contesting it is to set up either/or stereotypes, as Chaucer does here, and then collapse them, along with the whole *maistrye* issue. But it is undeniable that the narrative focus has shifted from the man knowing what the woman wants to the man getting what he wants.

The *Knight's Tale* and the *Wife of Bath's Tale* are not usually considered in close relation to each other. They belong to different fragments and they do not obviously refer to each other, as do the Tales of the Knight and the Miller or the Wife and the Clerk. They have in common that they are both romances, that their subject is love considered in the context of the chivalric life. Both present erotic episodes in grander epic stories which have generated many other narratives: the history of Thebes, the life of Theseus and the founding of Athens, the Arthurian fellowship and the Matter of Britain. Both poems discuss problems which are common in human experience but their method is not formally realistic and they include supernatural beings and intervention. Both open by setting the action in the distant past – 'Whilom, as olde stories tellen us' (I 859), 'In th' olde dayes of the Kyng Arthour' (III 857) – but both bring it up to the present with a grave climactic speech which solves the problems of the couple in the narrative and in its far-reaching moral and theological sweep has obvious didactic reference to any listener or reader. Both end with a blessing on the implied audience. The Knight issues a general and 'gentil' benediction: 'God save al this faire compaignye' (I 3108). The Wife pronounces a tendentious parody of a prayer: may women have 'Housbondes meeke, yonge, and fressh abedde' (III 1259) and may God shorten the lives of rebellious husbands and visit 'olde and angry nygardes' (III 1263) with the pestilence.

The Tales show similarities of form but great differences of feeling. In the *Knight's Tale* the official view predominates, though it can be questioned by the characters and belied by events. Theseus attempts to impose order and reason in the various spheres of international relations, private passion and philosophical enquiry. He conquers the Amazons and solves the problem of Emily's marriage, producing personal contentment and political stability out of tragic and mortal conflict. He defends the weak and ensures that the men slain in battle be given due burial. He forces the action back from forest to city, he builds a circular arena, he expounds the great chain of being. He creates personally and politically a happy ending, though along the way most of his plans have been abandoned or subverted. Theseus occupies a number of strong positions from which to deliver party lines: Duke of Athens, founder of cities, conqueror, tamer of the Amazons, middle-aged man, husband, success. The opposing voices are those of the victims of Fortune, poignant and plangent: the prisoners questioning the justice of the gods, the dying Arcite on the tragic brevity of his life and Emily in her one speech in the temple. Here the doubts, disagreements and questions are expressed. The spaces in the narrative – Chaucer's abbreviations of Boccaccio, the silence of Emily – are also eloquently and mutely expressive.

Theseus speaks for the establishment and presents its usual view, that what is 'stablissed' (I 2995) must be best for everyone. Male rulers have a strong interest in believing that. The *Knight's Tale* is situated on the far side of romance, where it borders on the epic, the repository of the received wisdom of a whole culture whose spokespeople and agents are usually men. The *Wife of Bath's Tale* foregrounds the counter-culture.[23] While it is critical of romance, it is still closer to the heart of the genre with its quests, enchanted forests, magical transformations, with its hospitality to the eccentric, the wayward, the magical, the marvellous. The answer comes from the forest and it comes from a woman. It is the women who are the figures of authority and the wife who delivers the authoritative sermon.

This speech is a kind of parallel to the First Mover speech and the views expressed in it are just as 'official'. But rather different selections from 'authority' provide the bases for the happy endings of the two Tales. Theseus chooses – or Chaucer chooses for him, as this is one of the passages which Chaucer adds to his source – to emphasise pattern, a hierarchical structure descending from the First Mover to the partial and corruptible. The mutability of life can be accepted when we see that it is not accidental but destined and predictable, that 'al this thyng hath ende . . . al goth that ilke weye . . . al this thyng moot deye' (3026, 3033, 3034). As in the speech of Egeus, no one ever lived who did not die, no one ever died who had not lived, and we see in the characters of this narrative the inevitable stages of human life – the young lovers, the mature ruler, the wise old man – through which the individual (Every*man*, male and aristocratic) passes in 'this worldes transmutacioun' (ı 2839).

The wife's counsel, on the other hand, emphasises unpredictability. Far from seeing a constant and recurring pattern in the cycle of human life, the wife argues that *gentillesse* may be found in unexpected places and may well not pass down through the generations of a noble family. Theseus's theological appeal is to the First Mover, who is exactly where you would expect to find him – at the top of the hierarchy. The wife's is to the incarnate God of Christianity who descended from heaven and chose to live his human life in 'wilful poverte' (ııı 1179). Even the predictability of the progression from youth to age is overturned in her transformation. Theseus is the voice of his society, speaking on a public occasion, squaring the desires of the individual with the public good. The wife speaks out of turn, in private, converting only her husband with her discourse, making real in the bedroom the answer and the undertaking that were mechanical in the court.

Both poems end with happiness in marriage after ordeals which were potentially tragic to the protagonists. The Knight seems to take the bracing view that Palamon's joy has been earned through suffering: 'And God, that al this wyde world hath wroght, / Send hym his love that hath it deere aboght' (ı 3100). The wife's final words to her husband, 'Cast up the curtyn, looke how that it is' (ııı 1249), suggest that the woe that is in marriage could be avoided by seeing more clearly, that there is no conflict of interest between the sexes. It is left to the audience to wonder if this solution exists only in the enchanted land of romance. The Wife of Bath's closing prayer brings us back to the war-zone of her own experience of marriage. The Knight does not compromise his happy ending – classical harmony modulates smoothly into Christian felicity – but the Tales that follow his in the first fragment give very different views of love, sex, marriage and women.

5

The Merchandise of Love: Winners and Wasters

I

'Why woldestow be deed,' thise wommen crye,
'And haddest gold ynough, and Emelye?'
CT I 2835–6

These lines occur at the most bitter moment in the *Knight's Tale*, when there is general grief for the death of Arcite, who is struck down by Saturn immediately after winning the tournament and the right to marry Emily. They are a wonderful example of Chaucerian hospitality to a range of voices and experience: for a moment the scope of the narrative widens to include a perspective on the story very different from the views of the main actors.

The main actors are aristocrats and gods. They are interested in questions of love, honour and philosophy rather than the vulgar problems of balancing the family budget. The soldier narrator is well aware of the underside of the chivalric world: he shows us the scene when the pillagers discover the half-dead bodies of the noble kinsmen in a heap of corpses on the battlefield. He recognises the knight's need for logistic support: he explains how Arcite, in disguise at the Athenian court, receives his own income secretly from Thebes, as well as wages from Theseus, and is careful not to rouse suspicion by spending it conspicuously. But, in general, in the *Knight's Tale* people have better things to worry about than money.

In this couplet we briefly hear the voices of the majority for whom financial problems are usually the major anxiety. It combines humour and pathos. The social level drops and the level of discourse drops with it. The cry seems undignified in its tragic context. The more usual breach of decorum in the *Knight's Tale* is for

66

tears to intrude on joy. Theseus's first speech complains that the widows, who kneel in his path as he rides from his wedding, 'perturben . . . my feste with criynge' (ı 906). But the reader can occasionally be guilty of the other indecorum, giggling at the funeral. This lament provokes at least a rueful smile. Yet one's sympathies are also momentarily engaged with the women: at the glimpse they give of lives of hardship and fear and at their generosity of spirit in being able to care about the griefs of the rich. Their question is quite as timeless and heartfelt as the prisoners' musings on the mystery of human suffering.

The comedy springs from the apparent incongruity with the context and with the concerns of the major characters. The women grieve that Arcite dies when he has gold enough and Emily, in that order, when we have been impressed for so long by the intense unwordliness of the passion of Palamon and Arcite for Emily above everything else. Yet there are senses in which the women's priorities mirror those of their 'betters'. Throughout the poem, as we have seen, Emily is relegated to second place in the phrase or sentence. There is a connection between gold and Emily, between the wealth of the aristocracy and the finer feelings they can afford. In the *Romance of the Rose* Poverty is painted on the outside of the wall of the Garden of Love and Idleness ushers the Dreamer within. Emily is finally bought, though, as her price is higher than that of a peasant or a bourgeois woman, nobody puts it that way. But Theseus finds the philosophical and emotional justification for her marriage to Palamon when he needs to cement his alliance with Thebes.

The economic basis of marriage is obvious in the *Miller's Tale* from the beginning. The link between the Tales prepares us for a contrast. All the pilgrims think the *Knight's Tale* 'a noble storie' (ı 3111) and 'namely the gentils' (ı 3113). It is a chivalric story, promoting aristocratic values, 'worthy for to drawen to memorie' (3112) to improve the mind and preserve a record of the epic works of the past and it appeals in particular to the pilgrims of gentle birth. The Host, mindful of protocol, invites the Monk, representative of the clerical estate, to tell the next tale. Perhaps a pious Christian story is to follow the courtly romance. But the drunk Miller elbows him aside and although Harry objects that a 'bettre man' (3130) of higher class should speak next, blusters that he knows a 'noble tale' (3126) with which he will 'quite' (3127) the *Knight's Tale*. The word 'quite' suggests retaliation, the word 'noble' suggests irony. The

Miller's Tale is a repudiation and a parody of the exalted feelings, values and diction of the previous story.[1] It is both a fabliau and a mock-romance.

The Knight is not the only pilgrim with whom the Miller finds himself at odds. He satirises the tale the Knight has told and displaces the tale the Monk might have told. Perhaps Harry Bailly expected a biblical story or the legend of a saint from the religious narrator. The Miller offers a 'legend and a lyf / Both of a carpenter and of his wyf' (3141–2): the joke glances at the hagiographers and at the Holy Family, as the story will evidently be a fabliau and tell 'how that a clerk hath set the wrightes cappe' (3143) and cuckolded the husband. The Miller mocks the idealism of those who fight and those who pray. But a pilgrim of his own estate, those who work, sees only a personal application. The Reeve, a carpenter by trade, bursts out angrily that it is wrong to defame men and to bring women into disrepute. Perhaps the Miller is suggesting he is a cuckold, though the Reeve's defensiveness is more revealing if he meant no such thing. But by the time the Miller has finished apologising, the Reeve's wife seems convicted of guilt by association. His reply is a masterly piece of insult disguised as mollification. Beginning 'leve brother Oswald, / Who hath no wyf, he is no cokewold, / But I say nat therfore that thou art oon' (3151–3), it manages simultaneously to suggest that all married men are cuckolds so that the Reeve need feel no particular shame about it, that he is crazed with misogyny and that he is guilty of a kind of sexual avarice. It becomes line by line more generous and more annoying. There are a thousand good women to set against every bad one, a remark made elsewhere by interested parties such as Proserpina and the God of Love and cold comfort if you are married to the exception. The Reeve must know this perfectly well himself, unless he is mad. (Have you stopped berating your wife?) The Miller is a married man himself: 'Yet nolde I . . . / Take upon me moore than ynogh, / As demen of myself that I were oon' (3159–61). There is no need to borrow trouble by deciding you are a cuckold, though the conclusion of this couplet – 'I wol bileve wel that I am noon' (3162) – implies that you probably are. But if so, would it matter? So long as you yourself have enough sex, why ask what is going on elsewhere?

> An housbonde shal nat been inquisityf
> Of Goddes pryvetee, nor of his wyf.

> So he may fynde Goddes foyson there,
> Of the remenant nedeth nat enquere.
>   3163–6

This counsel has many applications. The Reeve can, if he wishes, take it to heart and stop worrying about his wife's infidelity: the ground has shifted from the problem of infidelity to the problem of minding about it. But the lines reach far beyond the narrow concerns of the Reeve. They point back to the Garden of Eden itself, where Adam and Eve fell into excessive curiosity, were inquisitive about the secrets of God and the knowledge of the forbidden tree and committed the original sin. Being a complaisant husband somehow gets equated with being a faithful Christian. They also point forward. 'Privitee', in its various forms, is a word which echoes through the *Canterbury Tales*.

It is first used in the *General Prologue* in the portrait of the miserly Reeve himself ('Ful riche he was astored pryvely' – 1609)[2] and it can range in register from the 'privitee' of God to the privy into which May casts her love letter from Damian. It is a favourite word in the *Miller's Tale* and vital to the plot from the moment when the 'sleigh and ful privee' (1 3201) Nicholas first approaches Alison ('prively he caughte hire by the queynte' – 3276) and declares his 'deerne love' (3278) for her. Alison cautions him to 'been privee' (3295) in his lovemaking. John disregards his own warning, 'Men sholde nat knowe of Goddes pryvetee' (3454), when he falls for Nicholas's prediction, made to him 'in pryvetee' (3493), of a second Flood. He refuses to share 'Goddes pryvetee' (3558) with Alison, a dramatic irony since she is privy to the true plot, but later relents 'and to his wyf he tolde his pryvetee' (3603). He sends to his house 'pryvely' (3622) the tubs in which they are to spend the night of the flood and hangs them in the roof 'in pryvetee' (3623). The rival Absolon enquires 'prively' (3662) about John's absence and decides to knock on the window that night 'Ful pryvely' (3676), to be finally rewarded when Nicholas 'out his ers . . . putteth pryvely' (3802). The warning against curiosity encapsulates in one word divine mysteries, the reticences of private life, 'derne' loves and adulterous affairs, obscene practical jokes, a woman's private parts and what she does with them.

The Miller is also having his equable joke with the word 'housbonde'. It is the term both for a married man and for a man who practices husbandry or economy. In a sexually jealous and

financially prudent husband, such as Oswald the Reeve or John the
Carpenter, the meanings are combined. But the senses are synony-
mous only if a wife is a possession and sexuality is on ration.
Perhaps it is for the stingy and avaricious Reeve, who sees life itself
in terms of a limited commodity. He introduces his own Tale from
the bitter viewpoint of an old man: life has almost drained out of the
tun which Death broached when he was born. In the *General
Prologue* he seems a slightly sinister figure, withdrawn, obsessed
with profit, stealthily enriching himself at his lord's expense,
terrifying his inferiors 'like death' with his knowledge of their
secrets. He is physically spare; there is no excess to be seen. He is
'sclendre' (587), his beard is shaved as close as possible, his hair
close-cropped, his legs as lean and straight as a stick. The top of his
head is even tonsured 'lyk a preest' (590). Harry Bailly is irritated by
this mock-clerical air – 'The devel made a reve for to preche' (3903) –
when Oswald speaks of the hopelessness of age. But as usual,
Harry's interpretation misses the mark. The Reeve is a diabolic
parody of a priest not in his sermonising but in his sexuality. His
mock-tonsure suggests a celibacy of mean-mindedness rather than
of charity. In the Prologue to his Tale he explains that he is now
impotent but still full of frustrated desire.

The Miller's economy is a generous and profligate system. From
his viewpoint, it is good husbandry to enjoy as much as you can and
not grudge anyone else his pleasure, another parody of a more
spiritual attitude. Sex is God-given and so long as you can find
'Goddes foyson' in your wife's genitals and generosity, you need
not ask what happens to the rest of this abundance. Whereas the
Reeve's closeness suggests a loveless chastity, the Miller's openness
displays a licentious charity. The Miller could quit the Reeve's
despairing image 'hath so the tappe yronne / Til that almoost ai
empty is the tonne' (3893–4) with the text 'My cup runneth over'. He
has no desire to take on himself 'moore than ynogh' (3160), because
there is enough and to spare for everybody. The Wife of Bath uses
the same argument to her first three husbands to justify a woman's
infidelity: 'he is to greet a nygard that wolde werne / A man to lighte
a candle at his lanterne; / He shal have never the lasse light, pardee.
/ Have thow ynogh, thee thar nat pleyne thee' (III 333–6). It seems a
wonderful piece of special pleading, deftly belittling the emotional
realities of love and jealousy with a false analogy and turning the
tables so that the sin becomes not the wife's infidelity but the
husband's objection to it. Yet the same image in the *Book of the*

Duchess, describing White's radiant goodness, suggests the infinity of God's bounty: 'She was lyk to torche bryght / That every man may take of lyght / Ynogh, and hyt hath never the lesse' (*BD* 963–5). The Miller's expansiveness and tolerance are a profane analogy of divine creativity.

The Miller is duly grateful to his maker, though his application of the term 'Goddes foyson' is a comic surprise. For, if we translate the term as 'God's plenty', we see its philosophical origin in the term *plenitudo*. According to the principle of plenitude, the power and goodness of the Creator must be perfect: therefore everything that could exist must exist. There are no gaps in nature. Dryden used the phrase 'God's plenty' of the *Canterbury Tales* themselves,[3] the supreme compliment to Chaucer's supreme fiction. Chaucer parodies or parallels this theory of divine creativity with his defence of authorial responsibility. He purports to excuse himself for including the Miller's bawdy story 'for I moot reherce / Hir tales alle' (I 3173–4). Like God's, his creation must be as complete as possible. The audience, on the other hand, is free to select: anyone who does not like bawdy stories may skip the Miller's and find a pious tale. It is another version of the Miller's own reassurance: 'Of the remenant nedeth nat enquere' (3166). But for the author, the churl's tale has to be told as much as the Knight's. The churl and the Knight give different versions of *plenitudo*; the poet mimics God's activity by recording both.

The Knight's statement of the principle of plenitude is more orthodox and recognisable than the Miller's. Although it is partly made for ulterior motives, its purpose is to promote marriage rather than condone adultery. It is the 'First Mover' speech in which Theseus persuades Emily and Palamon to accept Arcite's death and find happiness with each other. A maker of patterns and prisons himself, he explains how the Creator binds the cosmos with a 'faire cheyne of love'. Every part derives from a perfect whole. Nothing is fragmentary or ill-fitting, everything is tied up and accounted for, there are no remnants. But the *Miller's Tale* is a story of loose ends. It is a tale about 'the remenant'. It is about the holes rather than the whole. John Leyerle points out a number of gaps and holes in the tale, from the orifices of the body to John's crucial 'shot-wyndow', which are 'a parodying inversion of *The Knight's Tale*: bonds and decorous order of love are turned into holes and wild chaos of licence almost as if Chaucer noticed that every link in "the faire cheyne of love" had a hole in it and wrote two poems as a result, one

on the links and the other on the holes'.[4] 'Goddes foyson' is equally
capable of inversion. To Theseus it means a totally ordered and
reasonable world of which love should be a microcosm and in
which marriage is a duty. To the Miller it means a world of casual
natural abundance in which one can use, misuse and not use up
natural gifts of God such as sex.

The opening couplet of the *Miller's Tale* introduces us to a world
sharply contrasting with the *Knight's Tale*: 'Whilom ther was
dwellynge at Oxenford / A riche gnof, that gestes heeld to bord' (I
3187–8). The first word is the same but the Knight's 'whilom'
gestures towards the distant past of classical mythology while the
Miller's is perfunctory: his story is set 'once upon a time' but in
the unheroic world of contemporary Oxford. By its bourgeois
standards the carpenter is 'riche', not by the standards of Theseus,
who is so rich that it is never mentioned. Money is not an issue in
the *Knight's Tale* for anyone except the mourning Athenian women,
minimal characters with a diminutive chorus. A truly rich man
would not need to take in lodgers. John scarcely makes a profit on
his: Nicholas recoups his rent in sex. It is obvious from the
beginning of the story that this will happen. The rich old man has a
beautiful young wife. The boarder has a room to himself, 'Allone,
withouten any compaignye' (3204), a bathetic replay of the tragic
complaint of the dying Arcite. There is a vacuum into which sex will
rush. The characters seem as much governed by the laws of
mechanics as the tubs and ropes of the farcical climax. They also
respond to a law of economics: the law of supply and demand.

Nicholas's solitary bedroom constitutes a demand, Alison's
nubile presence a supply. The student lodger also provides a
convenient supply for the restless wife. His rival Absolon cannot
compete with his proximity. Another law that governs this Tale is
summed up in the proverb: 'Alwey the nye slye / Maketh the ferre
leeve to be looth' (3392–3). Convenience is the last consideration of
the lovers in the *Knight's Tale*: they are willing to adore the
unattainable from a distance and to wait a lifetime. But Nicholas
and Absolon are not Palamon and Arcite and Alison is no Emily.
The energetic portrait of Alison has been much admired and its
sensuality often contrasted with the spirituality of the correspond-
ing description of Emily.[5] Emily is perceived exclusively in terms of
sight and hearing, Alison also in terms of touch and taste. She is soft
as the wool of a sheep, her mouth sweet as apples. The natural and
animal imagery parodies the conventional *effictio* of the courtly

lady. Emily sings like an angel, Alison like a swallow. She is as slim as a weasel and perhaps as slippery, as playful as a kid or calf or a jolly colt. But her appeal is not exclusively natural: she dresses smartly and plucks her eyebrows. One image is frankly commercial: 'Ful brighter was the shynyng of hir hewe / Than in the Tour the noble yforged newe' (3255–6). It punningly contrasts with the celestial brightness adored in the noble lady or the Madonna. The description of Alison's clothes concludes with her semi-precious purse 'of lether, / Tasseled with silk and perled with latoun' (3250–1), which hangs 'by hir girdel' (3250), the price John has paid for admission. There is a tension in the description between the images of weasel, swallow, kid and colt and the reminders of financial matters. All this vibrant, warm, sleek, soft, singing, skipping, playful, skittish sexuality is harnessed by another kind of power, that of money. The economic realities of what Alison can do with her sexuality are summed up in the concluding couplet: 'She was a prymerole, a piggesnye / For any lord to leggen in his bedde / Or yet for any good yeman to wedde' (3269–70).

These lines, which have been called the most snobbish in English Literature,[6] coolly presuppose that a double standard of sexual morality operates between the nobility and the working classes. More precisely, I think, Alison's price fluctuates. If we compare attitudes to sex in the *Knight's Tale* and the *Miller's*, we not not find a contrast between upper-class licence and lower-class respectability. We find instead shifting relationships between sex and money. The casual aristocratic munificence with money goes, in the aristocratic genre, with an intensely self-denying attitude towards sex. The noble characters of the *Knight's Tale* never give a second thought to money, which they take for granted as their right. But love and sex are earned: here they work, they worry, they fight, they make sacrifices, they save themselves. To use the Middle English terminology, the characters in the *Knight's Tale* are wasters about money and winners about sex. In the *Miller's Tale* things are the other way round. It is a world of hard work and hard-won money but fairly casual extra-marital sex.

The ethereal Emily is 'shene' (i 1068); Alison shines too, when she cleans herself up after her housework: 'Hir forheed shoon as bright as any day, / So was it wasshen whan she leet hir werk' (i 3310–11). At Theseus' bidding a stadium a mile in circumference is constructed to solve a personal problem. The *Miller's Tale* deals with the class who do the building: the plot is hatched while John works at the abbey at Osney and he himself makes the ladders leading to the latter-day arks. Estates satire operates between the *Miller's Tale* and the *Knight's Tale* and within the *Miller's Tale*. The genre, the setting, the plot, the characters, the values, the diction mock the courtly and philosophical romance which so pleased the 'gentils'. But the gap between high and low is a much less sensitive matter than that between the various shades of low and middle. Within this mock-courtly tale of bourgeois life another kind of estates satire is a motivating force: the mutual contempt of the clergy and the laity, the 'lerned' and the 'lewed'. Nicholas's seduction of Alison presents itself to him as a kind of clerical status symbol: 'A clerk had litherly biset his whyle, / But if he koude a carpenter bigyle' (3299–300), as if a course in cuckoldry had been included in his Oxford BA. His plan succeeds in part because the carpenter believes that it is better for your health to be stupid and ignorant and is all too prepared to believe that students study themselves into prophetic trances. But neither clerk exemplifies the clerical virtues. They are mock-courtiers in the mock-romance, aping courtly manners out of policy and pretension. They form a kind of parody leisure class, eager to lord it over the industrious dupe the carpenter. The studies and seductions of Nicholas are financed by 'his freendes fyndyng and his rente' (3220). He woos Alison while John is at work. She promises to engage in the sport of adultery 'whan that she may hir leyser wel espie' (3293). Absolon, the provincial dandy, has fine hair like his biblical namesake and he combs and cares for it like Idleness in the *Romance of the Rose* ('I entende to nothyng / But to my joye and my pleying / And for to kemb and tresse me' – *RR* 597–9).[7] He has the time to take a siesta to fortify himself for the traditional sleepless night of the courtly lover.

That climactic night of the adultery and its farcical aftermath is a Monday, the first day of the working week. Monday is presided over by Diana, goddess of chastity, an unlikely patron for the events of the *Miller's Tale*. The lovers of the *Knight's Tale* worship the planetary deities and Emily prays to Diana for a life of celibacy but Nicholas puts his astrological lore to baser uses. That night everybody except Absolon goes to bed early, to prepare for love, work or the Second Flood. The characters in the *Knight's Tale* also go to bed early on Monday in order to get up at dawn for Tuesday's tournament: 'by the cause that they sholde ryse / Eerly for to seen the grete fight, / Unto hir reste wenten they at nyght' (I 2488–90). Their entertainments are war games and they work hard at the grim business of enjoying themselves. In the working world of the *Miller's Tale* the characters have more fun. Nicholas plays the pop songs of the day, Absolon follows the sartorial fashions and takes part in the mystery drama: 'he pleyeth Herodes upon a scaffold hye' (I 3384) parodying and perhaps punning on the 'heraud on a scaffold' (I 2533) who opens the fatal tournament in the *Knight's Tale*. There work and play are almost indistinguishable. Which is the tournament? In the *Miller's Tale* play is given a sharper edge by its contrast with work. Alison and Nicholas make love until 'the belle of laudes gan to rynge, / And freres in the chauncel gonne synge' (I 3655–6). It is one of the funniest moments in the Tale. It has proved easy to point a moral but the clash is not only between the sacred and the sinful. Part of the pleasure for the sinners is the privileged feeling of being in bed when others rise to work or pray. The friars are not the only people whose vocation gets them up early. Gervase is in his smithy before dawn and is surprised to see the fop Absolon abroad at that hour. Absolon, of course, is up late rather than up early but he has been cured both of his love-longing and his leisure-class lounging by the 'misdirected' kiss. His immediate reaction to this insult is not to wash his mouth but to rub it with the sawdust and shavings round the carpenter's shop, cleansing himself of the illusions of love with the abrasive materials of work.

Absolon is punished for his illusions and pretensions, John for being stupid and Nicholas for being too clever by half. The successful seducer, the unsuccessful seducer and the jealous husband are all mocked. But in the vengeful world of the fabliau, Alison goes unscathed as if she cannot be blamed for wanting ways out of her 'cage'. The narrative seems to endorse the view that she, if not her husband, needs 'more than ynogh'.

The Miller's version of the fabliau genre is as expansive as his views on sexuality. Throughout the Tale he gives us, in every way, 'moore than ynogh'. The characters are generously elaborated beyond the mere types found in the French fabliaux, the wealth of biblical and literary allusion provides a rich background to the petty drama and the farcical ending itself is a kind of joyous comic overkill. The re-enacting of the story of Noah is far more than is needed to couple Nicholas and Alison. Since John often goes to work at Osney, they could easily jump into bed together. But they take advantage of his first absence not to commit adultery but to plan it. Like the troubadours and courtly poets, they make an art-form of it. Desire is delayed and narrative is retarded but the form is farce rather than romance.

The Reeve's fabliau, narrow and vengeful, is much more typical of the genre. Shorter and sparer than the *Miller's Tale*, it seems informed by a spirit of meanness. The Miller quits the Knight by offering an alternative and more cheerful view of life, comic instead of tragic, practical instead of idealistic, where sex is fun and easily available and courtly rhetoric a veneer upon the animal realities. The Reeve quits the *Miller's Tale* as revenge. The Miller has told how a carpenter is cuckolded by a clerk. The Reeve tells how a miller is beaten, sexually and financially, by two clerks. The carpenter in the *Miller's Tale* is stupid and bumbling but rather likeable. He bears no resemblance to the touchy Reeve. The miller in the *Reeve's Tale* is an evil character, dishonest, violent and even murderous. The description of him, one of the few passages where the Reeve elaborates beyond the demands of the plot, is a dark caricature of the Miller of the pilgrimage. He cheats the student customers of some of their corn by letting loose their horses to divert their attention: forced to stay the night, they retaliate by bedding his wife and daughter. The Tale is motivated by revenge and the clerks use sex as revenge.

The miller uses it for social climbing. He and his wife are a thoroughly nasty couple. They give themselves great airs but their village affluence is based on swindling and simony, to which the miller's name of Symkyn may allude. The wife is the illegitimate child of the parson and has been brought up nicely, like an upper-class girl, in a nunnery. Her father married her off to Symkyn with a dowry ('With hire he yaf ful many a panne of bras' – 3944), a literal example of 'the amorous effects of "brass"'),[8] presumably embezzled from church funds. She is exactly the kind of wife Symkyn wanted to acquire, 'wel ynorissed and mayde / To saven his estaat of yomanrye' (3948–9). Symkyn places a property value on the virginity of his bride and later on that of his daughter. Her grandfather the parson is prepared to endow her handsomely 'for hooly chirches good moot been despended / On hooly chirches blood' (3983–4) and hopes for a noble marriage into some ancient family. This, when the story opens, is causing difficulties and delays. It is like a parody of the dynastic alliances of the aristocracy. The girl, who is twenty and 'wel ygrowen' (3973) and whose 'kamus nose' (3974) may hint at a sensual nature, is getting restive. Like her mother, she enjoys her night of sex with the clerk and they say goodbye to each other at dawn in a brief travesty of the *aubade* of the courtly romance. Her father's first thought is that she has been 'disparaged', devalued by misalliance with a man unworthy of 'swich lynage' (4272). The miller's reaction suggests the thwarted pride of both the great lord and the owner of a pedigree cat.

Sex is a more complex force in the *Reeve's Tale* than the characters allow. It is not merely animal or economic or ambitious. There is a narrowness about their moral world exemplified by Aleyn's view that corn and sex are interchangeable – 'ther is a lawe that says thus, / That gif a man in a point be agreved, / That in another he sal be releved' (4180–2) – that he can recover in one 'point' what he has lost in another. John, the other student, earlier produces a proverb, 'Man sal taa of twa thynges, / Slyk as he fyndes, or taa slyk as he brynges' (4129–30), a stern piece of folk wisdom discouraging any aspiring hopes of having it both ways. (It occupies a similar position in the Tale to that axiom of pragmatic opportunism, 'Alwey the nye slye / Maketh the ferre leeve to be looth' – i 3392–3, in the *Miller's Tale*.) John produces it as a resigned reply to the miller's philistine jibe that, since the clerks are so clever, they can always expand his cramped house with arguments. But this common-sense view is inadequate. In fact, the clerks do take literally both what they find (sex) and what they bring (the daughter tells Alan where the stolen corn is hidden). Metaphorically, the narrow house is expanded. All the characters have to sleep in one room in which three times as many sexual relationships as before are generated. One of the relationships briefly expresses a little more tenderness than one expected to find among this disagreeable cast, so that one is glad that the frustrated thick-set girl has found some pleasure, despite the restrictions of her proud little family, and yet wonders if she is now unmarriageable, if she will grieve for her vanished clerk.[9] Sex proves to be a power that overcomes the laws of space and economics. Like the clerks' unbridled horses who gallop to the fen after the wild mares, it has a way of getting out.[10] The miller lets loose more than he bargained for.

The First Fragment moves forward in time, closer in space and down the social scale. It opens in mythical ancient Greece, continues in a contemporary English university town, shifts to a village near the other university and descends in the unfinished *Cook's Tale* to the underworld of the metropolis. It moves down the generic scale from epic and romance to the fabliau, from gods, aristocracy and founders of nations to the contemporary bourgeosie and down again to the flotsam and jetsam of the capital. The link between the

Reeve's Tale and the *Cook's Tale* promises an unsavoury story: the Host twits the Cook about his shop, where the flies buzz around, stale pasties are sold and the meat pies are reheated several times. The opening of the *Cook's Tale* seems to be leading to the most squalid of fabliaux but it breaks off after fifty-eight lines.[11] It is a fragmentary ending to a fragment. Even in those fifty-eight lines Perkin Revelour manages to be downwardly socially mobile. He is a riotous apprentice who loves to drink and gamble and whose master in despair dissolves their contract. So Perkin moves in with a friend of his own sort, who 'hadde a wyf that heeld for contenance / A shoppe, and swyved for hir sustenance' (I 4421-2) Perkin progresses from the respectability of the victualler's shop to the substratum of taverns and whorehouses.

The First Fragment also moves down a sexual scale, from the idealism of Palamon and Arcite to the cynicism of prostitute and pimp. In the *Knight's Tale* sex is for love, in the *Miller's* for fun, in the *Reeve's* for revenge and in the *Cook's* for money. As the Fragment proceeds there is more sex and it means less. The action of the *Knight's Tale* is fuelled by frustration. No sexual activity is possible until Palamon and Emily marry at the end of the Tale and live happily ever after. The stately pace of the narrative, with its balance, amplification and description, embodies this delaying of desire. It is also a highly formal narrative. Love gives structure to the lives of the characters, from the great chain which Theseus expounds as the binding cosmic force to the codified courtliness which civilises the aggressive sexual instinct. Theseus draws the anarchic passion of Palamon and Arcite back into the structures of society, the city, the tournament and the circular arena which he builds to contain it. Love, civilisation, poetry and theology give form and meaning to sex. The comic thrust of the *Miller's Tale* is to expose this as a sham. Courtliness and culture are a façade masking the real purpose of mating with Alison. The animal imagery describing her suggests which is the more powerful force. The cheerfulness of the Tale depends upon no deep emotions being involved. Yet the comic excess, as we have seen, produces its own complications and its own elaborations of desire. In the spare and severe *Reeve's Tale* there is, quantitatively, more sex but it is part of an arithmetical progression which reduces partners to ciphers. The Miller's carpenter is outwitted by one clerk, the Reeve's miller by two: one woman is seduced in the *Miller's Tale*, two in the *Reeve's Tale*. The logic governing the characters is also geometrical: the narrowness of the house, the moving of the cradle. Yet the clerks do expand the house, if not by arguments, the couplings are enjoyed and the *aubade* gestures towards the notion that sex should mean more than it does here.

The *Cook's Tale* has more sex and less plot than any other story in the First Fragment (or, indeed, of any of the *Canterbury Tales*). If emotional significance gives form to sex, this might explain why the Tale breaks off unfinished with the lines about the prostitute. There is an infinite amount of sex with countless clients and it means nothing. The concept of form traditionally had a sexual application. Aristotle proposed that in procreation the male contributed form and the female matter.[12] Chaucer alludes to this theory in the *Legend of Good Women*, though he reverses the roles of the sexes as they were defined by Aristotle and by his immediate source:[13]

> As mater apetiteth form alwey,
> And from forme into forme it passen may,
>   . . .
> Ryght so can false Jason have no pes.
> For to desyren thourgh his apetit
> To don with gentil women his delit,
> That is his lust and his felicite.
>
>   LGW 1582–8

Here male promiscuity rather than female passivity is degraded by the comparison to matter, though one might argue that the purpose is ironic at the expense of women rather than revisionary at the expense of men. Perhaps we are meant to realise that the narrator is departing from tradition. But the image of meaningless sex as mindless matter restlessly passing from form to form is apt either way in the *Cook's Tale*, to the wife with her multiplicity of clients or to the men who regard her only as a body, 'convertible' (to use the vocabulary of the Tale) with other bodies or with money. Mere matter has no story and the *Cook's Tale* appropriately ends here with meaningless sex, 'swyvyng for sustenaunce', formless fucking.

Sex at the end of the *Cook's Tale* has only economic meaning. But on matters of sex, class and money this fragmentary coda proves surprisingly complex. There are at least two voices in the Tale, expressing quite different economic attitudes.[14] The opening

description of Perkin is indulgent, even glamorous. He is as merry
as a goldfinch and as full of love as the hive is of honey. His
flirtations sound innocent, even beneficent: 'Wel was the wenche
with hym myghte meete' (4374). He dances 'wel and jolily' and
almost non-stop. The happiness of others is a spur to celebration:
'At every bridale wolde he synge and hoppe' (4375). His *joie de vivre*
cannot be contained in his master's shop: he leaps out when there is
riding to see in Cheapside and will not return till he has 'daunced
wel' (4380). He is popular with his own 'sort' (4381). He has plenty
of friends with whom to dance and gamble for he is an excellent
dicer and also very generous: 'thereto he was free / Of his dispense,
in place of pryvetee' (4387–8).

The loaded word 'pryvetee' sparks off another view of Perkin's
conduct. Presumably he is extravagant in private places, with all the
furtive and sexual connotations of the word. But he is also 'free of
dispense' instead of valuing 'privitee', the tight-lipped, tight-
arsed, close-fisted, lace-curtained ethic of the small shopkeeper and
his class. Now the voice of the master takes over. For twenty-four
lines the narrative grumbles about Perkin. We see his effect on
'chaffare', the 'bare box' and the 'shoppe'. The master's worldly
wisdom expresses itself in proverbs and maxims: linguistically and
conceptually he is unwilling to step out of line. Their content is as
unadventurous as their form: 'sikerly a prentys revelour / That
haunteth dys, riot, or paramour, / His maister shal it in his shoppe
abye' (4391–3); 'theft and riot they been convertible' (4395); 'Revel
and trouthe, as in a lowe degree, / They been ful wrothe al day, as
men may see' (4397–8). Finally he realises that Perkin's service is a
liability and he had better cut his losses and release him from his
contract:

> But atte laste his maister hym bithoghte,
> Upon a day, whan he his papir soghte,
> Of a proverbe that seith this same word,
> 'Wel bet is roten appul out of hoord
> Than that it rotie al the remenaunt.'
> So fareth it by a riotous servaunt . . . .
>
> 4403–8

The words 'pryvetee' and 'remenaunt' last appeared in close
proximity in the Link before the *Miller's Tale*. Perkin's master
means something very different by both. The Miller's philosophy is

permissive and extravagant. He does not believe in intruding on the 'privitee' of others or in worrying about the 'remenaunt'. In the master's view, you should guard your 'hoord' and the 'remenaunt' is exactly what you ought to worry about.

But in the narrative structure of the *Cook's Tale* the 'roten appul' (4406) which the master dismisses 'with sorwe and meschance' (4412) is precisely the interesting part of the story which we follow out of the careful shop and into the world of randomness. Although the narrative voice continues to sound disapproving ('Now lat hym riote' – 4414; 'ther is no theef withoute a lowke' – 4415; 'a compeer of his owene sort' – 4419), the prudential view is subverted by comedy. Attempts to punish Perkin are futile: he takes no notice of being 'snybbed' (4401) and positively wants to be dismissed. Skeat's note on the line 'And somtyme lad with revel to Newgate' (4402) might suggest how impervious Perkin is to rebuke: 'The point of the allusion lies in the fact that when disorderly persons were carried to prison, they were preceded *by minstrels* in order to call public attention to their disgrace'.[15]

But only respectable people like Perkin's master (or a Victorian clergyman) would care about the disgrace. The sort of person guilty of these misdemeanours would feel no shame: the line paints the picture of a medieval pop group revelling its way to Newgate. The punishers and the punished are living in different worlds. As usual, the winners do not have it all their own way. Their calculations are by no means as exact as they claim. 'Thefte and riot, they been convertible' (4395) in the master's economy. An absolute opposition is stated between two other terms: 'Revel and trouthe, as in a lowe degree', / They been ful wrothe al day, as men may see' (4397–8). But these qualities are only incompatible 'in a lowe degree'. Among the aristocracy they seem natural companions, as in the portrait of the Squire in the *General Prologue*. Perkin, a squire of low degree, is found wanting by the ethics of the bourgeoisie.

The Squire of the pilgrimage is the Knight's son. In him it is noble to dance and sing, follow fashion and court his lady. Perkin's behaviour, his dancing and dalliance, his enthusiasm for seeing the riding in which he cannot afford to join, his carefree generosity, are ironic echoes of the chivalric code. This last and least Tale of the First Fragment contains some incongruous reminiscences of its noble opening. Northrop Frye comments on the five literary modes he defines in *Anatomy of Criticism* that the lowest has something in common with the highest: 'Irony descends from the low mimetic: it begins in realism and dispassionate observation. But, as it does so, it moves steadily towards myth, and dim outlines of sacrificial rituals and dying gods begin to reappear in it. Our five modes evidently go round in a circle.'[16] Dim outlines of philosophy and romance form a misty penumbra around the antics of the 'propre short' anti-hero of the Cook's fragment. The prison reappears, but while the tower of the *Knight's Tale* provokes theological questions and expands into a grave definition of the world and all its suffering, the historical Newgate contracts into a joke. One of the most haunting lines of the *Knight's Tale*, 'al day meteth men at unset stevene' (I 1524), makes a general law of the unexpected meeting of Palamon and Arcite in the forest, 'unset' but probably predestined. Perkin and his riotous friends are disorderly but capable of making appointments for purposes they hold serious: 'And ther they setten stevene for to meete, / To pleyen at the dys in swich a strete' (I 4383–4). They make definite arrangements in order to commit themselves to chance.

The links with the larger world of the *Knight's Tale* suggest why the diminutive apprentice cannot be restrained within the boundaries of his master's shop. The master tries to contain with his 'box' (4390) and define with his 'papir' (4404) but finds the box bare and reckons it wiser to part with the paper. As in the *Reeve's Tale*, the categories prove too narrow for the human vitality that expands them. The two voices of the Tale favour, respectively, wasting and winning but these terms, like 'revel' and 'trouthe' prove not to be absolutely mutually exclusive. Perkin 'loved bet the taverne than the shoppe' and the shopkeeper despairs of his drinking, gambling and revelling. But shop and tavern coexist in the couple with whom the fragment ends: the husband 'lovede dys, and revel, and disport' (4420); the wife 'heeld . . . a shoppe' (4422–3) and under its cover of respectability plies a more lucrative trade as a whore.

Patriarchal systems are usually accompanied by the economic inferiority of women and the common desire to bequeath an estate to a legitimate (preferably male) heir. A way for a woman to improve her economic position is therefore to sell her sexuality. She can play with the system by marrying. She can play against it by trying to increase her own independent economic power. Prostitution, an illegitimate inversion of approved sexual activity, neatly combines both methods. In the *Canterbury Tales* Chaucer presents women, sexual relationships, strategies and aspirations of each kind in every stratum of society. The First Fragment opens with the arranged dynastic wedding of royalty and the victory of the male ruler over the warrior women. It ends with a rather squalid but apparently co-operative marriage in which the wife, for the first time in the First Fragment, has the power of the purse. The Fragment descends from the princess to the prostitute but the prostitute has more freedom than the princess. In later *Canterbury Tales* Chaucer explores the yet more disturbing theme of prostitution within marriage, the female use of sex as a commodity and the male exploitation of economic power for erotic purchase.

6

The Merchandise of Love: Wives and Merchants

I

A marchant whilom dwelled at Seint-Denys,
That riche was, for which men helde hym wys.
A wyf he hadde of excellent beautee;
And compaignable and revelous was she,
Which is a thyng that causeth more dispence
Than worth is al the chiere and reverence
That men hem doon at festes and at daunces.
Swich salutaciouns and contenaunces
Passen as dooth a shadwe upon the wal;
But wo is hym that payen moot for al!
The sely housbonde, algate he moot paye,
He moot us clothe, and he moot us arraye,
Al for his owene worshipe richely,
In which array we daunce jolily.
And if that he noght may, par aventure,
Or ellis list no switch dispence endure,
But thynketh it is wasted and ylost,
Thanne moot another payen for oure cost,
Or lene us gold, and that is perilous.

CT VII 1–19

The *Shipman's Tale* of French middle-class marriage deals with a very different milieu from the Cook's fragment but it opens with a similar technique. We hear two voices, those of the winner and the waster. The winner's voice is masculine, the waster's feminine and they speak for the husband and wife to whom we are introduced in these lines. The husband is a merchant, rich and therefore, in a world obsessed with money, held wise. His wife is beautiful, sociable and 'revelous' (VII 4), the word which gave Perkin his

84

nickname. The female voice expresses cheerful hedonism, the male voice killjoy thriftiness. His reaction to the sketch of her attractive qualities is to consider their cost-effectiveness: they are more expensive than the attention they provoke is worth. The returns do not justify the initial outlay. They, in a glancing travesty of Boethian values, are like passing shadows. He is a man of substance who must pay for them with real money. The female voice denies any conflict of interest. The husband clothes his wife 'al for his owene worshipe richely' (13) and she is perfectly happy to be a walking – or dancing – status symbol. It is a false economy to grudge the expenditure: if the husband will not pay for his wife's pleasures, someone else – as if it were a law of nature – *must*.

These opening lines present the views of both partners in a bourgeois marriage.They contrast sharply with the disreputable couple who close the First Fragment. Here the husband is the provider, the wife the consumer. We can see their descendants today in the suburbs. He is preoccupied with responsibilities, she is carefree. He is cautious, she is extravagant. But she has her own petty anxieties and he his own forms of largess. Although she complains about his stinginess, he is in fact generous with his wife, friends and household. One of his expenses is a mode of conspicuous consumption popular with the aspiring middle classes: entertaining. There is, perhaps, some justice in the wife's claim that she dresses smartly 'for his owene worshipe' (13) and 'for [his] honour' (421). The merchant is well aware that his financial success depends on his credibility – 'We may creaunce whil we have a name' (289) – and that his credibility depends upon an affluent style: 'We may wel make chiere and good visage / And dryve forth the world as it may be / And kepen oure estaat in pryvetee' (230–2). Traditionally, wasting was parasitical on winning (the industrious in *Piers Plowman* 'wonnen that [thise] wastours with glotonye destruyeth', B Prologue 22) but in the merchant's economy it can be productive. Some conservative categories are being redefined. So are some conventional attributes of the different classes: the merchant cares for his name as much as the aristocrat and for his 'privitee' as much as the shopkeeper. And he is almost monastic about his profession.[1]

Guests flock to the merchant's house, encouraged by his liberality and his wife's beauty. Among them is a young monk of whom he is fond. They come from the same village and 'the monk hym claymeth as for cosynage' (36), one of many heartless puns in the *Shipman's Tale*. The merchant treats him as a cousin but he is to be the dupe of the monk's cozening.[2] In this Tale all affective relationships can be converted into monetary terms.[3]

The relationship between the monk and the merchant is a curious one. They seem to have taken over each other's roles. The merchant is religious about his work. When the monk visits the couple, the husband entertains him for two days but on 'the thridde day' (75) he 'up ariseth' (75), as if resurrected, and goes up to his counting-house. It sounds like a rite of self-examination as he prepares 'to rekene with hymself' (78) and ascertain 'how that he despended hadde his good' (80). Worldly goods might be spiritual goodness and seem to demand similar self-denial. Preoccupied with the worldly, the merchant is prepared to renounce the world. For him a pilgrimage is another strategy 'to kepen oure estaat in pryvetee' (232), a temporary retreat from creditors and curiosity. This pretence is his version of 'pleye' (233). The austerities of his trade do not permit much other play. When he makes his business trip to Bruges, 'he neither pleyeth at the dees ne daunceth, / But as a marchaunt . . . / He let his lyf' (304–6). His puritanical devotion to his work is identified as the mark of the merchant profession. The other pleasure which he apparently denies himself until his business affairs prosper is erotic. He reminds the monk, 'ye know it wel ynogh / Of chapmen, that hir moneie is hir plogh' (287–8), ingenuously replacing the sexual symbolism of ploughing with a financial tenor. Perhaps, when he tells his wife that he has 'greet necessitee / Upon this queynte world t'avyse me ' (235–6), she feels that he is ignoring her and another sense of 'queynte'.

The monk, however, engages very congenially with the world and with the other sense of 'queynte'. Outside his cloister he no more feels like a fish out of water than the Monk of the *General Prologue*. He too is an out-rider, whose abbot allows him to leave the monastery and attend to the administrative business of its estate. This evidently allows him more time than the merchant to spend on pleasure and he also seems strangely affluent. He is a popular guest among the servants because he tips so lavishly and it is he to whom the wife turns for financial help. She is in debt through overspending on clothes. The monk agrees, with demonstrative affection, to bring a hundred franks when her husband is away. It is clear that he will supply the money in return for sexual favours.

The interview in which this arrangement is made is a parody of spiritual counsel. Estates satire is evident in the portraits of the monk and the merchant. In this scene gender satire is also playing on the authority of the man and the dependence of the woman. The wife confides her problems, sexual and financial, to the monk. He provides solutions, sexual and financial. The current of sexuality runs through this conversation from the beginning. The monk looks up from saying his prayers and his commendation of early rising soon turns into conjecture about what sort of night his companion has spent with her husband. She promptly responds that she has no pleasure in 'that sory pley' (117) and launches into complaints about her husband's failings and stinginess. Like a martyr, she could tell a 'legende' (145) of her life and her sufferings with him. The religious vocabulary highlights the mock-confessional quality of the scene. Both characters make vows of secrecy on the monk's breviary and continually swear by God in the course of their dubious dealings.[4] But they also use the gestures and language of romance: they kiss and address each other as 'my deere love' (158) and 'myn owene lady deere' (196). The monk is sexually emboldened by his promise to bring the hundred franks: 'with that word he caughte hire by the flankes. / And hire embraceth harde, and kiste hire ofte' (202–3).

The cousinship of sex and money throughout the Tale provides the basis for the monk's cozening of the merchant, his friend, and the merchant's wife, his mistress. Neither lover cares about the cousinship of affection which the merchant believes to exist between the two men. The wife dismisses 'cosynage' and 'alliance' (139) as a ground for confidence; the monk declares: 'He is na moore cosyn unto me / Than is this leef which hangeth on the tree!' (149–50). Her protestation of loyalty to her husband rings hollow between her assertions that he is the worst man since the beginning of the world and not worth a fly: 'But sith I am a wyf, it sit nat me / To tellen no wight of oure privetee, / Neither abedde ne in noon oother place' (163–5). But even in themselves the lines sound compromising, with the glance at her sex life and the hint that the verbal disloyalty she deplores might occur in a context of physical infidelity, if 'abedde' qualifies 'tellen' rather than 'privetee'. One version of 'privetee' is winning over another.

The conversation is an intimate one. Yet it does not take place in the 'privetee' with which the merchant conducts his financial affairs. The wife clearly counts on discretion when she interrupts the quiet monk at his morning prayers: 'This goode wyf cam walkynge pryvely / Into the gardyn, there he walketh softe' (92–3). The dialogue suggests the secrecy of the confessional, the garden setting the privacy of a meeting between lovers. Yet her small daughter is also present:

> A mayde child cam in hire compaignye,
> Which as hir list she may governe and gye
> For yet under the yerde was the mayde.
>
> 95–7

This child seems to be Chaucer's own addition to the story and she is never mentioned again. Nevill Coghill could see no point in these 'three lines of unused material . . . I do not find this little girl in Chaucer's analogues and cannot think what she is doing in this garden; she is a distracting irrelevance who never reappears'.[5] What she is doing in the garden is, of course, listening and the lessons she learns there will presumably reappear in her own adult life. She might well say then, like the Wife of Bath, 'My dame taughte me that soutiltee' (III 576). Her mother is governing and guiding her by example and the detail that she is 'yet under the yerde' (VII 97) underlines her *status pupillaris*. The subtle and suave courtesy of the *Shipman's Tale* covers a corruption far nastier than the honest dirt and robust vulgarity of Miller, Reeve and Cook.

The monk asks to borrow the hundred franks from the husband, saying that he needs to buy 'beestes' (272). The word suggests a different view of the transaction with the wife from the romantic phrases he used as he grabbed her 'flankes' (202). The merchant replies at once that his gold and his 'chaffare' (285) are at the monk's disposal. The generous dupe speaks more truly than he knows: he hands over the money and enables the monk to enjoy his wife as if she were a piece of merchandise for sale or hire. On his return from Bruges, he makes a friendly call on the monk, tells him about his business dealings and mentions that he is in immediate need of cash. The monk says that he has returned the hundred franks to the wife. The merchant raises the money from another source and concludes his deal with a handsome profit. His sexuality is closely bound with his finances. He goes home and makes love to his wife all night 'For he was riche and cleerly out of dette' (376). Finally, he voices his irritation about the loan to the monk: his wife should have told him the money had been repaid and spared him the embarrassment of having seemed to ask for it. The wife is furious with the monk but talks her way out of her debt. She claims to have supposed the money a gift in return 'for cosynage and eek for beele cheere' (409), she has already spent it 'on myn array, / And nat on wast' (418–19), she will pay her husband with daily sex 'and if so be I faille, / I am youre wyf; score it upon my taille' (415–16). Her husband forgives her but asks her to be more careful of money (and of sexual assets?) in future: 'be namoore so large. / Keep bet thy good' (431–2).

At the end of the Tale the couple accept their losses with realism and resignation. The monk has proved himself the most skilful operator: he has actually managed to make something out of nothing. He has purchased sex merely by moving other people's money around, a parody of the currency speculation conducted by the merchant. The wife has at least found a way of paying her dress bill and doubtless feels some satisfaction at the ingenuity of her solution. The merchant who, on the sternest view, has lost money, sex, wife and friend, prefers not to look at it that way. He can console himself by thinking that he has won a large sum of money elsewhere and is owed a large sum of sex at home. In both senses, the goods are his.

The battery of sexual puns with which the story concludes drives home the point made repeatedly by the words and actions of the characters. Sex can be used as merchandise, currency or credit. The wife converts her debt to her husband into sexual terms, a strategy encouraged by the letter, if not the spirit, of the Pauline texts about the marriage debt. She will employ her tail as a tally. She can pay her husband in sexual pleasure. Unlike the two men, she is simultaneously using and being used, because her sexuality functions as both money and goods. The good humour of the ending depends on several factors. One is the convertibility of the sexual and financial vocabulary which enables the characters to act falsely while speaking truly. Another is the traditional role of the woman as an object of exchange between two men: the complaisant husband is accepting the adaptation of an ancient system to a new world of financial speculation. But most important is the complaisance of the wife in welcoming this role for and with 'beele chere' (409). This is one reason why the story would be inadequate to the critical and questioning Wife of Bath.

II

Blood bitokeneth gold, as me was taught
                    CT III 581

It looks as though the *Shipman's Tale* was originally intended for the Wife of Bath. Although there are two voices in the opening lines, the woman's view is presented in the first person, which suggests a female narrator. This cynical tale of adultery is not suitable to either of the other women on the pilgrimage, who are both nuns. There are also specific similarities to the Wife's Prologue and Tale. The *Shipman's Tale* shares with her Prologue a bourgeois setting, an interest in sex, clothes and money, and an eye for the economic main chance in marriage. Like her Tale, it essays a definition of 'what women want':

> wommen naturelly
> Desiren thynges sixe as well as I:
> They wolde that hir housbondes sholde be
> Hardy, and wise, and riche, and therto free,
> And buxom unto his wyf, and fresshe abedde.
>
> VII 173–7

These lines supply an answer to the crucial question of the *Wife of Bath's Tale* and are couched in similar terms to its concluding prayer: 'Jhesu Crist us sende / Housbondes meeke, yonge, and fresshe abedde, / And grace t'overbyde hem that we wedde' (III 1258–60). Like the prayer, they may make one wonder whether these desires are entirely compatible, whether a man vigorous, powerful and 'fresshe abedde' is an obvious candidate for female domination.

The Wife of Bath's Prologue angrily exposes the conflicts of desire which the *Shipman's Tale* blandly ignores. The *Shipman's Tale* deals in deception, betrayal and prostitution within marriage, yet the tone is calm, the effect comic and the composure of the characters scarcely ruffled by their cynical transactions and accommodations. The Wife of Bath's Prologue is also comic but it is a record of violence, emotional and physical. In her five marriages she is both victim and aggressor. Her first three husbands, who 'were goode men, and riche, and olde' (III 197) fail to attract or satisfy her and she retaliates with constant nagging and abuse. Her fourth marriage to a vital and amorous man is tempestuous for other reasons. Her husband has a mistress and she retaliates by pretending to be unfaithful. Finally, when she can afford to marry a man much younger than herself, the tables are turned on her. Jankin batters her physically and verbally with the misogynistic anecdotes from his book of wicked wives. These wounding paradigms of oppression and destruction constitute an emotional assault. In contrast to the cool negotiations of the *Shipman's Tale*, this couple is reconciled only after a passionate fight. The characters of the *Shipman's Tale* evade the disturbing implications of their actions. Alison specialises in confrontation, gratuitously picking quarrels in her first three marriages over fabricated (or displaced) grievances. She has even been accused of murdering her fourth husband, a modern theory which emphasises the smouldering resentment in the Prologue and discounts the good humour and which recasts it in the mould of a modern genre, the whodunit.[6] In some sense, at any rate, the Wife of Bath kills off her husbands. If I were to view her through the eyes of a novelist, my vision would be more Jamesian than Holmesian: she successively drains her husbands of what they have and she lacks: money, property, vitality, education, articulacy, the various forms of power.

The *Shipman's Tale* would follow very naturally from the Wife's Prologue in describing marriage as sexual and financial transaction. But the Arthurian story which she does tell adds a romantic and philosophical dimension to its racy autobiographical 'preamble'. The *Shipman's Tale*, with its narrower concerns, would have underlined the cynical and prudential side of the Wife's Prologue. But there is more to Alison than cynicism and prudence. We see their obverse in her dream self, the faery wife of the Tale with her idealism and wisdom. The Wife's Tale effects an expansion of the ideas in her Prologue, whereas the *Shipman's Tale* would have represented a contraction. Though a gentler story in every sense, it is activated by the violence inherent in human nature and society. Its genre is romantic and its conclusion conciliatory but it opens with a rape and a death sentence and the threat of execution motivates the knight's enquiry. No such desperate possibilities menace the urbane surface of the *Shipman's Tale*. The Wife's Tale also contrasts with her Prologue and with the *Shipman's Tale* in its lack of interest in money. The characters' freedom from this concern is one of the most romantic aspects of their world. The subject surfaces briefly when 'richesse' (III 925) is volunteered as one of the 'wrong' answers to the knight's question and is disposed of authoritatively in the hag's sermon. Poverty, she instructs her snobbish husband, is no disadvantage: it was chosen by God himself in his incarnation, has been praised by venerable authors and confers benefits of clear-sightedness and detachment. Like most of her speech, this is idealistic in the extreme, but it plays its part in the Tale's emphasis on power rather than its trappings.

The wife in the *Shipman's Tale* has simpler ambitions than the Wife of Bath. She is far more frivolous. The story focuses on her desire for a good wardrobe, which she justifies as a prudent business expense for her husband. Alison also likes pretty clothes but frankly for her own sake ('ever yet I loved to be gay' – III 545). The merchant's wife in the *Shipman's Tale* is content to have her bills paid by her husband and to derive her status from him. She is happy to use her sex as a commodity and to accept her position as the beneficiary of her husband's success. 'The sely housbonde, algate he moot paye' (VII 11) is her opening maxim and she seems not to notice that she herself pays any other price than her 'debt' of sexual favours. But the Wife of Bath's most gruesome proverb, 'Blood bitokeneth gold, as me was taught' (III 581) suggests the true price payable for such transactions. Experience, her other teacher, proves that she needs money of her own.

By the time we first meet her in the *General Prologue* she is, by middle-class standards, rich. Her wealth comes from several sources. She has gained money from her marriages, by the traditional male route of annexing the spouse's property and by the traditional female route of widowhood. 'Oftetyme to be wydwe and wedde' (III 928) is one of the guesses made in her Tale at women's ruling desire. She is also running a business as a clothmaker. Her title of 'Wife' in the *General Prologue* was accepted without comment for centuries. Recent critics, more sensitive to this anomaly among the professions of the men and the profession of the nuns, have remarked on it.[7] Why is she not called the Clothmaker of Bath? Are we to understand her job as 'wiving'? She has, indeed, made a kind of career out of it. But her clothmaking is described before her marriages. This, rather than a husband's generosity, supplies her expensive clothes and fuels her pride, the next attribute in the description, which manifests itself in her uncharitable insistence on taking precedence at the offering. The other married women mentioned in the *General Prologue*, the wives of the guildsmen, are also jealous of their status but happy to derive it from their men:

Everich for the wisdam that he kan,
Was shaply for to ben an alderman.
For catel hadde they ynogh and rente,
And eek hir wyves wolde it wel assente . . .
It is ful fair to been ycleped 'madame',
And goon to vigiles al bifore,
And have a mantel roialliche ybore.

I 371–7

The Wife of Bath wants status in her own right and particularly enjoys 'vigilies' (III 556), with their romantic possibilities; when her husband is out of the way. Her 'mantel' (I 472) figures in her portrait between her buckler-like hat and her sharp spurs, the attributes of the parody knight. Defined as 'the Wife', living by the distaff, she apes the two professions, soldier and preacher, which were almost exclusively masculine.

Alison herself would explain the wife/soldier conflict as due to the contrary astrological influences of Venus and Mars. But this is only one of the tensions and inconsistencies revealed in her confessional Prologue. It is a document seething with potential contradictions from the first lines to the last. The apologist for marriage begins by presenting her credentials to speak of the 'wo' (III 3) in the condition and supports her argument from experience with a series of horrifying memories. She defends sex and marriage but accepts that virginity is the counsel of perfection. She describes three of her husbands as 'good' and two as 'bad' but she found the 'good' husbands unattractive and loved the 'bad'. She cared most for the one who treated her worst. The 'facts' about her marriages seem as confusing as the feelings. It is unclear, for example, whether she committed adultery. The critics who accuse her of murder base their case mainly on the gaps and indirections in her narrative. In the Tale the question of what women most want is solved by magic and all the ladies of the court agree that 'mastery' is the answer. But it is not so simple. Alison concludes her Prologue by showing how she won the battle with Jankin for dominance and then became kind and true. The end of her Tale recapitulates this as a paradox: the faery wife gains mastery and then obeys her husband in every respect. Then Alison's own voice resumes with the prayer that Christ kill off prematurely husbands who refuse to be governed by their wives. The Wife of Bath presents a series of conflicting views, as if the character is a focus for contradictory attitudes and aspirations.

Alison is particularly ambivalent on the relationships between sex and money. She classifies her husbands economically: 'I shal seye sooth, tho housbondes that I hadde, / As thre of hem were goode, and two were badde' (III 195–6). It is an economic description in two senses. The first three husbands are good because they are rich and perhaps also because they are old: she can drain them, dominate them and be detached from them. The fourth and fifth husbands are bad because they make their own bids for independence and domination. But, in other terms, the 'good' husbands are bad because repulsive and boring, the 'bad' husbands good because attractive and interesting. The first three marriages have nothing to recommend them but financial advancement, the fourth and fifth are stirring personal relationships. The Wife wants to make a simple equation between money and sex, as in the *Shipman's Tale*, yet her Prològue relentlessly complicates the issue. Here there is similar wordplay which suggests that the sexual and the financial are identical but it is the opening, rather than the closing, position. Early in the Prologue Alison claims to have picked the best husbands 'Bothe of here nether purs and of here cheste' (44b), punningly conflating scrotal and economic potency, heart and savings. But it is clear that in her five marriages these advantages have been serial, not simultaneous. The power of the chest is an irritation to her. The coffer or safe soon becomes a symbol not of pleasure and fertility but of dependence and imprisonment. The men's possession of money enables their possessiveness of her. She rages at her first three husbands:

> why hydestow, with sorwe,
> The keyes of thy cheste awey fro me?
> It is my good as wel as thyn, pardee! . . .
> I trowe thow woldest loke me in thy
>   chiste!
>   III 308–10, 317

and expresses her final victory over her fourth with this valediction:

> Lat hym fare wel, God yeve his soul reste!
> He is now in his grave and in his cheste.
>   501–2

At the end of the *Shipman's Tale* the merchant admonishes his wife:

'be namoore so large, / Kep bet thy good' (VII 430–1), asserting his ownership of her and her sexuality, while ratifying the identifications made during the Tale of erotic and economic hospitality, generosity, thrift and success. His wife is content to traffic in these terms. The Wife of Bath, however, insists that it is her 'good' (III 310), as well as her husband's. If sex is convertible into money, what is hers to bestow is also hers to reserve: 'Thou shalt nat bothe, thogh that thou were wood, / Be maister of my body and my good' (III 313–14). She wants first to limit male mastery to getting only what he pays for, finally to destroy that domination altogether. Unlike the merchant, she does not regard 'keeping' as prudent or 'largeness' as requiring caution. After surmising that her husband wants to lock her in his chest, she corrects him: 'We love no man that taketh kep or charge / Wher that we goon; we wol ben at oure large' (III 321–2). The characters in the *Shipman's Tale* want to play the system for all it is worth and rake in dividends of every kind. The Wife of Bath's conflicting desires implicitly question the system; the romantic genre of her Tale enables answers to be provided by magic.

The Wife sounds variously as profligate as the Miller and as prudential as the Reeve. As we have seen, she uses the Miller's argument, 'Have thou ynogh what thar thee recche or care / How myrily that othere folkes fare?' (III 329–30), against her first three husbands (though she does not seem to draw any comfort from it herself when her fourth is unfaithful to her). But she also claims that it makes sense to keep strict sexual accounts: 'Wynne whoso may, for al is for to selle' (414). In her opening defence of sex, she presents herself first as a channel for divine generosity and then as a creditor:

> In swich estaat as God hath cleped us
> I wol persevere; I nam nat precius.
> In wyfhod I wol use my instrument
> As frely as my Makere hath it sent.
> If I be daungerous, God yeve me sorwe!
> Myn housbonde shal it have both eve and morwe,
> Whan that hym list come forth and pay his dette.
>
> 147–53

'Precius' here is usually glossed as 'fussy' or 'fastidious' but it surely carries its economic sense too. Juxtaposed to 'frely', it suggests that Alison does not set a high price on her sexuality. But the metaphor of debt and her rebelliousness against her lack of freedom present a very different view of marriage. Here she laughs off the idea that she could be 'daungerous', distant and grudging. But later in the Prologue she advocates the use of 'daunger' as a sensible application of the law of supply and demand:

> With daunger oute we al oure chaffare;
> Greet prees at market maketh deere ware,
> And to greet cheep is holde at litel prys:
> This knoweth every womman that is wys.
>
> 521–4

These conflicting attitudes are apparently contradictory but psychologically and politically entirely plausible. In a world where sex is regarded as a sin, a pleasure and a commodity, the Wife defends, enjoys and trades in it. She is also defensive, disappointed and exploited. Since sex was in youth her only economic asset, she could use sex 'frely' in a free-thinking spirit only at the expense of other freedoms enabled by money. The concept of freedom is a problem which particularly interests Chaucer. 'Free', like 'gentil', has a large range of meaning, which Chaucer explores more fully in the *Franklin's Tale*. Free or generous action is possible only from an agent who has some freedom of choice. The conditions of marriage where one person is not free are such as to preclude the liberality which the Wife theoretically professes.

Both her grudging and her generous attitudes can be seen as perversions of orthodox theological positions.[8] In her opening defence of married sexuality, Alison gives St. Paul's teaching on the subject a new emphasis. He wrote of sex within marriage as a mutual debt between partners. Alison sees the indebtedness as entirely on the husband's side. She wants him to 'be bothe my dettour and my thral' (155). And Paul's metaphor, originally unhappy in its implications, keeps reliteralising itself with devastating effect. The wife in the *Shipman's Tale* is happy to become her husband's debtor and pay her account in sex, charging him again for what she promised at their marriage. When the concept of debt is used both literally and figuratively, applied to both money and sex, they become alternatives. The Wife of Bath understands it thus when she refuses to let her husband 'be maister of [her] body and of [her] good' (314). It would be foolish to give what she can sell.

Yet Alison expresses, almost simultaneously with the Pauline imagery of debt, a more generous theology of sex: she will use her 'instrument' as 'frely' as her 'Makere' gave it to her, whenever her husband wants to 'paye his dette' (149–53). Sex is to be given rather than sold, though Alison's energy suggests a threat as well as a promise. Sexual organs have been created by God and sexual generosity within marriage parallels the divine bounty. The argument is comically close to the Miller's and seriously close to the theologians' of the School of Chartres.[9] She dismisses as untrue to experience a clerical contention that the creation of 'oure bothe thynges smale / Were eek to knowe a female from a male / And for noon oother cause' (121–3). (A theory of meaning as difference could hardly go further.) The apparent contradictions of the Prologue – the longing and the distaste for sex, the profligate and the mercantile attitudes to lovemaking – are familiar enough now and entirely understandable in the intellectual and social context of the Wife's biography. The various Christian authorities on sex are not easily reconciled with each other or with the Wife's experience.

Alison's enjoyment of sex is a subject as ambiguous as her generosity with it. Her account of her first three marriages is a bitter record of frustration and disgust. This too she understands in contractual terms: 'Unnethe myghte they the statut holde / In which that they were bounden unto me' (198–9). She satirises her elderly husbands both for failing to satisfy her desires and for revolting her when they tried to. Fortunately, she manages to find the memories comic. She laughs when she recalls 'How pitously a-nyght I made hem swynke!' (202) and yet she did not even want them. Like many men, they were deceived by a pretence of female ardour:

> For wynnynge wolde I al his lust endure,
> And make me a feyned appetit;
> And yet in bacon hadde I nevere delit . . .
>
> 416–18

She wants from them sexual pleasure which they cannot give and financial profit which they can. So she is reduced to trading sex for money: these marriages would otherwise be a double loss to her. It is a grim business for both buyer and seller. She graphically describes how she would jump out of bed if her husband put his arm around her, unless he made his 'raunson' (411) to her in cash. She drives a hard bargain. As one study of her marriages and her money demonstrates, 'although her rights as a woman were quite limited and she was, legally, almost under the complete control of her husbands, Alisoun shrewdly managed her affairs and the affairs of her husbands so as to gain for herself the greatest possible benefit'.[10] Once the Wife has taken all that the first three husbands have to give, she sees no further reason to be kind to them.

> But sith I hadde hem hoolly in myn hond,
> And sith they hadde me yeven al hir lond,
> What sholde I taken keep hem for to plese
> But it were for my profit and myn ese?
>
> 211–14

Since their only attraction for her was economic, what else could they expect?

The story of her first three marriages reveals her frustration as well as her venality. Alison wants sex as well as its rewards and the ageing men cannot satisfy the young bride. Prudential considerations are abandoned in extra-marital desire:

> I ne lovede nevere by no discrecioun,
> But evere folwede myn appetit,
> Al were he short, or long, or blak or whit;
> I took no kep, so that he liked me,
> How poore he was, ne eek of what degree.
>
> 622–6

In her first three mariages Alison refuses to 'taken keep' (213) of the affective; extra-maritally she 'took no kep' (625) of the economic. This thoughtless sensuality, like the sublimations of romance, is an expression of the conflict between marriage and desire. The woman's wish discovered in the Wife's Tale for sovereignty 'as wel over hir housbond as hire love' (1039) is a yearning to reconcile them.

Desire is the basis of the fourth and fifth marriages. The first three husbands leave Alison rich and therefore free. In these respects a widow could be better off than a wife. A bride received her dower from her husband at the time of the marriage at the church door, perhaps the reason why that part of the ceremony, rather than the nuptial mass, is mentioned in both the Wife's Prologue and her portrait in the *General Prologue*: 'housbondes at chirche dore I have had fyve' (iii 6); 'housbondes at chirche dore she hadde fyve' (i 460). In the absence of specific instructions, the dower was deemed to comprise one-third of the husband's lands. Alison, however, extorts everything from her first three husbands 'they hadde me yeven al hir lond' (III 212). A wife's dower could not be alienated from her. But during her lifetime her husband had legal control over her body and her possessions. Alison, who boasts that she had her first three husbands 'hooly in myn hond' (211), again seems to be an exception to this rule. The benefits she gains from their deaths are quite clear. On being widowed, a woman took possession of her dower and was entitled to retain it even if she remarried.[10] A woman in Alison's position, the widow of several rich husbands, could accumulate considerable wealth. If affection had not cemented the marriage or developed during it, bereavement could be regarded as liberation, a release of capital and the opportunity to acquire more. It is an obvious consequence of the separation of the affective and the economic. No wonder that one answer suggested to the question of what women most desire is 'oftetyme to be wydwe and wedde' (928).

Money is scarcely mentioned in Alison's account of her fourth marriage. Presumably she now feels in a position to choose a mate with other attractions. But sex and power continue to be problematic and a sexually powerful husband proves harder to subdue. He is, in Alison's eyes, a waster, a cheerful profligate of romance: 'My fourthe housbonde was a revelour – / That is to seyn, he hadde a paramour' (453–4). Alison's jealousy reveals a degree of involvement lacking in her earlier marriages. Interestingly, though she takes her revenge in kind, making him 'of the same wode a croce' (484), causing him to fry 'in his owene grece' (487), it is only in emotional terms. She is not unfaithful but makes him think that she is. The issue is power rather than sex. Finally, she proves the winner, in both senses. Another husband bites the dust and is disposed of without undue expense: 'It nys but wast to burye hym preciously' (500).

Alison continues to talk about her relationship with Jankin in such terms. She explains the fact that of her husbands he treated her worst and she loved him best by the laws of the marketplace. Jankin was 'daungerous' of his love, women want what they cannot have, scarcity pushes a price up, the inexpensive is held cheap:

> With daunger oute we al oure chaffare;
> Greet prees at market maketh deere ware,
> And to greet cheep is holde at litel prys:
> This knoweth every womman that is wys.
> 521–4

But other values govern this relationship from the moment Jankin is first mentioned, with his 'crispe heer, shynynge as gold so fyn' (304). Alison is attracted by him physically and intellectually. She falls in love with a man half her age, a former clerk, child of Mercury rather than Venus. He is 'dangerous' to her in the modern as well as the Middle English sense. The battle of sexes is most violent with the man she most cares for. Yet the brief account she gives of their early friendship suggests an initial feeling of alliance, juxtaposing in her memories Jankin with the women she loved. In her quarrels with her husband, she 'took witnesse / On Janekyn, and on my nece also' (382–3). When her husband was away during Lent, 'That Jankyn clerk and my gossyb dame Alys, / And I myself, into the feeldes wente' (548–9). On this country walk in the spring Alison makes her feelings clear to Jankin, telling him that she would marry him if she were widowed.

She also tells him, falsely, that she has dreamed of him:

> I bar hym on honde he hadde enchanted me –
> My dame taughte me that soutiltee –
> And eek I seyde I mette of hym al nyght,
> He wolde han slayn me as I lay upright,
> And al my bed was ful of verray blood;
> But yet I hope that he shal do me good,
> For blood bitokeneth gold, as me was taught.
>
> 575–81

These lines offer a striking nexus of conflicting messages. Alison feels that she is in control, captivating Jankin with her fictitious dreams, telling him that he has enchanted her as she has been taught by an older woman. But the fictions we imagine reveal us as well as the fictions we dream and Jankin *has* enchanted her. Alison is conscious of the manipulative strategies she has been taught by female tradition, a sub-culture with its own murky education in survival techniques. But, critical though she is, she has absorbed some of the messages of patriarchy as if they were laws of nature. 'My dame taughte me' is the disingenuous boast of the graduate of the school of wives, calling attention to her skills in fabrication. By contrast, 'As me was taught' is such a mild and make-weight phrase that it helps to invest 'blood bitokeneth gold' with an air of neutral objectivity. But the terms of the maxim suggest the power of culture over nature: it demands deconstruction. The image of the bloody bed has associations more immediate than murder: puberty, menstruation, the rupturing of the hymen and childbirth. Blood is the sign of a woman's fertility, with the rewards and confinements it can entail, and the proof of her virginity, with the cash value which some societies place upon it. 'Blood bitokeneth gold' is, in this sense, a consoling proverb (compare 'Where there's muck, there's brass'), emphasising the price paid to rather than by a woman for her sexuality. The manifest content of Alison's imagined dream is terrifying, casting Jankin as her killer and anticipating the actual violence of their marriage. 'Blood bitokeneth gold' conveniently permits her to rationalise murderer into benefactor.

But she has not used the standard interpretation of such a dream in all its detail. It might suggest rather that she was to do Jankin good, since an obvious reading of the symbolism yielded a prediction of the death of the dreamer and the inheritance of the person who caused the bleeding.[11] This would give Jankin a motive for marrying a rich older woman, to drain and inherit Alison's money, as she drained and inherited from her first three husbands. It could even be a motive for murder. Alison's fears of Jankin's opportunism and violence are expressed unconsciously here and surface, with histrionic pathos, in their final quarrel, when she exclaims: ' "O! hastow slayn me, false theef?" I seyde, / "And for my land thus hastow mordred me?" ' (800–1).

In fact, Jankin is already in possession of her lands. On their marriage he would have been legally entitled to control the land she received as dower from her previous husbands and to draw the income from it. Alison, however, appears to have conveyed complete ownership to her young bridegroom ('to hym yaf I al the lond and fee / That evere was me yeven therbifoore' – 630–1) and lives to regret it ('But afterward repented me ful soore' – 632). The restitution of control over the land is a major clause in their reconciliation: 'he yaf me al the bridel in myn hond, / To han the governance of hous and lond' (813–14). Alison needs her own money and the independence it gives. The *General Prologue* suggests that she also needs her own work and the status that goes with success. But she wants love as well and, in her relationship with Jankin, is romantic enough to believe that it will make money irrelevant. Her Prologue is a strange record of contradictions, a story of the woe that is in marriage and a confession of the desire for it, an exhibition of attitudes to sex both generous and mercenary, a history of a woman's struggle for and surrender of mastery, an apology for realism and a yearning for the ideal. The romantic side of her nature triumphs in the magical romance of her Tale but the realistic conclusion of her Prologue is that a woman needs money as well as love.[12] Its closing harmony depends on both.

III

> And certeinly, as sooth as God is kyng,
> To take a wyf it is a glorious thyng,
> And namely whan a man is oold and hoor;
> Thanne is a wyf the fruyt of his tresor.
> Thanne sholde he take a yong wyf and a feir,
> On which he myghte engendren hym an heir . . .
> *CT* IV 1267–72

January, in the *Merchant's Tale*, buys a wife more blatantly than any other man in the *Canterbury Tales*.[13] Like the Wife of Bath's first three husbands and like John in the *Miller's Tale*, he is a rich ageing man who chooses a beautiful young wife. As in the *Miller's Tale* he is cuckolded by a younger man, a member of his own household, and we feel that this is inevitable. We know far more about January's initial motives than about those of the other elderly husbands and what we know is appalling. The story opens when he is sixty. He has been a great lecher in his time and now he is beginning to worry about the approach of death and his spiritual prospects. He sees a way of consolidating his assets after his reckless physical extravagance: 'I have my body folily despended; / Blessed be God that it shal been amended! / For I wol be, certeyn, a wedded man' (IV 1403–5). He fears that he will be damned unless he legitimises his sexual desires by marrying. He wants a wife as a sort of spiritual insurance policy. In the passage I quote the narrator ironically supports him and adds other reasons for marriage. A wife will, like interest on capital, be the fruit of his treasure. The mixed metaphor suggests the next advantage. A wife, unlike 'barren metal', can breed and a man of property needs an heir. One of the ironies in this passage is dramatic. In the final scene of the Tale May will ask January to help her climb a pear-tree because her condition has given her a craving for the fruit. There she and Damian make love and it is probably his child who will inherit January's estate.

January affects to consider marriage carefully but from the

beginning of the poem he is resolved on it. The narrator apparently supports him with his lengthy and ironic encomium on wedlock. Only an occasional caveat qualifies the fantasy of pure happiness. Theophrastus, who claimed that it was 'housbondrye' (1296) not to take a wife as a servant would be cheaper, a wife would expect a half-share of everything, would have an interest in her husband's death and might be unfaithful, is quoted and dismissed as a liar. January is so deluded about the absolute joy of the marital state that his only real anxiety arises when he tries to balance the books spiritually and wonders whether he will go to heaven when as a married man he has already enjoyed paradise on earth. Justinus reassures him on that score: a wife is more likely to be an earthly purgatory; January would be rash to marry and particularly to choose a bride much younger than himself. The case against marriage presents the economic aspects more frankly than the case for it. Justinus opens by quoting Seneca's advice on the need for caution in financial affairs as an analogy to the care needed in choosing a wife. One must ascertain what sort of person she is, including whether she will be a 'wastour of thy good' (1535). Justinus himself is thought to have the best possible wife but he finds marriage only 'cost and care / And observances, of alle blisses bare' (1547–8).

Justinus, the just man, gives sensible advice in contrast to Placebo, the flatterer. But Justinus is the just man and his counsel wise only in terms of this bitter and cynical poem. It is told by the Merchant, who is thoroughly unhappy after being married for two months to a woman completely different from the patient Griselda of the story he has just heard. Although both Tales are set in Italy, the Merchant presents a world very unlike the Clerk's. Walter's 'Saluces', is a feudal and conservative society, where the rights of the rich are unquestioned, the poor accept their station humbly and all are bound by mutual loyalties and obligations. The Clerk's grave tone and repetitive style underline its values. The Lombardy of the *Merchant's Tale* is geographically close but ethically a world away. It is a centre of banking and finance and high rewards in new careers. The style of the Tale itself, complex, decorative and ironic, continually engages in brilliant acts of double-dealing. January, the knightly protagonist of a story told by a merchant, combines the economic attitudes of both classes. His wife is to be a return on capital and a resource for providing family to inherit it. Yet the narrator purports to endorse his decision as, in Boethian terms, a wise preference for true happiness rather than the delusive gifts of Fortune, such as 'Iondes, rentes, pastures, or commune, / Or moebles' (1313–14). These will pass away like shadows; a wife will last – and perhaps longer than you want her to.

In fact, January indulges himself in the gifts of Fortune, courts delusion and entertains himself with the play of shadows. Now he is determined to marry:

> Many fair shap and many a fair visage
> Ther passeth thurgh his herte nyght by nyght,
> As whoso tooke a mirour, polisshed bryght,
> And set it in a commune market-place,
> Thanne sholde he se ful many a figure pace
> By his mirour; and in the same wyse
> Gan Januarie inwith his thoght devyse
> Of maydens whiche that dwelten hym bisyde.
>   1580–7

January believes he is inhabiting a romance which is finally rudely exposed as a fabliau. Here the image of the mirror in the market-place expresses both his narcissistic fantasy and its mercantile realisation. In concert with the mixture of genres, this strange simile conflating the imaginative and the commercial exposes the economic basis of romance which romantic conventions in their purest form conceal. Like a rich and acquisitive customer January finds it difficult to choose between all the goods on offer. Finally he settles on May, a girl of great beauty and small degree. Each can provide what the other needs and on marriage May is 'feffed in his lond' (1698) and later promised 'heritage, toun and tour' (2172) as the price for her fidelity.

The great absence in the debate on marriage, the choice of partner and the wedding itself is any consideration of the woman's feelings. The repetition of the phrase 'take a wyf' (1268, 1271) underlines masculine power and feminine helplessness. January has all the egotism encouraged in his sex and his class. He is sixty but is not prepared to marry a woman as old as thirty. It never crosses his mind that to a young wife he himself may be 'bene-straw and greet forage' (1422). Women are objects of consumption: "Bet is," quod he, "a pyk than a pykerel, / And bet than old boef is the tendre veel." ' (1419–20). The first half of the poem consistently looks at marriage from the man's point of view, though it consistently mocks his delusions. But the narrator's bias is also masculine: he condemns January as a fool rather than a knave, for expecting happiness in marriage rather than for approaching it with such motives. The discussion of marriage considers only its problems, advantages or cost-effectiveness for the man. The old knight wants a wife to ensure salvation, to gratify his lust with impunity, to provide an heir and he wants the best his money can buy. In the marketplace of January's imagination, he is the consumer, the women the merchandise.

May allows herself to be bought, presumably because her 'smal degree' (1625) is accompanied by poverty. We hear of January's thoughts, not of hers, during the negotiations. Her extreme quietness and passivity during the magnificent wedding and the gruesome wedding night indicate that January's only attractions for her are economic. She keeps her side of the bargain to the extent of giving January her body and nothing else. She complies with January's loathsome caresses on their wedding night and the narrator only allows us to guess her feelings: 'God woot what that May thoughte in hir herte' (1851). The first thought of May's to which we are admitted is her fantasy about Damian. The affair is a squalid one but the circumstances of May's marriage make it impossible totally to condemn her. In a similar position, the Wife of Bath tells her first three husbands that they shall not 'be maister of [her] body and [her] good' (III 314). May's private contract is that January shall not be master of her body and her love. Like an impressionable reader of romance, she makes a dichotomy between marriage and love, prudence and poverty. Althouth she is prepared to accept all the money and property January has to offer, she comforts herself with the fantasy of a world well lost for love: 'heere I hym assure / To love hym best of any creature, / Though he namoore hadde than his sherte' (IV 1983–5). May's dream of disinterestedness belongs, like Damian's love-letter, in the privy. She cannot afford to do other than prostitute herself to January and she cannot bear to do other than deceive him. The romance offers a plausible form for dignifying these arrangements but it is revealed in the garden scene as a fabliau, the genre in which sex and money are more frankly interchanged.

7

Real Women in Imaginary Gardens

The grete tour, that was so thikke and stroong,
Which of the castel was the chief dongeoun
(Ther as the knyghtes weren in prisoun
Of which I tolde yow and tellen shal),
Was evene joynant to the gardyn wal. . . .

CT I 1056–60

This forseyde Affrican me hente anon,
And forth with hym unto a gate broughte,
Ryght of a park walled with grene ston,
And over the gate, with lettres large iwroughte,
There were vers iwriten, as me thoughte,
On eyther half, of ful gret difference,
Of which I shal yow seyn the pleyn sentence:

'Thorgh me men gon into that blysful place
Of hertes hele and dedly woundes cure;
Thorgh me men gon unto the welle of grace,
There grene and lusty May shal evere endure.
This is the wey to al good aventure.
Be glad, thow redere, and thy sorwe of-caste;
Al open am I – passe in, and sped thee faste!'

'Thorgh me men gon,' than spak that other side,
'Unto the mortal strokes of the spere
Of which Disdayn and Daunger is the gyde,
Ther nevere tre shal fruyt ne leves bere.
This strem yow ledeth to the sorweful were
There as the fish in prysoun is al drye;
Th'eschewing is only the remedye!'

PF 120–40

When Emily walks and sings in the garden on a May morning, she appears like a vision of freedom to the knights immured in their prison tower. But, as we have seen, Emily is not free either. In the second half of the poem she is obviously much less at liberty than Palamon and Arcite and her own vision of freedom, expressed with poignant brevity in her prayer to Diana, is not of the garden, much less of marriage, but of walking in the forest. The opposition between joyful garden and hopeless prison is not absolute. Perhaps the 'wodes wilde' (I 2309) contrast with both. By the end of the poem life itself has been perceived as a 'foule prisoun' (3061). The prison is a microcosm of life, the garden part of a larger prison. Prison and garden are adjacent. Perhaps they even share a wall.[1]

Emily's garden has a long ancestry in both sacred and secular literature. Its archetype is, of course, the Garden of Eden, where there was perfect harmony between innocence and fertility, human love and divine blessing. According to Christian tradition, there was perpetual spring in Paradise and peace between God, man, woman and nature. The changing seasons, the carnivorous animals, the pain and toil of human life, the sinfulness of sex are results of the fall of Adam and Eve. Paradise was created directly by God: there nature in all its profusion cooperated with the man and the woman. Post-lapsarian gardens require work but have their own beauty as a meeting-place of nature and culture, a union which we also see in human sexual relationships.

Christian theologians were not agreed on whether there was sex in Paradise.[2] The biblical account seems to suggest that it was one of the effects of eating the forbidden fruit. The other famous garden of the Old Testament occurs in an exuberantly erotic context, the *Song of Songs*, an epithalamium attributed to King Solomon. The lovers express their devotion and desire in torrents of imagery drawn from the natural world, wild and cultivated. They are likened to wine, precious stones, a company of horses, a bundle of myrrh. The girl is a rose and a lily, her teeth are like a flock of sheep, her breasts like twin young roes, her belly like a heap of wheat set about with lilies. They make love in springtime but it is not the eternal spring of Eden: 'Rise up, my love, my fair one, and come away. For lo, the winter is past, the rain is over and gone; the flowers appear on the earth; the time of the singing of birds is come, and the voice of the turtle is heard in our land' (2: 10–12). They celebrate each other in a garden, like the royal lovers of Eastern painting. The woman is identified with the garden, full of fruit, plants and trees, fragrant and fertile: 'A garden inclosed is my sister, my spouse; a spring shut up, a fountain sealed. Thy plants are an orchard of pomegranates, with pleasant fruits; camphire, with spikenard, spikenard and saffron; calamus and cinnamon, with all trees of frankincense, myrrh and aloes, with all the chief spices: a fountain of gardens, a well of living waters, and streams from Lebanon' (4:12–15). 'Let my beloved come into his garden and eat his pleasant fruits' (4:16), she invites him. He answers: 'I am come into my garden, my sister, my spouse: I have gathered my myrrh with my spice; I have eaten my honeycomb with my honey; I have drunk my wine with my milk' (5:1).

The joyful sensuality of the poem attracted wholesale allegorical intepretation. Jewish exegesis held that the lovers symbolised the relationship between God and Israel, Christian that they represented the marriage between Christ and the Church. The arrival of the bridegroom prefigured the second coming of Christ. The words of the bride longing for her husband served as a particularly moving expression of female piety. Writing of contemplative nuns, for example, Jacques de Vitry quotes from the *Song* to illuminate their almost disabling extremes of devotion.[3] Images from the poem became traditional symbols or attributes of the Virgin Mary: the Tower of Ivory, the Rose of Sharon, the lily of the valleys. Chaucer's Prioress dedicates her Tale to Christ and 'the white lylye flour / Which that the bar and is a mayde alway' (*CT* vii 461–82). The 'well of living waters' (4:15) and the story of Rebecca inspire the tradition that the Annunciation took place beside a well. In the *ABC* the Madonna is the well of pity (126); in the *Second Nun's Prologue* she is the 'welle of mercy' (*CT* viii 37). In particular, the enclosed garden, the *hortus conclusus* of Jerome's translation, was revered as an image of the Virgin Mary in her purity and integrity.[4]

Like other religious motifs, especially those associated with the Madonna, the *hortus conclusus* has its counterpart in the love poetry of the Middle Ages. The Garden of Love is a favourite setting. Many subsequent poems allude to the elaborate allegorical earthly paradise of the the *Romance of the Rose*, part of which Chaucer translated from the French.[5] The narrator of the *Romance* falls asleep in Maytime and dreams of an enclosed garden:

> I saugh a gardyn right anoon,
> Ful long, and brood, and everydell

Enclosed was, and walled well
With highe walles enbatailled . . . .
RR 136–9

He hears birds singing 'daunces of love' (508) and longs to enter. He searches for a 'hole or place [o-] where / By which I myght have entre' (516–17), almost despairs, but finally discovers a wicket gate and is admitted by the porter, Ydelnesse. She is as carefree as her name implies: 'She ladde a lusty lyf in May: / She hadde no thought, by nyght ne day, / Of nothyng' (581–3). The Dreamer perceives the garden as a 'place espirituel' (650). He thinks it an earthly paradise, or even better than paradise:

For certys, as at my devys,
Ther is no place in paradys
So good inne for to dwell or be
As in that gardyn . . .

651–4

Sir Myrthe leads a dance of people so fair that they seem like angels to the Dreamer. At the invitation of Curtesie he joins the dance. It is accompanied by a carol from the lady Gladnesse; on one side of her dances Sir Myrthe and on the other the God of Love. Love too seems like 'an aungell / That down were comen fro hevene cler' (916–17): he is divinely beautiful and wears an amazing robe made from every kind of flower and a chaplet of red roses and birds fly around him. His squire, Swete-Lokyng, carries his bows and arrows. There are two bows, one crooked, gnarled and black, the other finely proportioned and beautifully painted, and ten arrows, of which five are golden and meant for the fair bow and five are black and suited to the foul bow. The golden arrows are Beaute, Symplesse, Fraunchise, Compaignye, Faire-Semblaunt. The black arrows are Pride, Vylanye, Shame, Wanhope, Newe-Thought. The Dreamer dances and then wanders on, stalked by the God of Love. The garden is shaded by great trees of every kind, fragrant with spices, abundant with fruit. It is full of animals, deer, leaping squirrels, playful rabbits. There are wells around which the grass is as thick and soft as velvet and the flowers look as if they had been painted. One well is identified as the place where Narcissus died: as a punishment for spurning the love of the nymph Echo, he was doomed to fall in love with his own reflection and drowned when

he tried to embrace it. The narrator looks into the well and sees there
two crystals. Like Narcissus, he is gazing at his own reflection and
into his own eyes. They reflect the enclosed garden and an
enclosure within an enclosure, 'a roser charged full of rosis, / That
with an hegge aboute enclos is' (1651–2). The God of Love shoots his
first arrow and the Dreamer falls in love with one of the roses.

The Garden of Love is a very ambiguous place. At first it seems
ideal. The Dreamer thinks it might be Paradise. It has in common
with Paradise the spring setting, the perfection of nature, the
radiant happiness of its inhabitants and the presence of the God.
But this God is the God of Love and his weapons are black as well as
golden. His worshippers have been chosen not for their virtue but
for their wealth, beauty, idleness, health and courtesy. Some of the
qualities excluded from the garden and painted on the outside of
the wall are sinful, some are merely unpleasant, and some – Elde
and Povert – are painful but could be seen as conditions of spiritual
opportunity. But all is hedonism within the garden – until one is
wounded by the black arrows. The well of Narcissus is a perilous
place: Narcissus died there and he died of self-love.[6] The name of
Narcissus, the allegory of the crystals, hint that there is something
narcissistic and self-projecting in the whole experience of romantic
love. Reason will soon appear to try to save the Dreamer from it.

The myth of Narcissus assigns different roles to the male and
female characters. His punishment is to fall in love with his
reflection, hers is to lose the power of independent speech and
become only an echo. These are suggestive images of masculine
egotism and feminine support. Formally, the *Romance of the Rose*
differentiates between the presentation of the man and of the
woman. He is voice, narrator and character; she is distributed
between the symbol of the rose and her various allegorical
attributes. Although these personified attributes add up to an
analysis of her mixed and changing feelings, the relationship is
presented entirely from the point of view of the lover. He, like his
patron the God of Love, is as predatory as courtly. His project is to
get into the garden and, as is spelled out in Jean de Meun's long
continuation of the poem, into the rose. He is hero, she is object.
The harmonious imagery of dancing and singing gives way to
figures of conflict and capture – plucking the rose, besieging the
castle – as if the couple were enemies. Perhaps they must be in any
society which is indulgent to male and repressive to female
sexuality.

The *Romance of the Rose* was a major influence on Chaucer's poetry, as he acknowledges in the early *Book of the Duchess*. Its narrator dreams that he wakes in a room whose walls are painted with the *Romance*. The spring morning, the birdsong, the flowers, trees and animals, the account of young love, owe much to the French poem. But the narrator emerges into the forest, not the garden, a fully natural background to this story of love and death. The Garden of Love recurs in two other dream poems but, in general, in his later poems Chaucer's use of the garden is sparing and suspicious. It is also highly evocative. The garden is, literally and metaphorically, seductive. When Pandarus tells Criseyde how he heard Troilus confess his passion to the God of Love 'in-with the paleis gardyn, by a welle' (*TC* II 508), the effect is stylised and parodic: Pandarus represents the religiosity of love and produces his courtly text, a miniature *Romance*, for the occasion. Criseyde tries to escape from thoughts of love into her own garden but there Antigone's text begins to work upon her. The garden is a wry location for the seduction in the *Shipman's Tale* where wife and monk, using the language of love, agree to trade sex for money. The Wife of Bath, significantly, prefers open settings: in her Tale the errant knight and the faery bride meet in the forest; in her Prologue she recalls how, one spring, 'Jankyn clerk, and my gossyb dame Alys, / And I myself, into the feeldes wente' (III 548–9) and she began to woo him. Chaucer sees what is lovely in the garden and what is wrong with it. In the *Knight's Tale* it is next to the prison, suggesting contrast and connection. In the Tales of the Merchant and Franklin, men attempt to trap women in gardens and in fantasies. In an earlier poem, the *Parliament of Fowls*, Chaucer analyses the symbolism of the Garden of Love, its joys and its miseries, its beauty and its artifice.

The *Parliament of Fowls*, like the *Romance* a dream-vision, is an examination of the nature of love which emphasises its ambiguity.[7] The poem opens with a tribute to the power of love by a narrator who has no direct experience but has read in books of 'hys myrakles and his crewel yre' (*PF* 11). 'God save swich a lord!' (14) is all he can say and the homage seems compelled more by the god's tyranny than his goodness. The vision, as in the *Book of the Duchess*, is prefaced by the reading of a book; the narrator, as in *The Book of the Duchess*, can make little meaningful connection between the two. The book, ostensibly, has little to do with love. It is the *Somnium Scipionis* from Cicero's *De Re Publica*, and, together with the commentary by Macrobius, it was popular and influential during the middle ages. The young Scipio dreams that his grandfather, Scipio Africanus, shows him the universe from a 'sterry place' (43), where he hears the music of the spheres and instructs him on the life after death. Those who love 'commune profyt' (47) will proceed to a 'blysful place' (48); 'brekers of the lawe' and 'likerous folk' (78–9) will whirl about the earth for aeons but will finally be forgiven and come too to the place of bliss. He advises his grandson not to delight in this world, so tiny from a celestial perspective, but to work for 'commune profit' (75) and earn eternal happiness at death.

The narrator feels dissatisfied with the book 'For bothe I hadde thyng which that I nolde, / And ek I ne hadde that thyng that I wolde' (90–1), perhaps because he wished to learn more about love. As if in answer to this desire, he has a dream which he attributes to Venus. Scipio Africanus tells him that he has behaved so well in reading 'myn olde boke totorn' (110) that he shall have some reward, and he takes him to the garden of love. It is a walled park with a double inscription on the gate. As if in parody of more eschatological works, the verses with their solemn opening 'Thorgh me men gon' (127, 134) recall the entrance to Dante's Underworld. But unlike the absolute prediction of the *Inferno*, the two sides of the same gate proclaim a vexingly ambiguous message. Like the God of Love's arrows in the *Romance of the Rose* one half is golden and the other black. The first inscription promises all one associates with Paradise: it leads to a 'blysful place' (127), the phrase Scipio used of his classical heaven, where there is perpetual May, a well of grace and the healing of all wounds. The other side of the gate threatens the exact opposite: a place of mortal wounds and barrenness, where Daunger and Disdayn preside, where the tree cannot bear fruit or leaves, where the fish gasps in a dry prison. The first inscription describes the joys of the garden of romance, the second the bitter reverse: fertility and barrenness, restoration and fatal injuries, the well of grace and parching thirst, 'al good aventure' (131) and imprisonment like that of Palamon and Arcite in their hopeless cell. Yet these are different aspects of the same experience. After the cosmic heights and depths of Scipio's vision and the clear moral choice it seemed to present, this dream suggests that human life offers its own version of heaven and hell and that the suffering and the joy are intertwined. No wonder that the Dreamer stands irresolute as if he were metal between two magnets. Then Africanus says briskly that this applies to Love's servants, not to him, and shoves him inside the garden. His first impression bears out the golden inscription. The garden is divinely beautiful. There is an abundant variety of trees with everlasting leaves, flowers in blossom, streams full of shining fish. As in *The Romance of the Rose* and the *Book of the Duchess*, squirrels and rabbits play, hinds and harts roam here. As if in rivalry to the music of the spheres heard by Scipio, the birds sing 'With voys of aungel in here armonye' (191), the gentlest of breezes accompanies them, and stringed instruments play so well that God the creator could never have heard better. But there are hints that the black inscription is also true. The God of Love, 'Cupide, oure lord' (212) is here, engaged in forging and filing his arrows, which his daughter, Will, tempers in the well. In attendance are allegorical characters – Pleasaunce, Aray, Lust, Curteysie, Beute, Youthe, Delyt – who suggest the loveliness but also the limitations of the romantic ideal. Beauty and youth are transient, desire can be for good or ill, the mere pleasure of 'delyt' is conventionally contrasted with the true spiritual happiness of 'felicitee'. Other more obviously dubious qualities inhabit the garden: 'the Craft that can and hath the myght / To don by force a wyght to don folye' (220–1), Foolhardyness, Flaterye, Messagerye, with its undertone of the go-between, and Meede. Outside a temple of brass sit Pees and Pacience but they are not the Christian virtues their names might imply. Pees is the discretion of the bawd; Pacience is pale and sits on a hill of sand, emblem of insecurity. She symbolises the weary frustration of waiting for ever for a love which will not be returned, one of the supreme virtues in the code of courtly love.

Inside the temple love seems worse again. Instead of the temperate breezes and harmony of strings and birdsong outside, the air here is heavy with passionate sights, inspired by the 'bittere goddesse Jelosye' (252), which fan the altars to oppressive heat. In pride of place stands Priapus, classical god of fertility, but rather than suggesting any innocent pagan delight in sex, his erect penis recalls a legend of frustrated violence and indignity. While the garden is bathed in perpetual daylight, it is almost dark inside the temple. When the Dreamer's eyes adjust, he can make out the figure of Venus sporting with her porter Richesse in a private corner: above the waist she is naked, below she is provocatively veiled with a transparent cloth. She is obviously profane, not sacred, love. A young couple kneel before her and cry for help. The power to whom Emily prayed, Diana, goddess of chastity and hunting, has been renounced here: the temple is hung with the broken bows of maidens who decided, after all, to waste their time in the service of Venus. On the walls are paintings of famous heroes and heroines ruined by love: Paris and Helen, Pyramus and Thisbe, Tristram and Isolde, Cleopatra . . . . It is like entering simultaneously a blue movie, a whorehouse, a madhouse and a graveyard.

The narrator emerges from the temple into the fresh air with relief. To comfort himself he walks on and comes upon Nature, whose court is a complete contrast to the temple of Venus. Unlike the fantastical goddess of dark corners, Nature is described in images of radiant light. In the temple instinct was elaborated into artifice. But Nature looks as Alanus de Insulis described her in his *Planctus Naturae*, a work defending natural sexuality. This gesture towards the poets and theologians associated with Chartres identifies Nature according to their views as the 'vicaire of the almyghty Lord' (379) and proper uses of sex as virtuous and god-given.[8] Instead of a temple of brass, an alloy, Nature holds court on a hill of flowers, her halls are made of branches and all the birds have flocked here to choose their mates. Her domain also differs from Cupid's despotic rule. The seasons do pass here: it is St Valentine's Day, so the birds are ready to mate. Nature's rule is more permissive and democratic than Cupid's: she allows free choice of partners and holds a kind of parliamentary debate to determine a disputed case.

A beautiful female eagle is loved by three males, one royal, the others noble and magnificent. Each claims that his love and service are the most deserving. Nature asks a representative of each order of birds to deliver the group's opinion. The falcon speaks for the aristocracy, the birds of prey. The suitors all seem equally meritorious, so it looks as though it will be decided by combat. 'Al redy!' (540) exclaim the warlike eagles in unison, but the falcon has a peaceful solution: let the lady choose her mate. All the other kinds of birds give characteristic replies: the goose cackles that if she won't love him, he should find someone else. The faithful turtle-dove blushes at the very thought of infidelity and counsels eternal loyalty, even to a dead beloved. The duck can see no sense in loving without reciprocation and the goose supports him with a quack and a proverb. The falcon issues the snobbish rebuke that they are to plebeian even to know what love is. The cuckoo suggests spitefully that the three suitors should remain celibate for ever and the merlin retorts that the world would be better off if the murderous ungrateful cuckoo stopped mating. The lesser birds are growing impatient and Nature asks the female eagle to make her own choice, adding that, if she were Reason, she would advise accepting the royal suitor. The lady eagle says she is unready to serve Venus and Cupid and asks for a year's respite, which is granted her. The other birds choose their mates by mutual accord and their choir sings a roundel in praise of Nature, summer and St Valentine. The song of the departing birds wakes the Dreamer and he returns to other books, hoping to have a better dream one day.

The interest and entertainment of the bird parliament lie in its variety. Like the Canterbury pilgrimage, it is a structure for expressing different points of view. The various birds, like the 'sondry folk' (*CT*1 25) represent different classes, different values and different experiences. The rival eagles live by the courtly and chivalric ideals. Their love is noble in its idealism and patience but it entails suffering and disappointment. The female eagle, like Emily, is not eager for love and, when she complies with Nature, will only accept one of her suitors. The other birds occupy a descending scale. At the bottom are those who are compelled by the instinct to mate, noisily impatient and unworried by the choice of partner. They seem in their 'lewednesse' (*PF* 520) considerably happier than their betters but perhaps they miss some of their refinements of joy as well of frustration.

The debate ranges through various attitudes to love. The poem as a whole has a cosmic range. It opens with a noble pagan philosophy in which those who care for 'commune profit' (75) are opposed to 'likerous folk' (79). This is the dream of Scipio, military hero of a very masculine culture and expanding empire. It ends with the domain of the 'noble emperesse' (319) Nature, vicar of the Christian god. She is tolerant and inclusive, ready to listen to the 'lewednesse' (520) of the lesser birds, whose desire to mate is their contribution to the 'commune profit' of their kind. In her macrocosm all human systems are microcosms. Among these lesser systems is the Garden of Love, refinement and sometimes perversion of her gifts.

II

This noble Januarie, with al his myght,
In honest wyse, as longeth to a knyght,
Shoop hym to lyve ful deliciously.

His housynge, his array, as honestly
To his degree was maked as a kynges.
Amonges othere of his honeste thynges,
He made a gardyn, walled al with stoon;
So fair a gardyn woot I nowher noon.
For, out of doute, I verraily suppose
That he that wroot the Romance of the Rose
Ne koude of it the beautee wel devyse;
Ne Priapus ne myghte nat suffise,
Though he be god of gardyns, for to telle
The beautee of the gardyn and the welle,
That stood under a laurer alwey grene.
Ful ofte tyme he Pluto and his queene,
Proserpina, and al hire fayerye,
Disporten hem and maken melodye
Aboute that welle, and daunced, as men tolde.

This noble knyght, this Januarie the olde
Swich deyntee hath in it to walke and pleye,
That he wol no wight suffren bere the keye
Save he hymself; for of the smale wyket
He baar alwey of silver a clyket,
With which, whan that hym leste, he it unshette.
And whan he wolde paye his wyf hir dette
In somer seson, thider wolde he go,
And May his wyf, and no wight but they two;
And thynges whiche that were nat doon abedde,
He in the gardyn parfourned hem and spedde.

CT iv 2023–52

The last act of the *Merchant's Tale* takes place in a walled garden.[9]
January creates this garden as a witness of his honour, a sanctum for
his lovemaking, a tribute to his marriage and, perhaps, a symbol of
May herself. Yet the enclosed garden is a prison: it has a lock. Like
John of the *Miller's Tale*, that other elderly husband of a young wife,
January hopes in vain to hold her 'narwe in cage' (i 3224). And all the
meanings within this symbolic enclosure are the opposite of those
January proclaims. It is introduced as a kind of status symbol.
January is trying to live up to the knightly style of his class, 'in
honest wyse as longeth to a knyght' (iv 2024) and he 'honestly'
(2026) builds the garden 'amonges othere of his honest thynges'

(2028). As in *Othello*, the repetitions of 'honest' and 'honestly' rouse our suspicions. The wealth and rank thus honoured have been the motive for May's loveless marriage and January's presumption that he can buy her. All he has is wealth. The garden is a travesty of the knightly honour to which January pretends. It is a kind of horticultural poem in the genre which celebrates January's class, the romance. Capability January is incapable in other respects. Too old to win honour in arms, he tries to compensate for his lack of knightly prowess and glamour by fabricating an atmosphere of romance. Too feeble to satisfy his wife, he is trying to make up with 'honest thynges' in the material sense for his lack of 'honest thynges' in the sexual sense. 'Thynges' are one of the Wife of Bath's many periphrases for genitals. January's 'thynges' are dishonest, promising more than they can perform. In the garden January will be dishonoured by his dishonest wife. In the most undignified of cuckoldings, the blind old man gives her a leg-up into the pear-tree where she couples with Damian.

The generic complexity and generic conflicts of the Tale culminate in a fabliau sexual exploit set in the garden of romance. Like the disposal of the love letter in the privy, it condemns romance as filth adorned with rhetoric. Like the pitiless vision of the repulsive January crowing on the morning after the wedding night, it displays married love as mere delusion. The generic paradox provides the structure for all the discordant details of the cynical-farcical climax.

At the close of this densely allusive poem, the garden is fertile with association. It parades its literary, theological and mythological sources and analogues. The author of the *Romance of the Rose* could not do justice to its beauty. Nor could Priapus, the phallic god who presides over the sultry temple of Venus in the *Parliament of Fowls*. It is January's romantic landscape, his erotic shrine and his attempt to recreate the sacred gardens of the Bible. He will call his wife into the garden in the vibrant and holy words of the *Song of Songs*. It is the conclusion of his programme to sanctify lechery by wedlock, a reification of his fantasy of marriage as the Earthly Paradise, his own 'personalised' Garden of Eden. But this is a landscape not of innocence but experience. Here, as in Eden, grows a tempting fruit tree: Damian and May will actually commit adultery in its boughs. God walked in Paradise and there are gods in this garden: the contentious Pluto and Proserpina dance and make music beside the well like symbols of harmony. But they also bicker, dispute and mirror the conflicts of human marriage in the celestial sphere. This is a walled garden, a literal *hortus conclusus* but a mocking symbol of chastity: within it May commits adultery and January forces unwelcome, even perverted, lovemaking on her.

The indescribably beautiful garden becomes uglier and uglier under the narrator's treatment. The fabliau mocks the romance, the squalid defiles the sacred, low style ruptures high.[10] The narrator's 'rude' (2351) speech at the crucial moment, 'in he throng' (2353), January's 'Ye, algate in it went!' (2376) compromise the elevated and allusive style of the rest of the Tale, as if the noble diction were merely a gloss on the vile reality. Understood properly, suggests the narrator, the wonderful cadences, sensuous imagery and holy symbolism of the *Song of Songs* are nothing but 'olde lewed wordes' (2149). In this re-vision of Paradise, words are the only covering for the creatures' nakedness and words are showily deceptive.

The garden is January's own creation and the finest expression of the 'fantasye' in which he has indulged throughout the poem. Every detail exposes his delusions. He has dreamed of having a young obedient wife who would be as pliable as 'warm wex' (1430). Instead, when he tries to keep May to himself in the enclosed garden to which only he bears a key, she takes an impression of it in warm wax for her lover to make a duplicate. The phallic symbolism of the key is obvious; there are two keys to this *hortus conclusus*. The 'heigh fantasye' that 'gan in the soule impresse / Of January about his mariage' (1577–9) is mocked by the impression in the wax. 'So depe may impressioun be take' (I 3613), as the narrator of the *Miller's Tale* remarks of another huband's unconscious collusion at another plot to commit adultery. The well hints at the fate of Narcissus. January's sexuality has always been narcissistic. The bright mirror of his mind has not proffered any true image of himself but a succession of auto-erotic fantasies. The laurel in the garden recalls another of his self-deceptions as a wooer, that he is essentially young: 'I feele me nowhere hoor but on myn heed; / Myn herte and alle my lymes been as grene / As laurer thurgh the yeer is for to sene' (IV 1464–6). In fact, his love-making is loathsome and perhaps impotent. The 'thynges which that were nat doon abedde' (2051) suggest that the garden provides a sexually enabling fantasy for January, the only place where he can reach a climax or act out particularly secret desires. January calls his wife into the garden in the lovely words of the *Song of Songs*: 'The turtles voys is herd, my dowve sweete' (2139). Yet January's view of the fidelity symbolised by the turtle-dove is entirely self-interested. Whereas the turtle-dove in the *Parliament of Fowls* swore that he would love his lady for ever, even if she were to die (*PF* 582–7), January uses the emblem to justify his own desire to possess May from beyond the grave:

> neither after his deeth nor in his lyf,
> Ne wolde he that she were love ne wyf,
> But evere lyve as wydwe in clothes blake,
> Soul as the turtle that lost hath hire make.
>
> 2077–80

Yet the garden is also the setting for a moment of self-awareness, when January apologises for his jealousy and attributes it to the gap in their ages (2160–84).

The young romantic hedonistic sexuality of the *Romance of the Rose* has its limitations but January does not even qualify to be among its dancers. He belongs with Elde, outside the wall. The God of Love is absent from his garden. Its tutelary deities are Pluto and Proserpina, Chaucer's own addition to the pear-tree story. They are bound – as the poem reminds us (2227–33) – in a union based on rape. Pluto carried Proserpina off to the Underworld, where she lives with him for the wintry half of the year and from which she returns for the spring and summer. Pluto, rapist, lord of the dead and god of wealth, is an apt patron for January. The story is an aetiological myth accounting for the procession of the seasons. The names of this couple symbolise their incongruity in seasonal terms. January is linked with Pluto, god of winter; 'fresh' May with Proserpina, goddess of spring. Unlike Eden, there is no perpetual spring in this garden nor any return to youth in the life of the individual. The laurel is evergreen in one sense, Paradise ever green in another, but January is not.

Pluto and Proserpina provide an alternative myth to balance the archetype of the Fall. The Gardens of Love allude to the Garden of Eden. January has always wanted an erotic 'paradys terrestre' (1332) and has created a version of it in his garden. But this paradise contains its own fall. January wants his wife, like his garden, to be a *hortus conclusus* but she unlocks both to the 'naddre' (1786) Damian. Their sin takes place in a tree and, like Eve, May longs for its 'fruyt' (2336) She is an Eve who poses as a Mary, trading on her pregnancy and swearing by the Queen of Heaven (2330–7). In a final irony, the narrator commends us in the last line to God's 'mooder Seinte

Marie' (2418). Such allusions place May in a tradition which condemns her deceit and sensuality. But the poem does not lock May into one traditional structure as January tried to lock her in his *hortus conclusus*. It alludes to the misogynist readings of the creation myth and quietly inserts its own revision. 'Allas, my syde' (2329) exclaims May, to explain her craving for pears. This suggests the grief of an Adam, from whose rib Eve was created, over the troubles she has caused him. Chaucer gives the complaint to the wife who, however imperfect, has equal reason to complain of men and of marriage. And he employs a myth which explains the changing seasons as the result of male lust, violence and possessiveness rather than female desire and disobedience. 'A woman in my plit / May han to fruyt so greet an appetit / That she may dyen, but she of it have' (2335–7), pleads May, with resourceful cunning. Yet her words are true, though she intends them to deceive. Walled in the garden, trapped in a loveless marriage, she is in a plight which craves the fruitful satisfaction of her appetite by Damian. January mirrors the cold barrenness of Pluto. May takes what fruit she can find, as Proserpina ate pomegranate seeds in Hades.

Pluto and Proserpina do not appear in any of the analogues to the *Merchant's Tale*. In the versions of the story which Chaucer might have known, God and St Peter intervene on the husband's behalf and restore his sight, divinely supporting the man and condemning the woman. Chaucer's introduction of pagan gods de-privileges their intervention. They have power but not authority. So blatantly made in human image that they have plausibly been interpreted as avatars of Jankin and Alison,[11] they side, all too humanly, with the partner of the same sex, wrangle over the alleged wickedness of all women and themselves cite authorities to support their opposing views. They suggest that the antagonism between the sexes is so deep that it is found among the gods themselves rather than that God the Father and St Peter, first Holy Father of the Church, will always avenge wrongs to patriarchy. Pluto restores January's sight so that he witnesses his wife's arboreal adultery, Proserpina inspires her with an excuse, and the story of January and May becomes another aetiological myth to explain why women can always talk their way out of any incriminating situation.

January is content to accept May's explanation, which will cover future as well as past infidelity, and presumably to accept Damian's child as the heir to his estates. In a sense he has everything he wanted: a beautiful young wife, an earthly paradise and an heir. In a sense. The *Merchant's Tale* deals in competing discourse and conflicting interpretations. It accommodates high style and low, pagan and Christian, clashes of genre, the knightly and the mercantile. The Merchant intends to savage the sacramental view of marriage and the romantic view of love. In his tale the sacrament merely dignifies sexual, financial and spiritual opportunism and the romance is exposed as a fabliau. He mocks January's folly in expecting good of marriage and of his cheap and sneaky wife. He dismisses the Canticle's lyrical invitation into the garden as 'olde lewed wordes' (2149). But the Tale also reflexively condemns the cynicism of the teller. His interpretation of the verbal, conceptual and institutional structures which his characters inhabit is partial. January's is even more partial. His attempt to create a stability of perfection in an earthly garden and his attempt to possess his wife entirely within it is a vain bid to control meaning. May, the prisoner of her own fantasy and limitations as well as his, chooses this structure to sabotage. The Tale's frequent description of her as 'fresh' is ironic in its suggestion of purity. But May does generate fresh meaning in January's closed system. The pluralism of the Tale invites the audience to construct better meanings than January's, May's or the Merchant's.

III

This squier, which that hight Aurelius,
On Dorigen, that was so amorus,
Of aventure happed hire to meete
Amydde the toun, right in the quykkest strete,
As she was bown to goon the wey forth right
Toward the gardyn there as she had hight.
And he was to the gardyn-ward also;
For wel he spyed whan she wolde go
Out of hir hous to any maner place.
But thus they mette, of aventure or grace,
And he saleweth hire with glad entent,
And asked of hire whiderward she wente;
And she answerde, half as she were mad,
'Unto the gardyn, as myn housbonde bad,
My trouthe for to holde, allas! allas!'

CT v 1499–1513

This must be one of the least romantic trysts in literature. Dorigen, the weeping heroine, is happily married to Arveragus. But she has made a foolish promise to sleep with the young squire Aurelius, if he can perform the seemingly impossible task of removing the black rocks from the coast of Brittany. When Aurelius hires a magician who makes the rocks seem to disappear, Arveragus tells his wife to honour her undertaking to his rival. Here they meet as she is on her way to the garden to keep her promise. Aurelius is so moved by her husband's generosity that he releases her from her pledge, leaving himself vainly in debt to the magician. But when the clerk hears the story, he emulates the generosity of knight and squire and writes off the debt.

This Tale has been seen as the conclusion of a 'Marriage Group', a theory which was influentially argued by G. L. Kittredge.[12] On this view, the Wife of Bath initiates a debate on marriage with her polemical Prologue and Tale, both stories of a wife's successful bid for 'maistrye' over her husband. Giving the lie to her complaint that no clerk will speak good of women, the Clerk retaliates with his Tale of an absolutely obedient wife. The Merchant, embittered by his own brief experience of marriage to a woman who could not be more different from Griselda, tells a savagely ironic story of female treachery and male fantasy and folly. The *Franklin's Tale* repeats the knight-wife-squire triangle but with better-natured characters and a happy outcome. It also opens quite differently, with a genuinely good marriage between unselfish people who negotiate a kind of equality. The Merchant's ironic encomium of marriage is echoed and answered in the Franklin's sincere praise. He repudiates both the Wife of Bath's doctrine of female sovereignty and the theory of male dominance embodied in the Clerk's Walter. Kittredge concludes that the Franklin offers not only the solution to the marriage debate but also Chaucer's own view of the subject and, indeed, ours: 'We need not hesitate, therefore, to accept the solution which the Franklin offers as that which Geoffrey Chaucer the man accepted for his own part. Certainly it is a solution that does him infinite credit. A better has never been devised or imagined.'[13]

However, many subsequent readers have hesitated to accept the theory of the 'Marriage Group' or the *Franklin's Tale* as the 'certain solution' to the issues raised by the other stories. The four Tales deal with marital problems but also with other topics, such as 'gentillesse'. They allude to each other but as a sequence they are interrupted by the stories of the Friar, Summoner and Squire, and they also allude to other *Canterbury Tales*. Most of the *Canterbury Tales*, not only the 'Marriage Group', deal with marriage; several – the Tales of Knight, Miller, Shipman, Manciple – like the *Franklin's Tale* present a love-triangle composed of two men and one woman.

It is difficult to see the *Franklin's Tale* as concluding a debate. Rather, it begins with a 'solution' and ends with a question. It is perhaps the most ambiguous of the multifariously ambiguous *Canterbury Tales*. A feminist or a sexist reading can be supported from the Tale. One may be moved and convinced by the passage in which the narrator supports the young couple's private marriage contract and argues that love and 'maistrye' cannot co-exist. Or one could see the problems that follow as the result of the husband's surrender of authority to the wife. On this view, the culminating irony is that Arveragus does finally assert his authority over Dorigen in, paradoxically, telling her to sleep with another man. The story hinges on Dorigen's rash promise to love Aurelius when he removes the black rocks: here a statement intended metaphorically, that she will never love him, is taken literally and understood to mean the opposite. The turning-point in the story, when Aurelius entrusts the task to the magician, is presided over by Janus, the double-headed god 'with double berd' (v 1252), lord of exits and entrances, facing both ways. The poem even opens in a land described as verbally plural, 'In Armorik, that called is Britayne' (729) or Brittany, and has to correct potential confusion with 'Engelond, that cleped was eek Briteyne' (810).

The Franklin's Prologue, describing the Tale as a Breton lay composed by one of the 'olde gentil' (709) poets of Brittany to be read or sung to musical accompaniment, seems to herald a very traditional work. The *Tale* opens with a conventional situation conventionally described. It introduces the couple, who are not named for nearly a hundred lines, as the desperately love-stricken knight and the superlatively beautiful lady familiar from romance. These apparently stock characters initially play their usual parts. He is too in awe of her to tell her of his love but he performs 'many a labour, many a greet emprise' (732) for her. Finally she rewards 'his meke obeysaunce' (739), takes 'pitee . . . of his penaunce' (740) and accepts him as her husband and her lord.

The events of a standard romance plot have been compressed into the opening lines. The poem begins with a happy ending and immediately presents it as problematic. Before marriage the knight has served the lady and she has had all the power of decision. In marriage, on the orthodox view, the husband becomes her lord. However, the poem at once raises the question of definition: the husband's lordship consists 'of swich lordship as men han over hir wyves' (743). It is analogous to but not the same as political lordship, it may bestow legal rights without personal domination and it will vary from couple to couple. This particular husband abrogates any right to exert force or authority over his wife. He will obey her, like a lover his lady, but with one proviso: 'Save that the name of soveraynetee, / That wolde he have for shame of his degree' (751–2). The theory of the alternative system, like the theory of the orthodox, is expressed in words, which are slippery of definition and apt to generate unexpected meanings. Arveragus, indeed, wants to claim merely a word, 'the name of soveraynetee' (751), for the sake of appearances, 'for shame of his degree' (752). He does not clarify which 'degree' he means, that of knight, man or husband, and probably he cannot subdivide his identity into separate compartments of this kind. He has been conditioned, because of his class and his sex, into a kind of pride which can accept service but not shame. The narrator, after explaining that liberty and tolerance are essential between friends, insists that this couple can unite the values of romance and of marriage without contradiction.

> Thus hath she take hir servant and hir lord, –
> Servant in love, and lord in mariage,
> Thanne was he bothe in lordshipe and servage.
> Servage? Nay, but in lordshipe above,
> Sith he hath bothe his lady and his love,
> His lady, certes, and his wyf also . . .
>
> 792–7

The conflicting theories of the relations between the sexes seem to have been reconciled. But words have a life of their own and appearances a kind of reality, as Dorigen finds when her rash promise is taken seriously, the rocks apparently vanish and Arveragus exerts his 'soveraynetee'.

Perhaps the different roles which Arveragus has to play are not so easily combined. When he goes to England 'to seke in armes worshipe and honour' (811), as befits a knight, he leaves his wife in a state of dejection so deep that she even questions the goodness of God who created the rocks that imperil his passage home. Her friends try to console her by taking her to a garden of surpassing beauty. The garden is a triumph of nature and art, full of leaves and flowers and cultivated by 'craft of mannes hand' (909) so that no other could compare with it but Paradise itself. It is May, the season of love. Among the dancers in the garden is the young squire Aurelius, who is already secretly in love with Dorigen. He is the perfect lover in the perfect setting, 'fressher . . . and jolyer of array' (927) than the month of May itself. He sings and dances better than anybody in the whole history of the world. He is a poet, discreetly bemoaning his unrequited love in 'many layes, / Songs, compleintes, roundels, virelayes' (947–8). He has adored Dorigen in silence for more than two years. He is as virtuous as attractive: 'Yong, strong, right vertuous, and riche, and wys, / And wel biloved, and holden in greet prys' (933–4). Like Arveragus, he is the more sympathetic (or quixotic?) in seeing himself in terms which cross the boundaries of traditional gender roles: he compares his hopeless love to that of Echo rather than Narcissus.[14] But the effect of love will be to degrade the character of Aurelius.

In the garden he at last tells her of his passion and begs for her mercy. Dorigen's reply is decisive.

> Ne shal I nevere been untrewe wyf
> In word ne werk, as fer as I have wit;
> I wol been his to whom that I am knyt.
> Taak this for fynal answere as of me.
>
> 984–7

Unfortunately, it is not her final answer, Her absolute 'No' modulates into a playful, conditional, unintended 'Yes'. She promises 'in pley' (988) to love him when he removes the rocks. This, she thinks, is impossible and she tells him so: 'Lat swich folies out of youre herte slyde' (1002). But the promise is foolish too and why does Dorigen make it? At one level, it demonstrates her love for her husband: the first image that comes to mind is the rocks that endanger his return. But she should not wish them away. Her questioning of the adversity they represent brings her close to heresy or atheism and her marriage is actually threatened by their disappearance rather than their presence. At another level, it is one of the social compromises which women are conditioned to make. Dorigen wants to be nice. (The Prioress also wants to be nice, with sexual connotations even less appropriate to her vocation than to Dorigen's rebuff of her suitor.) It is as if Daunger had briefly assumed the guise of Fair Welcome. Dorigen softens the blow and gives Aurelius's imagination something to work on.

Imagination and fantasy are as suspect in the *Franklin's Tale* as in the Merchant's. When he comes home, Arveragus is generously free from wondering what approaches may have been made to his wife in the meantime: 'No thyng list hym to been ymaginatyf' (1094). But during his absence Dorigen has been consumed by her 'derke fantasy' of longing and anxiety. Aurelius is the major victim of fantasy but he tries to turn it to his own advantage. From the moment that his brother decides they should consult a magician, Aurelius deals in illusion. The narrator reminds us that the story is set in a pagan time and that the audience's Christian faith 'ne suffreth noon illusioun us to greve' (1134). The magician displays his skill by conjuring up within his house phantasms of the noble life, forest and deer parks, hunters, falconers on a river and jousting knights. This dream-like masquerade culminates in an image of reciprocated love: 'he hym shewed his lady on a daunce, / On which hymself he daunced, as hym thoughte' (1200–1). But this emblem of sexual harmony properly applies to the relationship between Dorigen and Arveragus. In the earlier garden scene Aurelius joins the dance but in her husband's absence Dorigen has no interest in dancing and no pleasure in watching: 'For she ne saugh hym on the daunce go / That was her housbonde and hir love also' (921–2). Now Arveragus is back and enjoys in reality what Aurelius imagines: He 'daunceth, justeth, maketh hire good cheere' (1098). Aurelius has become more irrelevant than ever.

The clerk fulfils his contract and 'thurgh his magik, for a wyke or tweye, / It semed that alle the rokkes were aweye' (1295–6). The magician deals only in appearances and so, it proves, does Aurelius. He breaks the news to Dorigen as if the disappearance of the rocks were a reality: 'wel I woot the rokkes been aweye' (1338). This is the climactic last line of a speech which alternates between a smooth courtly surface and a threatening ultimatum. Aurelius approaches 'his sovereyn lady deere' (1310) with proper nervousness and humility, 'with dredful herte and with ful humble cheere' (1309), and uses all the correct rhetoric of the religion of love. He wants to displease her less than anyone in the world (1313), he would not claim anything from her as 'of right' (1324), he is quite unworthy of her love (1330) *but* she must remember the promise made in the garden. And he claims that he says this more to save her honour than his own life (1331–2). It is a thoroughly slimy performance, coercion and blackmail posing as courtliness and concern.[15] Is this the reality under the romantic façade? To underline the disjunction between romance and reality, the season is now midwinter and the green of the May garden is gone.

Dorigen sees no way out of his trap except suicide. She meditates on a long catalogue of chaste women and faithful wives of the past, most of whom took their own lives rather than be sexually dishonoured. But the more Dorigen talks about suicide, the longer she delays, until Arveragus returns and tells her to keep her promise to his rival.

All three characters have been criticised for their behaviour at this point in the Tale.[16] Aurelius has only made the rocks seem to disappear and has no right to trap Dorigen into unwilling adultery. Dorigen did not mean her promise literally and neither he nor she should consider it binding. Both she and Arveragus should know that the troth she plighted him at their marriage has priority over the contradictory troth plighted to the squire. Dorigen, further-more, is too weak a character to cut the Gordian knot by suicide. Arveragus does finally assert over her the mastery he forswore at the opening of the poem in, of all things, telling her to accept another man and break her marriage vow. Are not all these characters deceivers or self-deceived?

The *Franklin's Tale* is a story in which plans go awry – and it is usually better that they do. It is also a story in which events, arguments and promises are not taken to their logical conclusion. The stereotype knight and lady of romance turn into the husband and wife negotiating a new relationship. The balance which they reach proves inadequate to the strains placed upon it. Dorigen seems ready to die of grief at her first separation from Arveragus. She weeps and sighs 'as doon thise noble wyves whan hem liketh' (818), a comment which suggests indulgence in as well as nobility of sentiment. But she does survive and is even gradually comforted by her friends. She charmingly and foolishly qualifies her rejection of Aurelius. Theologically, her moment of greatest danger is when she questions God's creation of the rocks but she stops short of the ultimate heresy in a prayer for her husband and a relegation of the problem of suffering to the clerks. Unlike the pugnacious Wife of Bath, Dorigen has no wish to usurp their prerogative.

In the soliloquy about suicide, which is also, fortunately, not taken to its conclusion in action, Dorigen is very docile in her consideration of clerical authority. She perceives herself as facing the ancient dilemma of the virtuous wife. Should a women prefer death to dishonour? Many of the women in the books have chosen to kill themselves rather than suffer or risk sexual defilement. But her examples are classical, which may suggest, in this poem about pagans but interpreted by Christians, values which need questioning. One of the examples is Lucretia, whose suicide had provoked controversy in the early Christian period because it suggested a mechanical view of sexual virtue.[17] If Lucretia did not assent to her rape, in what sense could she be considered guilty? Her suicide seems to place more importance on the body than the will. (A modern audience might add that it fits a view of a wife as her husband's property and a raped woman as damaged goods.) Dorigen arguably bears more responsibility for her plight but what purpose would her suicide serve? Why should she be sacrificed on the altar of an ancient masculine idea of honour? It proves not to be Arveragus's concept of honour and her suicide would be a wry gesture of loyalty to him.

The narrator anticipates criticism of Arveragus and intervenes to tell his audience to be patient and judge by the event. Arveragus is justified by the event but can we make any less pragmatic defence of him? Perhaps justification by the event is not merely pragmatic. The narrator suggests that the characters may, without realising it, be in the hands of God. The winter setting symbolises 'Nowel' in a bleak landscape (1245–55) and the encounter of Dorigen and Aurelius in the street may be due to mere chance ('aventure') but possibly to grace (1508). The world is at a turning-point and Arveragus, at the end of the poem as at the beginning, both criticises and conforms to tradition. His action is ambiguous in that he simultaneously surrenders and asserts his rights over his wife. It is also a confrontation of ambiguity, of what the resonant words 'truth' and 'honour' mean when applied to a woman. These words traditionally have a much narrower field of reference for women than for men.[18] They are usually synonymous with chastity, sometimes held to be the *only* female virtue. According to this usage, Arveragus's masculine honour, in complement to his wife's, might be saved by fighting a duel with Aurelius. This would be his equivalent of her hypothetical suicide. Instead, the husband acknowledges that his wife's 'truth' is as important as his own and should operate in the public world of contracts and social life, not only in the private sanctum of the marital relationship. And the lover is forced to learn this lesson: that Dorigen is a person independent of her relationship with him and his fantasies about her. Their final interview takes place not in the garden of romance but in the busiest street in town.

Like other absolute conclusions, a meeting in the garden is avoided. Aurelius takes his leave of Dorigen in a crowded street, the real and unromantic world, which will provide no beautiful and enchanted memories of their parting. (Chaucer is sterner and more consistent than Dickens, who changed the original ending of *Great Expectations* from a hasty chance meeting and parting between Pip and Estella in Piccadilly to an ambiguous reconciliation in the evocative and still-walled garden of vanished Satis House.) The romance proves broad enough to accommodate an attack on romance. It moves on from the love problem to the money problem, from the knight's surrender of his wife, from the squire's renunciation of her, to the clerk's refusal of payment. The Tale reflects the common sense of the Franklin, his bourgeois concern with status, his comfortable sublimation of materialism in generosity.[19] He is aware that he is not as 'gentil' in the social sense as the Knight and his son is a disappointment compared with the Squire. The characters in his story do not go to the extremes of Palamon and Arcite. Nobody dies. Dorigen alludes to the tragedies of the classical past but does not finally emulate them. A classic finale is posited – the compromised wife resolves to commit suicide – but averted as a false solution. Dorigen inhabits a romance rather than a classical genre – the Franklin's expression of modesty in his Prologue includes the disclaimer that he never slept on Mount Parnassus or studied Cicero –, a romance in which the logic may be gentler and more forgiving than in tragedy, whose compromises have an element of common sense. It is characteristic of Chaucer to eschew the absolutes of tragedy in favour of the fluidities of romance or the deflations of comedy. Even in his 'tragedye' (*TC* v 1786) *Troilus and Criseyde* he denies us the finalities and satisfactions of the tragic mode, such as the fatal symmetry of revenge on the battlefield with its dubious restoration of honour. It would have been formally gratifying if Troilus had killed Diomede but Fortune – the unfinished business, the inelegant contingencies of real life – did not permit this perfect close.

One of the stories left unfinished at the end of *Troilus* is Criseyde's. The heroine drops out of the poem while we follow the hero to his death and beyond. Like Criseyde, Dorigen fades out of her story and is forgotten. Husband, lover and perhaps author confer on her an authority and autonomy which are belied by the event. Husband, lover and wife are successively marginalised but husband and lover are restored to a central position at the close. The poem opens with a couple – knight and lady. They are defined as Arveragus and Dorigen, particular people with their particular relationship based on equality. The couple becomes a triangle – husband, wife and lover. Finally, this triangle is replaced by another all-male triangle – knight, squire and magician. As usual, in groups of men, competition surfaces. 'Which was the mooste fre?' (v 1622) asks the narrator. Who was the most generous? I find myself asking 'Who was the least free?' and, despite the vows of service made to her throughout the poem, answer 'Dorigen'. She escapes the *hortus conclusus* and is excluded rather than enclosed.

8

The Saints

I

'Fader,' she seyde, 'thy wrecched child Custance,
Thy yonge doghter fostred up so softe,
And ye, my mooder, my soverayn plesance
Over alle thyng, out-taken Criste on-lofte,
Custance your child hire recommandeth ofte
Unto youre grace, for I shal to Surrye,
Ne shal I nevere seen yow moore with ye.

'Allas! unto the Barbre nacioun
I moste anoon, syn that it is youre wille;
But Crist, that starf for our redempcioun
So yeve me grace his heestes to fulfille!
I, wrecche womman, no fors though I spille!
Wommen are born to thraldom and penance,
And to been under mannes governance.'

CT II 274–87

Three of the *Canterbury Tales* – those of the Man of Law, the Clerk
and the Second Nun – present adult women of amazing virtue.
Their virtues are specifically Christian: between them they
illustrate charity, patience, constancy, faith, fortitude, chastity, self-
sacrifice and missionary zeal. The Nun tells the story of the saint
and martyr Cecilia. The long-suffering heroine of the *Man of Law's
Tale* is aptly named Constance. The Clerk tells the tale of that
byword of wifely obedience, patient Griselda. All three stories are
set in the past, the age of miracles. Two take place in the early
centuries of the Church. Saint Cecilia probably lived in the first,
second or third century, the time of conversions, catacombs,
persecutions and martyrdom. The *Man of Law's Tale* opens
'whilom', once upon a time, in the vague past, though some of its
characters derive from late sixth-century originals: in the Tale,

131

Rome is now a Christian empire, Islam is already an established religion in the Middle East and Christianity is gaining ground in Anglo-Saxon England. The Clerk also opens his narrative with 'whilom' and concludes by setting it and its values firmly in the past: 'Grisilde is deed and eek hire pacience' (IV 1177).

The *Man of Law's Tale* is delivered on the first or second morning of the pilgrimage. If on the first day, it stands in a climactic position at the end of the first group of stories.[1] If it opens the storytelling of the second day, it is a new beginning, introducing another genre and another view of life. In the link between Fragment I and the *Man of Law's Tale*, Chaucer produces a kind of comic 'signature' when the lawyer lists the work of the hack poet who has pre-empted most of the stories. Here the Host lectures the pilgrims on the dangers of procrastination and idleness, as if the time has come to turn to something serious and improving. After the *Knight's Tale*, a story of pagan virtue and suffering, the Man of Law tells 'with a sobre cheere' (II 97) a story of Christian virtue and suffering. The Knight depicts male heroism, the lawyer female heroism. Constance has as little say in her destiny as Emily, but her religion enables her to turn her passivity to positive effect. The Tale follows three fabliaux, in which adultery is seen as comic and women as sexual objects or sexual opportunists. Here, by contrast, extra-marital desires are inspired by the devil and punished with direct intervention from heaven. Sexuality is presented in the service of marriage and marriage in the service of the Christian life.

The story begins with a marriage and a conversion. The Sultan of Syria hears of the beauty and goodness of Constance, daughter of the Emperor of Rome. He is so overcome with the desire to marry her that he is prepared to renounce his religion. Constance, therefore, sets out, in great pomp, as the representative of Christianity against Islam, against the force that was in Chaucer's time seen as the greatest threat to Christianity. However, when we first see Constance, her bearing is hardly that of the triumphant envoy of Empire and Christendom. Rather, on the 'woful day fatal' (II 261) of her departure, she is pale and overcome with sorrow but resigned to her future. Our first impression of Constance, tearful, frightened, helpless but resolute, is typical. Throughout the Tale she will accept danger and disaster in this spirit. Her first speech, which I quote above, expresses her sorrow, outlines her values and hints at the strength she will salvage from weakness. She bids farewell to her father and mother and commits herself to Christ. She submits to the authority of God, her parents and her future husband.

These mirrored hierarchies – sexual, social, familial and spiritual – present analogies which disturb me in this Tale and which will be explicitly denied in the *Clerk's Tale*.[2] The woman of noble birth is handed from father to husband for political reasons, just as the lower-class girl is sold for financial reasons. Emily cements the alliance between Athens and Thebes. Young Alison is married to elderly John. But there is a further dimension to the marriage of Constance. Her mission is to claim for Christianity the Sultan and all his subjects. Her second marriage, to the Anglo-Saxon King Alla, will repeat this pattern. Constance, in her total submission to the will of God, is an exemplary Christian for this purpose. And this relationship provides her with a model for the relationships between parent and child, ruler and subject, husband and wife, and man and woman.

The narrator comments that Constance's grief is hardly surprising when she has to leave her family and country and be 'bounden under subjeccioun' (II 270) to someone about whom she knows very little. 'Housbondes been alle goode, and han ben yoore; / That knowen wyves; I dar sey yow na moore' (272–3), he comments, with heavy irony. The irony, apparently directed against all the bad – or even all the – husbands in the world, seems rather beside the point here. Both Constance's husbands will love her and her troubles will rather be caused by assorted mothers-in-law, would-be rapists and false witnesses. The narrator, sympathetic to women, cynical about men, seems to generalise from Constance, even when her particular experience does not quite fit his generalisation. I think the irony is rather directed against the fact that the official voice of the culture is masculine, which the narrator first parodies and then subverts with 'I dar sey yow na moore' (273). Constance herself, however, endorses the official view. Her speech tempers the plaintive with the docile and culminates in her statement of male supremacy. The suggestion is that the narrator, albeit in a veiled and vulgar way, is more critical of this hierarchy than is Constance.

In Syria, Constance falls victim to the first villain of the Tale, her mother-in-law. The Sultaness is not prepared to renounce her faith, and she devises a plot against the Christians. She tells her son that she is willing to convert and offers to give a feast to celebrate his marriage. The Sultan and all the Christians are massacred at the table. Only Constance escapes, and she is put to sea in a rudderless boat.

The Sultaness is a monstrous archetype. She is the terrifying older woman, the 'bad mother' of psychology, the malignant stepmother of folk-tale, the witch, cousin to the queens in *Cymbeline* and *Snow White*. She is animated by our deepest and oldest terrors, of being rejected, deceived, assaulted, where we depended on being loved. She greets Constance on her arrival 'as any mooder myghte hir doghter deere' (397). 'Thou Semyrame the secounde' (359) exclaims the narrator to her, reminded of the Assyrian queen who killed her husband. The Sultaness – like Medea and Agave – kills her own child. Her method is particularly frightening. She slaughters a large number of people, including her son, at a banquet she herself has arranged. Her treachery equals that of Lady Macbeth, who conspires to murder her royal guest after feasting him, or Clytemnestra, who murders her husband in the welcoming bath on his return from ten years at war. Although the Sultaness kills by the sword, like a man, she is metaphorically the female poisoner, stealthily producing death instead of nourishment. Like Lady Macbeth and Clytemnestra (both wives of soldier husbands), her wickedness as a woman is fuelled by her usurpation of a masculine role: she is a 'virago' (359). She is a rebel against male authority and her crimes are finally attributed to personal ambition rather than religious conviction: 'She herself wolde al the contree lede' (434). But it hardly matters which is the 'real' reason. These motives, whose coexistence might trouble a Christian conscience, are perfectly consistent for the Sultaness. Her refusal to renounce her faith, which would be admirable in a Christian, is symptomatic of the total perversity of this character. Her false religion, her false values, her false appearance, her false assumption of a masculine role are all intertwined in the symbolism of the Sultaness. Constance harmoniously unites the roles of Christian, daughter, wife, mother, subject, victim. The Sultaness inverts all the decent roles available to a woman: she is infidel, rebel, murderer, a travesty of a mother. The Sultaness is an Eve figure opposed to the Madonna-like Constance. The gap in their ages is emphasised. By contrast with the affectionate tone in which the youth of Constance is emphasised – 'O my Custance, ful of benignytee, / O Emperoures yonge doghter deere' (446–7) – the Sultaness is repeatedly described as old. The narrator, protective and exclamatory, finds the submissive young Constance more appealing than the domineering older woman. But the claims of symbolism and sexuality combine here. 'Old' and 'new' have their standard Christian values. The Sultaness represents the old Eve of female sinfulness in opposition to the new law of Christianity. Constance knows that the blood of the Lamb has washed the world clean of its 'olde iniquitee' (453). The Sultaness, however, would rather have her son die than convert and leave his 'olde sacrifices' (325). Satan knows the 'olde way' (367) to women, as he did to Eve, and makes his 'instrument . . . of wommen' (370–71) now, as he did then. The Sultaness is compared with Satan, too. Like him, she is the 'roote of iniquitee' (358). As in the medieval pictures of the Temptation where the snake has a woman's face, she is a 'serpent under femynynytee' (360). A series of apostrophes links the two in consecutive stanzas which begin 'O Sowdanesse' and 'O Sathan' (358–71).

The Sultaness attacks the Church through its members and its sacraments. Marriage provokes her to murder, baptism provokes her to mockery. Marriage, baptism and murder dissolve into each other as in a witches' brew, when the Sultaness outlines her plot to her henchmen: 'We shul first feyne us cristendom to take' (351). The Sultaness has no understanding of the sacrament of baptism. To her it is a little cold water, rather than the crossing from the old life to the new. The wastes of cold water over which Constance will be wafted before she returns to Rome symbolise the Christian life in its earthly exile. Her safe passage is compared with the Israelites' crossing of the Red Sea, a figure of baptism, but the Sultaness is blind to such spiritual meanings. Her 'Coold water shal nat greve us but a lite!' (352), is as briskly dismissive as Lady Macbeth's 'A little water clears us of this deed'. Whereas Constance perceives that the 'Reed of the Lambes blood' (452) washes the world of its sin, the Sultaness plans that her baptism will let loose a flood of blood which a fount of baptismal water will not cleanse: 'thogh his wif be cristned never so white, / She shal have nede to wasshe awey the rede, / Thogh she a font-ful water with hire lede' (355–7). This ghastly joke simultaneously derides the Christian symbolism of white and red (baptism and martyrdom) and the courtly (the lilies and the roses of the lady's complexion, her chastity and her love). But her murderous literalism will be belied by the event.

Constance is put to sea in her rudderless boat, emblem of the Church, allegory of the fact that we do not control our own destinies, and reminder of other perilous journeys of apostles, saints, martyrs, missionaries and chosen people.[3] She accepts it in an exemplary Christian spirit, commending herself to the cross

of Christ. After several years, she is cast up on the coast of
Northumberland, kingdom of Alla, in an England where there are
only a few covert Christians. She kneels on the shore and thanks
God for sending her there. She is found by a constable and his wife,
Hermengyld, who are both pagan. Constance first converts the wife
to Christianity; then, through a miracle of healing which recalls the
ministry of Christ or the acts of the apostles, the husband. Satan,
however, is in wait. He causes a young knight to fall in love with
Constance 'of foul affeccioun' (586) (this narrator has no sympathy
with the courtly tradition). The knight woos her in vain for 'she
wolde do no synne, by no weye' (590). Disappointed, he tries to
frame Constance by murdering Hermengyld and setting the blood-
stained weapon by Constance. But when the knight swears in court
on the gospel that she is guilty, he is miraculously struck down and
the voice of God convicts him of slander. King Alla, who has
presided over the court, is converted and marries Constance.

Constance's second mother-in-law is as evil as her first. Like the
Sultaness and unlike 'faire Custance, that is so humble and meke'
(719), Donegild is 'ful of tirannye' (696), another virago, domineer-
ing and satanic. In an apostrophe to her which rhetorically echoes
those to the Sultaness and Satan, the narrator exclaims that he has
no words to describe her 'malice and . . . tirannye' (779). He can only
consign her to the devil with the rebukes 'Fy mannysh, fy! . . . Fy
feendlych spirit!' (782–3). While Alla is away at war, Constance has
a son and Donegild informs him that his wife has given birth to a
monster. Alla, a husband after Constance's own heart, writes back
that whatever Christ sends him is welcome. Donegild then forges a
letter, purporting to come from Alla, with orders that Constance
and her son be put to sea in the same rudderless boat which brought
her to Northumberland. When Alla arrives home and learns the
truth, he kills his mother.

Constance voyages for more than five years, her journey broken
only by another brush with an unwelcome lover. She is cast ashore
at a heathen castle where the steward, an apostate, boards the ship
and tries to rape her. Constance screams, her child screams, and the
Madonna comes to her aid: the rapist, for all his greater strength, is
overcome like Goliath and Holofernes, falls into the sea and is
drowned 'for vengeance' (923). Meanwhile another act of venge-
ance is taking place. The Roman Emperor hears of the slaughter at
the wedding feast in Syria and sends a senator there with a punitive
force to burn and slay. Finally all paths converge on Rome. The

senator, on his way back from Syria, meets the ship of Constance and conveys her to Rome. Alla, in remorse over the murder of his mother, arrives to do penance. The face of his child Maurice reminds him of Constance and all are reunited: Constance, Alla, their child, her father, and her aunt, who happens to be the wife of the senator. When Constance left Rome at the beginning of the Tale, she was handed passively from father to husband. Now in the joyful recognition scene, it is made clear that the highest political power will be transmitted from her husband to her son and the narrator has to recall the story back to his heroine. Constance and Alla return to England, where they live together in great happiness. But, as the narrator points out, worldly joy is brief. Alla dies a year later and Constance returns again to Rome and her family and remains there until her death.

The most obvious feature of this narrative is that it is very repetitive. There are three long sea-journeys, two of them in a rudderless ship and lasting several years. There are two marriages and two wicked mothers-in-law. There are many conversions and both Constance's husbands are converts. There are two foreign lands in which Constance is an exile. There are two unwelcome and unscrupulous lovers. There are two attempts to traduce Constance. There are four acts of vengeance, two committed by men close to Constance, two occurring by God's direct intervention. There are a number of miraculous escapes. There are two reunions in Rome. Constance's response to all her sufferings is always the same: she is constant.

Behind the eventful monotony of this story are important moral claims. As much is implied through the narrative as is explicitly stated through the speeches and prayers, actions and reactions of the central figure. And speeches are less vital than prayers, actions than reactions. Constance suffers more than she acts. Her story is full of adventure, travels to exotic lands, plots, intrigues, murder and mass murder, courtroom drama and recognition scenes but its meaning is inward and spiritual. It is about self-subjection, not self-assertion. It is a tale of Christian heroism, the subject Milton would maintain should be celebrated more than the military glories of classical epic: 'argument / Not less but more Heroic than the wrauth / Of stern Achilles on his Foe pursu'd / Thrice fugitive about Troy Wall' (*Paradise Lost* ix 13–16).

In the *Man of Law's Tale*, the narrator's rhetoric presents us with such comparisons. When Constance leaves for Syria, he comments that more tears could not have been shed at the sack of Troy or the fall of Thebes or the Punic Wars. He does not think the triumph of Julius Caesar could have been 'roialler ne moore curius' (402) than the fatal wedding feast of Constance and the Sultan. But classical allusions soon give way to biblical. How did Constance survive the massacre at the feast? By the same power that preserved Daniel in the lions' den. Who kept her from drowning? God, who saved Jonah in the whale's belly and the Israelites at the crossing of the Red Sea. Who kept her from starving? Christ, who fed five thousand with the loaves and fishes. Constance, like David and Judith, exemplifies the strength of the apparently weak. Cast out to sea a second time with her young son, she resembles the Madonna to whom she prays. Her courage is to endure. She never acts in her own defence. She cannot fight and has no champion but Christ (631–7). Like Christ, she does not even speak in her own defence, and she is Christ-like in the most powerful stanza of the poem, when she stands out from the crowd like the pale face of a man led to execution.

Throughout the Tale, the supreme virtue is to accept what God sends. 'Send', in its various forms, is a key word in the poem. When Constance is cast up on the coast of Northumberland, she would like to die but 'she kneleth doun and thonketh Goddes sonde' (523). When Alla learns the false news of his child's deformity, he replies: 'Welcome the sonde of Crist for everemoore / To me that am now lerned in his loore! . . . Crist, whan hym list, may sende me an heir / Moore agreable than this to my likynge' (760–1, 766–7). When Constance is put out to sea again, 'she taketh in good entente / The wyl of Crist, and knelynge on the stronde, / She seyde, "Lord, ay welcome be thy sonde!"' (824–6). In Rome, Alla, who supposes his wife and child drowned, meets his son, is struck by the boy's resemblance to Constance and wonders: 'What woot I if that Crist have hyder ysent / My wyf by see as wel as he hire sente / To my contree . . . ?' (1041–3). The narrator's final prayer for the audience is that they be governed and guarded by 'Jhesu Crist, that of his myght may sende / Joye after wo' (1160–1). The verb also has human as well as divine subjects. The poem is full of embassies, messages, banishments and invitations. The Emperor sends Constance to the Sultan. The Sultan sends for his council to discuss the marriage. The Sultaness sends for her council to disclose her opposition to it. Donegild and Alla send letters to each other about his child. The Emperor sends the senator to Syria on his mission of vengeance. The senator sends for Constance to reunite her with Alla.

Constance, however, is always the object. Throughout the poem, she accepts being sent, what she is sent and where she is sent. The only moment when her natural feelings break out – and its pathos is therefore more striking – is near the end of the poem. When she is at last reunited with her father, she says 'Sende me namoore unto noon hethenesse' (1112).

At one level, Constance's story is an amazing one, with its marvels and miracles. Her travels recall the missionary journeys of St Paul and the apostles (also, etymologically, the 'sent'). At another, they are a metaphor for the universal human voyage over the sea of life. There is a divine plot and purpose in Constance's wanderings, the ship is an emblem of the Church and all the lines of the story finally meet in Rome, the base of Constance's earthly and spiritual family. Yet the Tale is not allowed to conclude at the climactic moment of reunion and recognition. Life is all vicissitudes. We are repeatedly told that woe follows joy and the narrator's final prayer is for heavenly joy to succeed upon earthly woe. The double story of the two exiles, the two marriages and the two voyages dramatises the alternations of the human lot. Like Pericles in Shakespeare's play, which owes as much to Chaucer as to Gower, Constance endures not one tragic adventure but a lifetime of loss and travail. Constance is intended as an example to all Christians, to Everyperson, male and female. All Christians experience adversity, all believe that they should co-operate with the will of God. Nevertheless, the story of Constance is in many ways a tale of female suffering.[4] She is subjected to a woman's trials: her arranged marriage far from her home; sexual assault; double vulnerability with her small child. Her association with the Madonna suggests a specifically female version of Christian heroism: caring and suffering for others rather than occupying the central place in one's own story. Despite its many dramas, this Tale is anti-dramatic. And its respect for the quiet acceptance of suffering links it not only with a tradition of Christian thought but also with a tradition of writing by and about women. For example, *Middlemarch*, with its care for the tragedy of frequency and its acknowledgement of our debt to those who lie in unvisited tombs.

A verbal echo in the Tale connects the suffering of Christians with the suffering of women. Constance concludes her farewell speech to her parents with the submissive couplet: 'Wommen are born to thraldom and penance, / And to been under mannes governance' (286–7). When the Sultaness declares her opposition to

Christianity she asks: 'What sholde us tyden of this newe lawe / But thraldom to oure bodies and penance?' (337–8). The unregenerate Sultaness has perceived a truth about Christianity but without understanding it. Suffering, humility and self-denial are prized. But this is no pointless espousing of 'thraldom and penance'. It is an imitation of Christ. In the Christian view the Lord's service is perfect freedom, the poor in spirit are particularly blessed and the meek shall inherit the earth.

However, the political and sexual-political consequences of this ethic can be pernicious. These convictions frequently find expression in political and economic metaphors (service, slavery, 'thraldom', freedom, poverty, inheritance, etc.). The paradoxes they generate have been employed to persuade the poor and the oppressed to regard their condition not as an injustice but as a kind of spiritual privilege. The *Man of Law's Tale* extends this vocabulary to define gender roles. The virago Sultaness objects to the 'thraldom and penance' of Christianity, the submissive Constance accepts it as the birthright of women. The Sultaness has an unfeminine and unChristian desire to 'lede' (434). Constance's second mother-in-law is repeatedly described as full of tyranny (696, 779). But of Constance we are told 'Humblesse hath slayn in hir alle tirannye' (165). But is 'humility' the obvious alternative to 'tyranny'? A modern reader would probably supply 'equality' as the opposite term. Is God's relationship with the Christian soul reasonably imaged in a tyranny of husband over wife? The narrator of this Tale, eloquently sympathetic to Constance's fortitude, does not question this analogy. In his tale of patient Griselda, the Clerk does.

II

> This storie is seyd nat for that wyves sholde
> Folwen Grisilde as in humylitee,
> For it were inportable, though they wolde;
> But for that every wight, in his degree,
> Sholde be constant in adversitee
> As was Grisilde; therfore Petrak writeth
> This storie, which with heigh stile he enditeth.
>
> For sith a womman was so pacient
> Unto a mortal man, wel moore us oghte

Receyven al in gree that God us sent;
For greet skile is, he preeve that he wroghte.
But he ne tempteth no man that he boghte,
As seith Seint Jame, if ye his pistel rede;
He preeveth folk al day, it is no drede.

CT IV 1142–55

The Clerk also tells a story of a woman who is constant in adversity.[5] But unlike the ordeals of Constance, the trials of Griselda are inflicted on her by her husband. The Tale is, at the literal level, about marriage. When the story opens the young marquis Walter appears to have all the qualities desirable in a ruler and he is loved by his subjects but there is one serious drawback. He devotes himself to the immediate pleasures of hunting and hawking and, worst of all, has no desire to marry. At last his people come to him in a group and through a tactful spokesman beseech him to wed. Walter reluctantly agrees, making the proviso that he shall choose his own wife and that they are to worship her as if she were an emperor's daughter. Unlike the tale of Constance, an Emperor's daughter married to kings, this story will present a union between two partners from opposite ends of their society. Walter chooses Griselda, a virtuous peasant girl whose father is the poorest in their village. He first asks her father for her hand and then proposes to her, making it his condition that she will always comply with him in everything. Griselda agrees and promises never to disobey him.

Griselda proves an excellent wife, not only in domestic matters but also in helping rule the country. She has a daughter whose birth they welcome, although they hope to have a son in due course. Then Walter decides to test Griselda. He has her daughter taken from her, apparently to be killed, but really to be brought up far away by his sister. Griselda accepts this without resisting. Her manner to Walter is unchanged and she never mentions her daughter again. Some years later Griselda has a son. Unsatisfied with the first test, Walter tells her that the people resent the idea of peasant blood succeeding him, so that the boy must go the same way as his sister. Griselda's reaction is the same as before: her will seems to be identical with his. Walter still desires to test his wife. When his daughter is twelve years old, he tells Griselda that the pope will allow him to repudiate their marriage and take another wife. He sends her back to her father's house, but recalls her to make the preparations for the second wedding. He brings his children back, pretending that his daughter is to be his next bride. Griselda willingly makes the preparations for the marriage and at last Walter is satisfied. He reveals the truth and restores her children to her.

As in the *Man of Law's Tale*, the pathos and power of the story depend on narrative repetition and accumulation. Our indignation with Walter and our sympathy for Griselda mount as he piles needless test upon test and she consistently submits. She is as constant as Constance, 'sad', 'pacient', 'stidefast', 'ay oon, 'ever in oon' (IV 564, 677, 711, 754, 1047). But the scope and the atmosphere of the narrative are very different. Although Constance, like Griselda, is subjected to repeated ordeals, the effect of the *Man of Law's Tale* is far less oppressive and less intense. The worst injustices are not imposed upon Constance by her husbands; she responds to them throughout the Tale as God-given. Griselda is more analogous to the torture victim who suffers not only pain and injury but the trauma of the way they are inflicted. Despite the pathos of Constance's exiles and wandering, she is in the hands of the Lord. God steers the rudderless ship. And, for the reader at least, her story is one of dreary adventure. Constance voyages to the fringes of the Christian world and beyond and the future of Christendom hangs in the balance with her. Spiritually constant, she is also mobile in a world of flux. Christianity is spreading, the Middle East is poised between two rival religions, Anglo-Saxon England is in the process of conversion. Upward spiritual mobility is the route of the converts. The image of the Christian life is the long sea-voyage.

By contrast the *Clerk's Tale* is almost claustrophobic. Griselda's peasant origins and trial by marriage permit little freedom of movement. Her life exhibits a *stabilitas loci*, as if her promise to conform her will to Walter's were taken in the spirit of a monastic vow. The only development possible is further trial, demonstration and exploration of her stability. Griselda's whole world reinforces her submission to Walter. We are introduced in the *Clerk's Tale* to an intensely conservative and hierarchical society. As if to set the mood, the Clerk expresses his 'obeisance' (IV 24) to the Host, who has the 'governance' (23) of the storytelling and under whose 'yerde' (22) he professes himself for the duration of the game. 'Obeisance' to Walter will be sworn again and again in the Tale by all his subjects, as well as his wife.[6] The setting, under the mighty Appenines and 'Mount Vesulus', suggests that the geographical heights and depths provide a God-given context and analogy to human hierarchies. Walter rules over 'Saluces' as his 'worthy

eldres' (65) did before him and as his son will do after him. It is to
ensure this proper succession that his people dare presume to
advise him to marry. He is 'drad' (69) as well as 'biloved' (69). They
approach him 'flokmeele' (86), as if they were mere sheep and he
their shepherd, even perhaps a representative and image of the
Good Shepherd who appointed him in his supreme position. A
spokesman, carefully chosen, pleads with him as cautiously as
possible. He assures Walter that for him marriage will be a 'blisful
yok / Of soveraynetee, noght of servyse' (113–4). Walter is moved to
pity by the 'meek preyere' and 'pitous cheere' (141) of his people.
He assents and 'with humble entent, buxomly, / Knelynge upon hir
knees ful reverently' (186–7) his subjects thank him.

The second part of the *Clerk's Tale* narrates Walter's choice of
Griselda, her acceptance of his demand and their early marriage. It
emphasises the extremes of rich and poor and sets the stage for the
extremes of behaviour it will display. The action moves from the
court to the country, from the palace of Walter to the cottage of
Janicula, the poorest man in an impoverished village. Walter has
often noticed Griselda on his hunting expeditions and has admired
her 'wommanhede' (239) and her virtue. She is chaste, temperate,
industrious and devoted to her father. She cherishes him 'with
everich obeisance and diligence / That child may doon to fadres
reverence' (230–1). A system of interlocking duties is being set out,
of subjects to rulers, children to parents, wives to husbands and
Christians to God.

Janicula is almost at the bottom of Walter's society in being the
poorest man in his village. Griselda is humbler still, as a woman and
a daughter. Yet Walter recognises that he should ask Janicula's
permission for the marriage and Griselda's assent to its terms.
Janicula agrees, in words which anticipate his daughter's: 'Lord,
. . . my willynge / Is as ye wole, ne ayeynes youre likynge / I wole no
thyng' (319–21). When Walter asks Griselda to promise never to
oppose him, she replies, 'as ye wol youreself, right so wol I. / And
heere I swere that nevere willyngly, / In werk no thoght, I nyl yow
disobeye, / For to be deed' (361–4). Janicula declares that his will is
identical to his lord's. Griselda affirms her total submission to
Walter in thought as well as work, not only to obey him but to want
only what he wants. The word 'will', in its various forms, is
emphasised throughout the second half of the poem. When Walter
first tests Griselda, he says that he must do with their daughter 'Nat
as I wolde, but as my peple leste' (490). Griselda replies that both

she and her child are his: 'werketh after youre wille' (504) with
them. 'This wil is in myn herte' (509), she assures him. When Walter
announces that her son is to be taken away, seemingly to his death,
Griselda answers, 'I wol no thyng ne nyl no thyng, certayn, / But as
yow list' (646–7). She recalls that when she first came to him, she left
'my wyl and al my libertee' (656) at home, as she left her old clothes.
If she had prescience to know his 'wyl' before it was expressed, she
'wolde' perform it (659–61); now she knows what he 'wolde', she
will concur in it because she 'wolde' gladly die to please him (662–
5). Finally it seems as if 'of hem two / Ther nas but o wyl' (715–16).
Griselda 'shewed', as if demonstrating a conviction which the
narrator does not necessarily share, that 'A wyf, as of hirself,
nothing ne sholde / Wille in effect, but as hir housbonde wolde'
(719–21). Constance's version of saintliness is to accept what God
sends and her pain and fear in doing so are always evident.
Griselda's vocation is a yet more arduous task of unselfing, of
actively making over her very will in the image of another.

The religious allusions in the Tale suggest that Griselda is a saint
and martyr and imitation of Christ. Her humble birth is Christ-like.
When the narrator describes her home, he reminds the audience
that 'hye God somtyme senden kan / His grace into a litel oxes stalle'
(206–7). Griselda is at once reminiscent of Christ, his mother, his
disciples, the patriarchs and their wives when she crosses her
threshold and is called by Walter. She comes from a well, a
traditional setting for the Annunciation to the Virgin. She sets
down her waterpot, like Rebecca at her meeting with Isaac, or like
the Apostles Simon and Andrew, James and John, leaving their
fishing nets at the summons of Christ, or like the Samaritan woman
when she recognises the Messiah. The words which recall the
Nativity, 'in an oxes stalle' (291), are repeated at this moment.
Griselda promises her loyalty to Walter in the same terms as the
centurion's profession of faith in Jesus which became a prayer of
the Eucharist: 'Lord, undigne and unworthy / Am I' (359–60; cf.
Matthew 8: 8). When she commits herself to Walter, Griselda leaves
her old clothes behind, like one entering the religious life. Her
absolute obedience to Walter resembles the unhesitating faith in
God of the patriarchs: like Abraham and Jephthah, she is willing to
sacrifice her son and daughter in this cause. The Clerk compares her
humility to Job's and Griselda echoes the words of Job when Walter
tells her to leave, taking the 'dowry' she brought with her: ' "Naked
out of my fadres hous," quod she, / "I cam, and naked moot I turne

agayn" ' (871–2). She asks Walter only if she may keep her smock to cover her nakedness. As she walks back to her village, barefoot and silent with a weeping crowd following her, she seems to re-enact Christ's progress to Calvary. The religious allusions encourage us to understand Griselda's marriage as an election to a martyrdom of willing suffering and humiliation.

But the Christian allusions suggest a radical as well as a conservative interpretation. In descending to an ox's stall God's grace obliterates the absoluteness of the social hierarchies in the Tale. Walter may tower above Griselda like the mountains above the valley but in the prophecy every valley shall be exalted and every mountain and hill made low. Walter's people urge him to take a wife 'born of the gentilleste and of the meeste' (131), from those most noble and greatest in rank, as if *gentillesse* were synonymous with high birth. But Walter replies that children do not necessarily resemble their 'worthy eldres' (156) and that goodness comes from God, not from genealogy. In this, at least, Walter concurs with the magic lady of the *Wife of Bath's Tale*. Griselda repays his trust, not only in her obedience, affection and domestic skills ('wyfly hoomlinesse' – 429) but also in her ability to help him rule his country. She proves capable of contributing to the 'commune profit' (431) and in Walter's absence can arbitrate and resolve disputes between his subjects. Doubly a subject herself through her low birth and her female sex, she is also a natural ruler. The Clerk implicitly opposes the belligerence with which the Wife of Bath argues the case for women's rights but he agrees with her that *gentillesse*, wisdom and intelligence observe no boundaries of rank or gender.

He also agrees with her that women do not get credit for their virtues. When the Clerk compares Griselda to Job, he himself points out the masculine bias in literature of which the Wife of Bath complained:

> Men speke of Job, and moost for his humblesse,
> As clerkes, whan hem list, konne wel endite,
> Namely of men, but as in soothfastnese,
> Though clerkes preise wommen but a lite,
> Ther kan no man in humblesse hym acquite
> As womman kan, ne kan been half so trewe
> As wommen been, but it be falle of newe.
>
> 932–8[7]

Clerks concentrate on men and take Job as the paragon of humility but in fact no man can equal women in the Job-like virtues of 'humblesse' and truth. The Wife of Bath has also adapted the example of Job to her own uses, though she prefers to recommend its imitation to the men who preach male superiority. She bounces back this exemplar from masculine homiletic at her husbands: 'Ye sholde ben al pacient and meke ... Sith ye so preche of Jobes pacience. / Suffreth alwey, syn ye so wel kan preche' (III 434–7). In her hands the preaching of patience becomes a weapon. It is a wonderfully comic manoeuvre, yet it exposes that the orthodox use of the example can often do something similar when it is employed to encourage the oppressed to accept their subjugation. Driving the example at a different target reveals clearly that it can function as an attack. The Clerk's use of the example is more pacific, but he too revises it with a feminist emphasis and an awareness of the masculine bias in the tradition.

The *Clerk's Tale* is, in part, an answer to the Wife of Bath, and he both agrees and disagrees with her. Like the Wife, he gives a platform to the view that *gentillesse* does not automatically follow from gentle birth, though, unlike the Wife, he does not present any reordering of society as a consequence of that recognition. The Wife believes in an entrenched and perhaps inevitable hostility between clerks and women. The Clerk sees the evidence for this generalisation and wishes to prove an exception to the rule. The Wife points to centuries of anti-feminine satire produced by the clergy and denies that they have anything positive to say of ordinary women: 'For trusteth wel, it is an impossible / That any clerke wol speke good of wyves, / But if it be of hooly seintes lyves' (III 688–90). The Clerk admits that clerks have said little in praise of women, so himself produces an encomium of a wife and mother. Yet the Wife of Bath's proviso – 'But if it be of hooly seintes lyves' – surely applies here. Griselda is no ordinary or even credible woman: her story is virtually, if not technically, a *miraculum*, or saint's life. The Clerk also intends it as a rejoinder to the Wife's defence of female domination. The Wife relates in her Prologue how she opposed and subdued her five husbands and in her Tale how the knight was educated into submission by his wise lady. Griselda's views on marriage are exactly the opposite. Whereas the knight in the Wife's Tale is schooled and punished into learning what women want, Griselda's programme is to renounce any individual desire and conform her will to Walter's until they are identical. The cost could not be higher and the humble peasant woman pays it with a fortitude which qualifies her to be praised like the patriarchs. The Clerk simultaneously defends women against being defamed by the unjust attacks of the clerical tradition and against being implicated in the militant anti-clerical self-seeking defence of the Wife of Bath.

But with such friends, who needs enemies? At its literal level, the *Clerk's Tale* appears to celebrate a woman for uncritically accepting a position of slave-like submission. Griselda abandons her will to Walter's even to the extent of conniving in his apparent murder of their children. Not even the most bigoted proponent of wifely obedience would have recommended her tacit collusion in grave sin. In so far as the story has any psychological plausibility, we may reasonably feel that Griselda shares in her husband's guilt. The powerless have their own bitter sources of power. Griseldas produce Walters. It it were realistic fiction, we would suspect in her silent acceptance a stubbornness which goads him on in the hope of producing a reaction. The Tale does not invite such a psychological interpretation. But it compels a political reading. At the political level the concept of humility is being enlisted to do double duty both as Christian virtue and as force for maintaining social categories. As in the story of Constance, the suffering of the Christian heroine is not only an inspiration but a problem, a question of sexual politics as well as a statement of awesome sanctity. The religious value placed on patience and self-abnegation can be used to condone injustice and vindicate the suffering of the poor as a kind of spiritual opportunity. On this view the suffering of women can qualify them as poor in spirit and therefore blessed. Christian resignation is not the only good response to inequities of gender and class. In a much later text which considers the oppression of women in the context of Christian society, a woman writer points out the dangers of quietism: when Helen Burns preaches the 'doctrine of endurance' in traditional religious terms, Jane Eyre objects, 'If people were always kind and obedient to those who are cruel and unjust, the wicked people would have it all their own way: they would never feel afraid, and so they would never alter, but would grow worse and worse.'

But the Clerk does not intend his Tale to be taken literally. At the end of the narrative he explains that it is an allegory. 'This storie is seyd, nat for that wyves sholde / Folwen Grisilde as in humylitee'

(IV 1142–3): it is not told as an exemplum for women so that they may imitate the humility of Griselda. That would be intolerable ('inportable' – 1144) even if they wanted to. 'Though they wolde' (1144) may suggest that it is impossible for the will of one individual to be subsumed, Griselda-like, in another's. Rather, the story teaches that the Christian should accept the trials sent by God as willingly as Griselda endured the tests imposed by Walter. Griselda serves as an allegory of the faithful spirit. But there the resemblance ends. Griselda may be like the resolved soul but Walter is not like God. His role is indeed more like Satan's in the story of Job. He is tempting Griselda rather than testing her. He is trying to discover her quality – and his behaviour suggests a perverse desire for her to fail the tests. God, however, has no need to experiment to ascertain the true nature of his creatures. He knows everything already. But he may allow them to suffer as a discipline and a means of development and he does not send adversities beyond what they can bear.

The Clerk is specifically dismantling some of the analogies which can make the ideal of humility work as a force for oppression. The Tale is only acceptable as an allegory: it is 'inportable' (1144) at the literal level. Chaucer takes this moral from his source, a Latin prose version by Petrarch of the last story in the *Decameron*, but whereas Petrarch prefaced his story with this interpretation, Chaucer places it at the end of the narrative. This has the effect of making the literal level of the Tale even more outrageous. A new reader does not know until the close of the story that Griselda's extreme behaviour is to be repudiated and the Tale always produces considerable indignation in the classroom. Throughout the poem Chaucer ensures that the literal level will arouse discomfort. He adds to his source passages which sharply criticise Walter's trials of Griselda. Where Petrarch is restrained, merely describing Walter's desire for the first test as 'more strange than laudable', Chaucer's narrator intervenes to condemn: 'as for me, I seye that yvele it sit / To assaye a wyf whan that it is no nede, / And putten hire in angwyssh and in drede' (460–2). At the second test he finds Walter's conduct not 'strange' but all too typical of married men. He exclaims: 'O nedelees was she tempted in assay! / But wedded men ne knowe no mesure, / Whan that they fynde a pacient creature' (621–3). It has sometimes been objected that censure of Walter is improper, since he represents God, and that these discontinuities in the allegory are a blemish. But the Clerk makes it clear that Walter is not God. There is a deliberate disjunction between the levels of the story so that the allegorical should excite emulation and the literal should excite horror.[8]

Chaucer makes other adaptations to Petrarch's version of the story. As well as adding a criticism of men, in claiming Walter as typical, he omits some misogynistic details in his source. Petrarch introduces his heroine by praising her 'masculine' qualities – 'the vigour of manhood and the wisdom of age lay hidden in her maiden bosom' – and his Walter perceives 'in her a virtue beyond her sex and age'. Chaucer cuts this. His Griselda typifies her sex in her virtue as Walter typifies his in his vice. Although Griselda's amazing patience is dead and gone, barely credible and not to be imitated, the Clerk generalises from her to defend her sex: no man can equal women in humility. In the *Clerk's Tale* the narrator criticises Walter but his people are more demonstratively servile to him than in Petrarch's story: Chaucer adds, repeats and intensifies their gestures and expressions of devotion and obedience. They provide a dignified and archaic background to the drama of Griselda, and her story can be read as nostalgic celebration or veiled critique of their society with its corresponding hierarchies.

Writing of the marriage in the *Nun's Priest's Tale* Sheila Delany aptly comments on the power and political significance of these correspondences between marriage, society and religion. 'When Engels wrote that within the family the husband is the bourgeois and the wife represents the proletariat, he was paraphrasing a perfectly traditional medieval topos: the system of correspondence which privileged God, king, husband and reason over nature, populace, wife and passion. (In neither case, of course, is the idea merely metaphorical, for the institutional structures of religion, state, family and education did and do reinforce one another's hierarchies.)'[9] This seems to me a true account of the system but Chaucer did not inhabit the system uncritically. In the *Clerk's Tale* the tension between the two levels of the fiction and the sympathies and protests of the narrator suggest that he disputes the God/creature, husband/wife, ruler/subject analogies which he leaves unexamined in the *Man of Law's Tale*. In the *Second Nun's Tale* they have no force at all.

III

> And right so as thise philosophres write
> That hevene is swift and round and eek brennynge,
> Right so was faire Cecilie the white
> Ful swift and bisy evere in good werkynge,
> And round and hool in good perseverynge,
> And brennynge evere in charite ful brighte.
> Now have I yow declared what she highte.
>
> *CT* viii 113–19

The *Second Nun's Tale* of Saint Cecilia was probably written before both of these *Tales*, since of the three only 'the lyf . . . of Seynt Cecile' (*LGW* F 426) is mentioned in Alceste's list of Chaucer's works in the Prologue to the *Legend of Good Women*. But it comes later in the *Canterbury Tales* as we have them and presents another view of female heroism. Like Constance, Cecilia is a paradigm of the Christian witness and missionary activity of the early Church but, while Constance is swept and sent passively on her epoch-making journeys, Cecilia is a militantly active heroine. The Man of Law sympathises aloud with the helplessness of his victimised protagonist: 'Allas! Custance, thou has no champioun, / Ne fighte kanstow noght' (ii 631–2). But Cecilia is well able to defend herself, proves almost indestructible and makes no claim on our pity.

From the moment the Second Nun begins to speak, her emphasis is on activity. This Nun is not described in the *General Prologue* and we never learn her name. In these and other ways she contrasts with her companion and superior, Madame Eglantyne, the Prioress. We know how the Prioress looks and what impression she takes care to create. But her entourage, the Second Nun and the Nun's Priest, is invisible. (If there are 'preestes thre' – i 164 – with her, two are also inaudible.) We know about the Prioress's feelings but about the Second Nun's function. Whereas almost everything in the portrait of the Prioress seems irrelevant to her calling, the Second Nun is perceived only in terms of the obligations of her profession: prayer, work and study. She presents herself in that traditional monastic role of translating and transmitting sacred material.[10] She is the woman with the book. Her heroine is likewise a woman dedicated to preaching and teaching. And she is invincible. While some of the preachers among the Canterbury pilgrims patronise the Wife of Bath for trespassing on their domain, nobody dares bring an *ad feminam* argument against Cecilia.

The Nun opens her Prologue with a repudiation of the diabolical vice of Idleness, 'that porter of the gate is of delices' (vIII 3), suggesting a particular condemnation of one vain expense of time and spirit, romantic passion. This is the Idleness of the *Romance of the Rose*, who admits the Dreamer to the garden and to the idolatrous and erotic view of women which is cultivated there. But in Cecilia's story the rose symbolises martyrdom. The section against idleness concludes by turning to the subject of the poem, 'Thou with thy gerland wroght with rose and lilie – / . . . mayde and martyr, Seint Cecile' (27–28).

Like the Prioress's Prologue, the Second Nun's Prologue contains an Invocation to the Virgin Mary. But whereas the Prioress leans passively upon the bosom of the Madonna, the Second Nun asks for the Virgin's help in her activity of translating. The Prioress compares herself to a baby a year old or less who cannot speak and needs guidance in her song. She is clearly identifying herself with the child in her Tale whose faith moves him to sing a hymn he does not understand. The Second Nun writes about an articulate adult, declares that faith is dead without works and prays for enlightenment in her task. The *Prioress's Tale* is, on the kindest interpretation, a work of affective piety. Profound emotion is the response it invites, from the characters in the Tale who weep and fall prostrate at the miracle and the Canterbury pilgrims who for once are hushed and 'sobre' (vII 692) at its conclusion. The Second Nun welcomes a more critical audience, points out that she has attended primarily to the 'sentence' (vIII 81) of the story and invites them to emend any stylistic imperfections in her version (84).

The Prologue concludes with a series of etymological explications of the name 'Cecilia'. All the etymologies are false but each reveals another aspect of the wisdom and power of the saint. She is in her chastity 'hevenes lilie' (87), the flower that symbolises the purity of the Virgin. Because of her Christian teaching she is 'the wey to blynde' (92). Or her name may be a conjunction of 'heaven' and 'Leah', symbol of the active life to which the Nun pays honour. Or, because of her example of good and wise works, her name may mean 'the hevene of peple' (102–4). Throughout this exposition, the emphasis is on Cecilia's teaching, actions and effectiveness. The lily whiteness of her 'chaastenesse' (88) and 'honestee' (89) does not imply a sequestered life untouched by experience. The meditation on her name also valorises her works and wisdom, her 'good techynge' (93), her 'lastynge bisynesse' (98), her 'grete light / Of sapience' (100–1), her 'goode and wise werkes' (105), her 'cleernesse hool of sapience, / And sondry werkes, brighte of excellence' (111–12). It culminates with a comparison of Cecilia to the *caelum* itself, 'swift and round and eeek brennynge' (114), swift and busy in good works, perfect in perseverance and always burning with the fire of charity.

The story opens on Cecilia's wedding day. Like Constance and Griselda, the first thing the heroine does is marry. But whereas they were explicitly transferred from father to husband, Cecilia's father is not mentioned. We learn only that she 'was comen of Romayns, and of noble kynde' (121) and, although she marries, she has a will of her own and her own ideas about the marital relationship. She has always prayed for perpetual virginity and her marriage to Valerian does not affect her resolve. On her wedding night, she goes to bed with her husband 'as ofte is the manere' (142). The phrase seems faintly comic, as if the narrator were explaining something we all take for granted. But Cecilia will prove that there is nothing absolute about these general rules of human behaviour. If there is a moment in which the audience might be tempted to smile at the heroine's chastity, it is soon forgotten as Cecilia retains her virginity and successively proves stronger than all the men in the story. There is none of the slight prurience at the expense of the saintly heroine in which the Man of Law indulges.

> They goon to bedde, as it was skile and right;
> For thogh that wyves be ful hooly thynges,
> They moste take in paicence at nyght
> Swich manere necessaries as been plesynges
> To folk that han ywedded hem with rynges,
> And leye a lite hir hoolynesse aside,
> As for the tyme – it may no bet bitide.
>
> ii 708–14

John Fisher comments on the convergence in the *Second Nun's Tale* of such traditions as the use of marriage as a 'means for securing converts', 'the early Church's emphasis on celibacy' and 'the sort of militant feminism that enabled female saints like St. Catherine of Siena and Joan of Arc to have such enormous influence on political affairs.' He finds in this tale of early Christianity a primitive and uncompromising quality: 'By the time these traditions had reached the tales of Constance and Griselda and the Wife of Bath's Prologue, they had been watered down. In the martyrdom of St Cecilia, we witness them in their awful pristine purity.'[11]

Clearly, Cecilia's chastity is one of her greatest strengths. It gives her both political and spiritual advantages. She seems not only equal with all the men in the story but actually more powerful than most. In a patriarchal society she remains unbowed under the 'yok / Of soveraynetee' (IV 113–14), the term in which marriage is ominously recommended to Walter. Cecilia's celibate marriage neatly gains her independence from her unnamed father as well as safeguarding her from being her husband's possession. Instead of producing children, its effect is to gain two more souls for Christ: Valerian, who converts and agrees to remain celibate, and his brother Tiburce, who also becomes a Christian and a martyr. Cecilia's choice to remain 'unwemmed' (VIII 137), undefiled, preserves her integrity in a religious tradition which usually considered sexual experience polluting. Her celibacy is always seen in positive terms, as a choice of a better life rather than as a discipline or deprivation. At her marriage, Cecilia hardly hears the playing of the organ because she sings an interior song to God, and she unwaveringly puts her heavenly love first throughout the poem.

Valerian initially suspects a human rival when, on their wedding night, Cecilia tells him that a guardian angel will protect her from his embraces. He agrees to refrain only if he may see the angel. Cecilia replies that he must first become a Christian and sends him to Pope Urban. The Pope is in hiding on the Via Appia among the burial places of the saints, the catacombs. The Church is underground, persecuted and intense. Its members must be prepared for arrest, interrogation, torture and execution. In these terms, Cecilia commands absolute respect: she is like a heroine of the Resistance. The social setting combines with the austerely spiritual judgements in the Tale to make her gender no disadvantage to her. A new world is struggling to emerge amid the structures of the old. These revolutionary times contrast sharply with the conservatism of the world of the *Clerk's Tale*.

Although the Clerk emphasises that God's grace and God-given *gentillesse* can cut straight through all the social strata, yet the coherence and antiquity of the society he describes encourage its members to know their places and honour their traditional roles. The sexual politics of Walter's domain mirror the social politics. Patriarchal structures receive no such support in the *Second Nun's Tale*. The civil authority is corrupt, idolatrous and repressive:

disobedience is a Christian virtue. When Cecilia is questioned by
the prefect Almachius, she is unimpressed by his reminder that
'myghty princes' (vii 444 and 470) have outlawed Christianity and
have given him powers of life and death. On the subject of
Christianity, 'Yowre princes erren, as youre nobleye dooth' (449)
she replies; as for his power, it extends only to being 'ministre of
deeth' (485).

Beside Cecilia's courage and chastity, the quality most em-
phasised is her intelligence. Her use of it to argue and to preach is
never criticised as unwomanly. In her first speech, she tells Valerian
that she has 'conseil' (145) for him. The word could open the door to
a familiar controversy about women which Chaucer explores in
other poems. 'Wommennes conseils been ful ofte colde', says the
Nun's Priest, 'Wommanes conseil broghte us first to wo / And made
Adam fro Paradys to go' (vii 3256–8). A long section of the *Tale of
Melibee* is devoted to the question of whether Melibee, a man,
should heed the counsel of Prudence, a woman: his wife demon-
strates resoundingly to him that he should. But the question is not
even raised in the *Second Nun's Tale*. When Valerian returns from
his visit to Pope Urban, the angel commends him and 'for thou so
soone / Assentedest to good conseil' (viii 232–3) offers to grant him
any wish. Valerian asks for conversion of his brother Tiburce. Cecilia
instructs Tiburce in the folly of idolatry and the wisdom of the
doctrines of Christianity. Her explanation of the Trinity is charac-
teristic: it is analogous to the three 'sapiences' of the human
intelligence, 'Memorie, engyn, and intellect' (339). As C. David
Benson points out, her main objection to the idols is that they are
stupid:[12] 'They been dombe, and therto they been deve' (286). She is at
her most polemical and contemptuous in her interrogation by the
prefect Almachius. She opens her defence in almost pedantic terms:
'Ye han bigonne youre questioun folily / . . . that wolden two
answeres conclude / In o demande; ye axed lewedly' (428–30). She
does not conceal her contempt for an adversary who disputes
foolishly and ignorantly ('lewedly' – 430). The princes he represents
'erren' (449); he himself is 'confus in . . . nycetee' (463), confounded
in stupidity; every word in their interview exposes his 'nycetee'
(493–5); he is a 'lewed officer and a veyn justise' (497), people will
'scorne' (viii 506) him and laugh at his folly in blindly believing
stone idols to be gods. Almachius may well ask how she dare speak
so proudly to him, upon which Cecilia explains that Christians hate
the sin of pride and, redefining the terminology, assures him that

she speaks not proudly but steadfastly. Some of Cecilia's prototypes are men, Moses disputing with Pharaoh and leading the chosen people to the Promised Land, the prophets opposing the idols of paganism, Daniel unharmed in the lion's den. But she is also the ancestor of a particular kind of formidable career-woman, the terror of schools, colleges and hospitals. The *Second Nun's Tale* has the grace to present this character as more impressive than repellent.

Almachius sentences her to death but Cecilia still proves unstoppable. He first orders her to be scalded to death in her own house in a bath. This is fuelled for a day and a night but Cecilia sits coolly in it, feels no pain and does not even sweat. Then Almachius sends a henchman to cut off her head but three blows, the legal maximum, fail to sever it. Undeterred by the executioner's boiling water and bungling sword, Cecilia lives on for three days, continuously preaching and teaching the Christian faith. Almost her last word is 'work'. She sends for Pope Urban and bequeaths her house, 'that I myghte do werche / Heere of myn hous perpetuelly a cherche' (545–6). Constance and Griselda leave sons behind them, to become rulers like their fathers. Cecilia achieves a different kind of perpetuity: her house in Rome is a church 'into this day' (552).

9

Criseyde

The double sorwe of Troilus to tellen,
That was the kyng Priamus sone of Troye,
In lovynge, how his aventures fellen
Fro wo to wele, and after out of joie,
My purpos is, er that I parte fro ye.
Thesiphone, thow help me for t'endite
Thise woful vers, that wepen as I write.

now wol I gon streght to my matere,
In which ye may the double sorwes here
Of Troilus in lovynge of Criseyde,
And how that she forsook hym er she deyde.
TC i 1–7, 53–6

These are the opening and closing lines of the Proem to Book i of
Troilus and Criseyde. In the Retraction to the *Canterbury Tales*
Chaucer refers to the poem as 'the book of Troilus'. This introduc-
tion gives the same emphasis. The story is to be about Troilus and
his double sorrow. The parabola of his fortunes 'fro wo to wele, and
after out of joie' (i 4) places him, according to a medieval definition,
among the ranks of tragic heroes. Appropriate rhetoric, an invoca-
tion to one of the Furies, heralds the relation of the fall of a great
man. Already it stirs profound emotion in the narrator: even the
verses weep as he writes. As the Proem develops, the story of
Troilus is invested with a quasi-religious significance, an occasion
for prayerful contemplation in the audience. The narrator presents
himself as a priest of love and delivers a kind of bidding prayer for
lovers in their various circumstances, happy or sorrowful. He is
apparently thinking mainly of male lovers: 'Have he my thonk, and
myn be this travaille! . . . preieth for hem that ben in the cas / Of

Troilus . . . sende hem myghte hire ladies so to plese' (I 21, 29–30, 45), though he does specifically include women when he considers lovers as the victims of slander, 'that falsly ben apeired / Thorugh wikked tonges, be it he or she' (38–9). This Proem lasts for eight stanzas but the heroine is not named until the penultimate line. The narrator returns from the prayer to the story, 'the double sorwes . . . Of Troilus in lovynge of Criseyde, / And how that she forsook hym er she deyde' (54–6). Criseyde appears in this outline only as the object of Troilus's love, the cause of his double sorrow before winning and after losing her, and the guilty party. But this stark and sexist outline will soon be complicated.

Next, the narrator briefly sketches the public background to the private story. It takes place during the Trojan War. The Greek army is besieging Troy and in the end the city will be destroyed. Criseyde enters the poem as a potential casualty of the siege. Her father, the prophet Calchas, foresees the fall of Troy and defects to the Greeks. In the ensuing outcry the citizens say that Calchas and all his family deserve to be burnt to death for his treachery. Criseyde, who has known nothing of his plans, is terrified. Her isolation is emphasised. She has no idea what to do 'for both a widewe was she and allone / Of any frend to whom she dorst hire mone' (I 97–8). Then comes the poem's first description of the heroine:[1]

> Criseyde was this lady name al right.
> As to my doom, in al Troies cite
> Nas non so fair, forpassynge every wight,
> So aungelik was hir natif beaute,
> That lik a thing inmortal semed she,
> As doth an hevenyssh perfit creature,
> That down were sent in scornynge of nature.
>
> 99–105

The introduction presented Troilus as the protagonist and Criseyde as secondary, merely the cause of the hero's suffering. Now the entire focus shifts. The narrator is equally interested in Criseyde, is indeed partisan about her. She is superlatively lovely, in his opinion the most beautiful woman in Troy. Her attractiveness has even drawn the narrator into his narrative, so that he becomes a character in the poem himself. Often he claims only to be following his sources but here the phrase 'as to my doom' (100) transports him back into history. It produces a jolt between the different levels of the fiction, as when John Fowles confides in his experimental novel *The French Lieutenant's Woman* which of the girls in the story he finds the prettiest.[2] At this moment in *Troilus* the narrator repositions himself, fictively, historically and emotionally. He is closer to Criseyde than he appeared to predict. But he does not know much about her. In this stanza the phrase 'semed she' (103) is not emphatically dubious. But the verb 'seem' (so vital to the argument of the *Franklin's Tale*) will appear in more vexing contexts. Here it suggests that Criseyde's heavenly appearance could cause confusion, giving the impression of a being less human and vulnerable than she is, but, for the narrator it makes her pre-eminent among the mortal women of Troy. He empathises with Troilus but he admires Criseyde. He looks at her appreciatively, as varying people with varying degrees of interest will do throughout the poem. She may find this flattering or threatening, dislike or exploit it or both. ('Lord! so faste ye m'avise! / Sey ye me nevere er now?' (II 276–7) she snaps to Pandarus. But a little later she reflects, with a mixture of embarrassment and self-satisfaction, that it is no wonder if Troilus loves her 'for wel woot I myself . . . / Al wolde I that noon wiste of this thought – / I am oon the faireste . . . / And so men seyn, in al the town of Troie' (II 744–8).) The unearthly quality of her beauty hints that she may be immune to ordinary human desire, 'scornynge . . . nature' (I 105). Like Emily she is 'aungelik' (I 102) and 'hevenyssh' (I 104). But the narrator, however moved, does not make Palamon's mistake of thinking the lady a goddess, though Troilus initially does ('But wheither goddesse or womman, iwis, / She be, I not' –I 425–6). Her 'aungelik . . . beaute' (102) is 'natif' (102), she only 'semed' (103) like 'a thing inmortal' (103), and the *topos* of the heavenly artefact scorning nature is a simile, not a statement. Criseyde is a real woman, not an angel sent from heaven nor the erotic nemesis implied in the invocation to the Fury.

But she is a stranger. How are we to decode the information given us in this stanza? Perhaps it tells us more about ideals of women than about the woman herself. To coin a word for an activity frequent in the annals of love, are we to intrapolate? Does outward beauty mirror inward virtue? We do not yet know whether Criseyde's angelic appearance accords with her character. But we do know that it contrasts with her circumstances. The lady who seems 'lik a thing inmortal' (103) is in actuality in fear for her life. The downward movement begun in this stanza, comparing her to a perfect creature sent down from heaven, reaches earth in the next.

Criseyde, distraught with terror, falls to her knees before Hector to
ask his protection, an exact inversion of the courtly motif of the
knight kneeling before his lady.[3] Hector is prompt to pity, a sign for
Chaucer of the noble disposition. Touched by Criseyde's suffering
and by her beauty (would a plain woman be less deserving of pity?),
he promises that she will be safe and respected in Troy. Criseyde
thanks him humbly, returns to her home and 'held hir stille' (126).
The political realities of her situation are very different from the
images of freedom and power in the first description.

II

> She nas nat with the leste of hir stature,
> But alle hire lymes so wel answerynge
> Weren to wommanhod, that creature
> Was nevere lasse mannyssh in semynge;
> And ek the pure wise of hir mevynge
> Shewed wel that men myght in hir gesse
> Honour, estat, and wommanly noblesse.
>
> I 281–7

Criseyde emerges from her seclusion to attend the feast of the
Palladion, the image of Pallas Athene, a goddess to whom she feels
particular devotion. Despite the war, the Trojans continue to hold
their religious ceremonies devoutly and place their trust especially
in this image. However, there are natural as well as spiritual reasons
for observing this holiday. Although Athene is a virgin goddess,
her festival occurs in the season of renewed fertility. It takes place in
April, amid the colour and fragrance of the spring blossom. The
green of the meadow and the red and white of the flowers recall
Emily's walk in the garden and its aphrodisiac effects. Like the
'sondry folk' (*CT* I 25) who journey to Canterbury in April, the 'folk
of Troie' (I 160) come to worship at their temple 'in sondry wises'
(159) and with a similar mixture of motives. Everyone – except
Criseyde – has dressed smartly 'bothe for the seson and the feste'
(168), both for the religious rite and for the coming of spring. People
want to see and to be seen. Even Troilus, who scorns love, is there
with other young knights, looking at the girls and thinking himself
superior to their charms.

Criseyde, in her widow's black, is out of place. Throughout the poem, except during the brief happiness of her affair with Troilus, she feels at odds with her circumstances. Here she stands out from the joyful crowd in her mourning, her beauty and her sense of insecurity. She stands near the door, behind other people, taking up little room, and covers her nervousness with an air of disdain: 'What, may I nat stonden here?' (292). Her looks are a double-edged advantage, exciting affection and compassion but also drawing attention to her. Nobody has ever seen so bright a star hidden under so black a cloud, the first of the images of dimmed radiance associated with the heroine.

Troilus, the target of the vengeful God of Love, takes one look at Criseyde and falls in love with her. In the next stanza, quoted above, we too are invited to look at the heroine, though we may have some difficulty in visualising her. It is both vague and emphatic. It gestures towards qualities which Criseyde may or may not possess and is decisive on the ambiguous subject of 'femininity' or 'wommanhod' (283), which may or may not exist. Here and at other crucial moments during the story the femininity of the heroine is underlined. Like the Prioress, who 'was nat undergrowe' (*CT* i 156), Criseyde is not small, but she corresponds so successfully to the image of womanliness that nobody could look less masculine. There the likeness ends. The Prioress is Chaucer's comic study of femininity, Criseyde is his tragic. The Prioress is adept at exploiting the notion of femininity and salvaging what fun there is to be had from the limitations of her position. She even manages to dress up her nun's habit. Criseyde – 'simple of atir' (i 181) – seems to dress down her widow's weeds, sensing that her gender and her beauty make her doubly vulnerable.

From Criseyde's beauty and bearing one could intrapolate the qualities of character to be expected in a noble lady. Would one be right? Probably, but this most ambiguous of Chaucerian narrators does not commit himself to an answer. He does not even ask the question, but the obliquity of his description suggests it. This stanza of positive celebration begins with two negatives and proceeds with a neatly poised example of the vexing Chaucerian 'but'. Criseyde was not ('nas nat' – 281 – the double negative does not cancel itself, though we have to wait for a moment for this to become clear) among the least (does 'leste' – 281 – mean 'smallest physically' or 'lowest socially'?) in stature (so 'nat . . . leste' – 281) refers to her height, though leaves unclear whether this was average or above) 'but' (282 – but tall? but majestic? but attractive none the less? Is her height an advantage or not and, if a disadvantage, does she carry it off?) perfectly feminine with it. The very manner of her movements ('the pure wise of hire mevynge' – 285 – does 'pure' suggest 'chaste, virtuous' or only 'mere'? Is intrapolation endorsed or not?) implies her noble class and her nobility of character. The question of intrapolation seems to be left open. Criseyde's movements are moving. At first sight she evokes emotional responses which may not be justified. But perhaps they are, since the description is now concerned with the expressive aspect of the heroine's person. Her appeal resides as much in her demeanour and in what it seems to show of her personality as in her beauty. It was apparent ('shewed wel' – 286 – was it obvious or did it only appear so?) that one ('men' – 286 – one, as I have just translated, or men, the sex more susceptible to her appearance?) could suppose ('myghte' – 286 – sounds conditional and 'gesse' – 286 – speculative) 'Honour, estat and wommanly noblesse' (287). The stanza ends on resounding terms of praise, yet the method of arriving at them seems questionable.

The climactic phrase 'wommanly noblesse' (287) introduces the idea of feminine honour which Criseyde will eventually compromise. 'Wommanhod' 'wommanly' and related words re-echo throughout the poem, though their meaning sometimes seems rather nebulous. When the lovers first meet, Troilus addresses Criseyde as 'wommanliche wif' (III 106), a tautology which, whether due to nerves or to the calculated rhetoric of pleonasm, testifies to her overwhelming effect on him. On the night when they first make love, he repeats this phrase: he vowes his faith and service to the 'fresshe wommanliche wif' (III 1296) on pain of death 'If that it like unto youre wommanhede' (1302). At the height of their happiness Troilus continually talks to Pandarus and 'wolde . . . a proces make / Hym of Criseyde, and of hire womanhede, / And of hire beaute' (III 1737–41). In Book IV, when Criseyde is about to be sent off to join her father in the Greek camp, she tries to calm Troilus with a display of her feminine intuition and practicality. 'I am a womman, as ful wel ye woot', she says meaningfully, 'And as I am avysed sodeynly, / So wol I telle yow' (1261–3). Troilus, however, is sceptical about how effectively feminine stratagems will work on her father: 'Ye shal nat blende hym for youre wommanhede' (IV 1462). When they are separated he imagines the pallor of her 'fresshe wommanliche face' (V 244) and rereads her letters, 'refiguryng hire shap, hire wommanhede' (V 473). In Book V, when Criseyde has finally betrayed

Troilus by taking the Greek Diomede as her lover, she laments that she will for ever more be emblematic of the faithlessness of her sex (1054–68).

Criseyde does indeed become an emblem. As Shakespeare's Pandarus puts it: 'Let all constant men be Troiluses, all false women Cressids, and all brokers-between Pandars' (*Troilus and Cressida* III ii 202–3). Yet Chaucer's Criseyde does not share the faults and foibles attributed to women by the clerks and satirists. She is not vain, flirtatious, garrulous or indiscreet. She is not interested in dressing well: at the beginning of the poem she apparently prefers the camouflage of her widow's habit; after this her clothes are never described and her beauty is next celebrated in a nude scene. The satires charge women with frivolity and extravagance: Criseyde lives quietly at home and her reading-matter is serious. Women allegedly cannot keep secrets and betray to each other the confidences of husbands and lovers. But when women friends visit the distraught Criseyde in Book IV and chatter 'nyce vanite' (729) about her departure from Troy, she scarcely hears 'tho wordes and tho womannysshe thynges' (694) and does not speak a word herself. Although she becomes an exemplar of infidelity, she is not promiscuous, or even very susceptible. She is slow to accept Troilus's love and her dispirited surrender to Diomede is only made possible by the chance of war. There is no reason to suppose that she would have deserted Troilus had she been able to stay in Troy.

Nor does Criseyde fit into the established roles for women. She is neither wife nor nun. After all, I am not a nun ('I am naught religious' – II 759), she reflects, when she debates with herself whether to love or be loved by Troilus. She gestures towards the nun-like aspects of the widow's role: it is proper, she tells Pandarus, only for wives and girls to dance but for a widow like herself to read the lives of saints (II 113–19). In Book IV she resolves that, separated from Troilus, she will form her own 'ordre' (782) and her rule will consist of sorrow, complaint and abstinence (782–4). In neither case does Criseyde persist in a life of nun-like chastity. Yet she does not conform to that other stereotype of the widow, sexually sophisticated and predatory. The Wife of Bath is much married and much widowed and her talk is all of sex, marriage and the hope of remarriage. Criseyde, in sharp contrast, appears to use her widowhood as an excuse for no further sexual involvement, though it proves, as she becomes involved with Troilus and later with Diomede, to have been only an excuse. Except for this purpose her husband seems forgotten and we know nothing about their relationship. Since Criseyde feels that her love for Troilus 'al com it late, / Of alle joye hadde opned hire the yate' (III 468–9), her marriage was evidently not a love-match. Although a widow, she seems at first emotionally virginal. She does not become a wife again. That role would have saved her from being parted from Troilus. She is the daughter of an absentee father: since he is a traitor, the relationship is a disadvantage to her. Her uncle Pandarus is no substitute: he prefers the role of pimp to protector. The fact that she is his niece is revealed, rather belatedly, by Troilus to point out the impropriety of his love being presented to her by her uncle (I 1022). And, as if to achieve further blurring of female categories, the narrator remarks that he does not know her age or whether she had children (V 826; I 132–3).[4]

Criseyde, the representative of faithless women, eludes category in this poem. Yet she is continually characterised as intensely feminine. It is as if here Chaucer discards all the stereotypes of femininity which he so brilliantly redeploys, animates and criticises in the Prioress and the Wife of Bath. Remove those distorting lenses and what do we see? Chaucer's longest and most complex study of a female character. The portraits of the Wife and the Prioress have their own trenchancy and truthfulness, since women are influenced, moulded and deceived by the stereotypes. I speculated in Chapter 1 about the effects on women of being constantly told by men and in books written by men that they are wicked. I do not know first-hand because that accusation is not made now. Women do not assume that they are morally worse than men. If anything, they think they are better and fear that they pay too high a price for it. Women do not seem more sensual than men but deeply inhibited. They are not more fickle: they tend, because of a history of economic dependence on marriage, to be more monogamous. The stock medieval calumnnies now seem weirdly inapposite. And for most of the poem they have little application to Criseyde, who finally turns into a stereotype. Chaucer's investigation of the predicament of her femininity is more existential than essentialist. He charts how she becomes 'false Cressid' through the social pressures without and the psychic pressures within. This is the double sorrow of Criseyde.

Criseyde is living in a man's world. The besieged city of Troy is a patriarchal society at war, when masculine strength is most prized. The war is being fought for the possession of a woman. Apart from

Criseyde, the major characters are men, wielding various kinds of power, social, familial, military and political: Troilus, Pandarus, Hector, Calchas, Diomede. The other women characters are Helen, symbol of female destructiveness, Cassandra, whose prophetic wisdom is always ineffectual, Andromache, who is to lose her great husband to the war, Criseyde's nieces and maids and the women who vainly try to comfort her in Book IV. They form an inner circle of love and friendship within the outer circle of power and politics. The affair of Troilus and Criseyde is the secret innermost circle of the poem.[5] The outer circle is even more powerful than usual, because of the political crisis. It increases in power as the threat to the city increases. The atmosphere darkens as the fortunes of Troy decline. The sanctum of personal relationships becomes less and less sacred and the value placed on women as people plummets. 'We usen here no wommen for to selle' (IV 182) declares Hector, when the exchange of Criseyde for Antenor is proposed, but she is exchanged or sold.

The poem is a man's world in another sense. It is written by a man and presented by a masculine narrator, who keeps reminding us of the fact. He knows more about Troilus than about Criseyde. Indeed, he knows everything about Troilus: he can tell us when he is lying (II 1077). But he stresses his ignorance about Criseyde, even about such facts as her age and whether she had children (V 826; I 132–3). He foregrounds the difficulty of representing her feelings (II 666–79). In the area where facts and feelings intersect, the narrator at crucial points in the poem professes himself at a loss. In Book I, while Troilus languishes with love for Criseyde, the narrator says that he does not know whether Criseyde was ignorant of this or feigned ignorance (I 492–7), though it is evident in Book II that the news comes as a complete shock to her. As the seduction of Book III approaches, he claims that his source does not reveal whether she believed Pandarus's story that Troilus was out of town (III 575–8). In Book V he temporises about her infidelity: he refuses to say that she gave her heart to Diomede (V 1050) but a few stanzas later is merely insisting that no sources record how long it was before she forsook Troilus for him (V 1086–92).

Chaucer presents Criseyde as both subject and object, examining both her mind and her world, the social and political pressures upon her from outside, the emotional problems within. 'I am myn owene womman' (II 750), claims Criseyde. But she is not her own creator. She is a 'creature' (I 283). The narrator disclaims the responsibility or the freedom to create her: he is under the obligation to follow his source and the end of the story is determined from the beginning. Nobody in the poem is self-created: all are shown as under the constraints of nature and society. The poem raises questions about choice and freedom and so do the characters.[6] The influence of Fortune is emphasised. Astrological causes are suggested. Troilus wonders lengthily in Book iv whether we have free will at all and 'proves' that his tragedy was pre-determined. Even the horse, proud Bayard, thinks about the subject: 'Yet am I but an hors' (i 223), he concludes and accepts 'horses lawe' (223). Criseyde, neither wife nor nun, feels that her position is one of relative freedom. But in being human she is under many constraints and in being a woman she is under more.

The Bayard simile occurs just after the God of Love lets fly his arrow at Troilus. Despite his contempt for lovers, he falls in love instantly and involuntarily. Like Bayard, he is bound by the 'lawe of kynde' (i 238). No one can withstand the God of Love. There is no volition involved and love is repeatedly described in images of captivity. Troilus should be an 'ensample' (i 232) to those who 'scornen Love, which that so soone kan / The fredom of youre hertes to him thralle' (234–5). 'Love is he that alle thyng may bynde' (237). Do not refuse to be 'bonde' (255) to Love, since he can 'bynde' (256) you at his own will. Troilus reflects on this punishment for his earlier presumption: 'O fool, now artow in the snare . . . Now artow hent, now gnaw thyn owen cheyne!' (507, 509). Now he is 'ykaught' (534). His love is exemplary in other ways too. He is a textbook lover, doing and suffering all that is codified in books of love. He falls in love at first sight. He becomes ill and fears he will die. He dare not tell his beloved of his devotion. He writes poems full of conventional tropes, such as the oxymora which expresses his paradoxical extremes of feeling. Like the lover in the *Romance of the Rose*, he is finally persuaded to confide in one friend, Pandarus, who undertakes to help him. Troilus is an absolutist of love. All this is in contrast to the way in which Criseyde falls in love in Book ii.

III

Whan he was come unto his neces place,
'Wher is my lady?' to hire folk quod he;
And they hym tolde, and he forth in gan pace,

And fond two othere ladys sete, and she,
Within a paved parlour, and they thre
Herden a mayden reden hem the geste
Of the siege of Thebes, while hem leste.

ii 78-84

In Book ii we meet Criseyde at home. Book i opened in the public world with the long reaches of European literary tradition, the political state of Troy and the defection of Calchas. We saw the heroine only briefly and mainly through the eyes of others: a name in a programme or a history, a suppliant to Hector, a visitor to the temple, a reflection in the mirror of Troilus's fantasy, a challenge to Pandarus's romantic expertise. The structure of the poem ensures that our first perspective on Criseyde is from a distance. Now we move into her house, into her private circle, into her thoughts and, after she falls asleep, into her unconscious mind.

The action of Book ii begins, indeed, at the threshold of consciousness. The spring has advanced further and its effects are more potent. Pandarus, who claims to have been hopelessly yet buoyantly in love for many years, wakes on 3 May determined to visit Criseyde on Troilus's behalf but feeling lovesick on his own account. Half-asleep, he drowses until the chattering of the swallow at his window becomes too insistent. Mythologically, she is Procne, who laments the rape of her sister Philomela by her husband Tereus. The radiant April scene of Book i also contained the sombre figure of Criseyde. Book ii has a similar setting. It opens with a stanza in praise of spring with its flowers and scented meadows. But as well as celebrating the beauty of fertility, it alludes to the dark side of sex, to betrayal, violence, rape and mutilation.[7]

Criseyde is unaffected by any May madness. Pandarus finds her sitting in a parlour with two other ladies, listening to a maid read from a book about the siege of Thebes. The Proem to Book ii has pointed out that the people of other times had other customs and yet might be expressing feelings similar to our own. There the narrator attempts to close the gap between the audience and the extreme and stylised behaviour of Troilus. Here we are implicitly invited to sympathise with Criseyde. She is doing something similar to us. She is attending to the story of Thebes, a tragic history of siege and warfare. In view of the threat that hangs over Troy, it is a specially grave subject to be chosen only by an earnest and responsible audience. The narrator of the *Nun's Priest's Tale* sneers that women are foolishly devoted to fiction and romance: 'This story is also trewe, I undertake, / As is the book of Launcelot de Lake, / That wommen hold in ful gret reverence' (*CT* vii 3211–13). But Criseyde's reading-matter is serious, historical, sobering and exemplary.

It is Pandarus who is unserious, who jumps to the conclusion that the book is erotic ('Is it of love?' – ii 97) and who idiotically describes his mysterious news as five times better than the lifting of the siege! He is impatient with her reading. He tells her to let her book go, throw off her veil, dance and do observance to May. Criseyde seems as immune to spring fever as she did in the temple. She retorts that it would be more becoming for a widow like herself to sit in a cave and read the lives of saints, a genre even farther from the love stories Pandarus hoped for. We have here another vignette which revises the motif of the Man with the Book. It is the male character who displays the 'feminine' penchant for romance, fantasy and gossip and who myopically concentrates on personal and ignores public affairs. Criseyde, a heroine of romance, is anti-romantic in her tastes. Persuasion by literature will work upon her from quite another source.

As well as being a frustrated lover, Pandarus is something of a frustrated author. Troilus and Criseyde are to enact his desires, by acting out what he cannot and by acting at his direction. In this conversation he produces his own essay in romance: he describes a garden scene where he heard Troilus confess his passion to the God of Love. His quasi-literary ambitions have some comically proleptic effects. For modern readers the bedroom scenes he stage-manages have their farcical associations. He anticipates the epistolary novelist, both in his voyeuristic intrusiveness and in his sense of the possibilities of this medium: both lovers write letters at his suggestion and he gives Troilus the added benefit of some instruction in composition and literary theory. Pandarus finally achieves a satisfying compound of action, literature and vicarious sex, when he brings the couple together for their first night of love. 'He drowe hym to the feere, / And took a light, and fond his contenaunce, / As for to looke upon an old romaunce' (iii 978–80). Is Pandarus reading a book, pretending to read it, observing or averting his gaze from the new version of the old romantic story being enacted in his house?

In this first conversation on the subject, however, there is little to encourage the hope that Troilus's love will be returned. Criseyde's initial reaction to the news is dismay. Pandarus's presentation apparently does little to further his commission. He is at first tantalising and portentous, then emotionally blackmailing and aggressive. If she does not show compassion, Troilus will die – and he, Pandarus, will die too! When she asks his advice, he tells her that she should love Troilus because age is eroding her beauty every hour and pleasantly quotes the taunt of the king's fool to proud women: 'So longe moot ye lyve, and alle proude, / Til crowes feet be growen under youre ye' (ii 402–3). Criseyde bursts into tears and says that she wishes she were dead. She speaks bitterly of her sense of betrayal. Pandarus, whom she thought her best friend, is urging her into love, when she would have expected him to protect her and to disapprove. He acted as if he were bringing wonderful news and this turns out to be 'al the joye and al the feste' (421) and her 'blisful cas' (422). After such a build-up, 'Is al this paynted proces seyd – allas! – / Right for this fyn?' (424–5), she asks, voicing a common female disgust at the elaborate male overtures which prove to mask a simple purpose. It seems like a revelation to her of the treachery of life: 'of this world the feyth is al agoon . . . This false world, allas, who may it leve?' (410, 420). The structure of the poem is circular, with its movement from public to private and back to public, from Troilus's first sorrow to his happiness and on to his second sorrow, with the narrator's Prologue on the God of Love and his Epilogue on the Christian God. Within this larger structure there are many anticipations and echoes in the opening and closing books. Here Criseyde expresses the contempt for the world which Troilus feels on leaving it and with which the narrator takes his leave of his book. But unlike the poet she knows no Christian faith to compensate for the faithlessness of this life and she has nowhere to live but the poem. Her pessimism is far-reaching and it makes Pandarus's romantic errand look trivial.

But Criseyde is a complex character and what she says is only part of what she is thinking. From the opening of this scene, she both clashes and harmonises with Pandarus. She emerges as a more serious person in the exchange about the book but she falls easily into Pandarus's joking mode on the subject of love:

> 'Is it of love? O, som good ye me leere!'
> 'Uncle,' quod she, 'youre maistresse is nat here.'
> With that thei gonnen laughe . . .
>
>   ii 97–9

She is curious to hear his news and her technique for detaining him is to invoke gender roles, first teasingly, then practically. She asks him: 'What aileth yow to be thus wery soone / And namelich of wommen?' (211–12), requests him to sit down and 'speke of wisdom' (214) in private with her, and tells him a 'tale . . . of hire estat and of hire governance' (218–19). Book II opens with a revisionary vignette, of a woman listening to a tragic history while a man wants to gossip about love, but it soon offers the conventional picture of a woman seeking advice from a man about business matters. Like Pandarus, she is trying to play her cards right. Their conversation is interspersed with the phrases 'quod Pandarus' (85, 93, 106, 120, 155, 168, 190, 220, 429, 490), 'Pandarus seyde' (208–9, 254–5, 505–6), 'quod he' (79, 125, 227, 278, 491), 'hire uncle . . . seyde' (250–1), 'he seyde' (264–6, 276, 327), 'quod she' (104, 113, 122, 127, 136, 162, 183, 210, 225, 239, 310, 388, 475, 494, 499, 589, 595), 'she seyde' (89, 145, 275–6, 408–9, 463). But in both there is another level of unspoken thoughts from the moment that Pandarus intimates he has intriguing news. Criseyde is titillated: 'tho gan she wondren' (141), although she affects indifference and says that she will not pester him with questions. Pandarus inwardly plans his strategy for revealing it ('Than thoughte he thus' – 267). Criseyde, whose outward response to his news is tears and despair, has been thinking 'I shal felen what he meneth, ywis' (387). Pandarus's interview with Criseyde is in sharp contrast to his conversation with Troilus in Book I. Troilus has his secret but, when he finally speaks, he says exactly what he is thinking. Criseyde, like Pandarus, simultaneously conceals and reveals.

One of Criseyde's characteristic thoughts is 'What will people say?' Pandarus has lengthily assured her that no dishonour is intended and that no one will think visits from Troilus mean more than friendship. Criseyde then inwardly turns to the possibility of scandal in the alternative course, if she rebuffs Troilus and Pandarus's threats of suicide are genuine. Suppose he were to kill himself in her presence, 'What men wolde of hit deme I kan nat seye: / It nedeth me ful sleighly for to pleie' (461–2). She anounces that she will choose the lesser of two evils. She often has recourse to proverbs, as if they offer the support of objective wisdom in her maelstrom of uncertainty and indecision. Rather than cause her uncle's death, she will, within the bounds of honour, be kind to Troilus. But the terms in which she states her resolve are devious and delicate:

> 'Now wel,' quod she, 'and I wol doon my peyne;
> I shal myn herte ayeins my lust constreyne.
>
> 'But that I nyl nat holden hym in honde;
> Ne love a man ne kan I naught ne may
> Ayeins my wyl, but elles wol I fonde,
> Myn honour sauf, plese hym fro day to day.
> Thereto nolde I nat ones han seyd nay,
> But that I drede, as in my fantasye;
> But cesse cause, ay cesseth maladie.'
>
> 475–83

This is a puzzling speech for several reasons. Criseyde, like the narrator, is a virtuoso of the double negative. But the cautious effect of the speech stems as much from its conceptual oddity as from its multiple negations. Troilus's love is a textbook example of the passion and he expresses it in highly stylised and conventional terms. Criseyde is far more individual and her thoughts and feelings diverge from such paradigms. Here she constructs a small allegory in which 'herte' and 'lust' are, strangely, on opposing sides and the heart has to be constrained towards positive feeling for a man rather than from excessive emotion. Her 'fantasye' does not create imaginary love scenes but the case against them. She cannot love – against her will, though Troilus's experience and most poetry about love suggest that it is an involuntary passion, as perhaps Criseyde acknowledges when 'ne kan' modulates into 'ne may', the impossible turning into the impermissible. These searching but subtle variations on the accepted senses of moral and psychological terms suggest an uncertainty about her own volition and desire far more complex and profound than the traditional disdain of the courtly lady.

When Pandarus leaves, Criseyde withdraws to her closet to sit 'as stylle as any ston' (600) and review every word of their conversation. She continues to overestimate the power of her own will: she comforts herself with the thought that there is nothing to fear

> For man may love, of possibilite,
> A womman so, his herte may tobreste,
> And she naught love ayein, but if hir leste.
>
> 607–9

But events immediately bely her confidence in her self-control. A cry of praise breaks out in the street for Troilus returning victorious from battle. Criseyde looks out of the window and begins to fall in love. 'Who yaf me drynke?' (651) she asks herself, as if intoxicated or enchanted by a love potion. No wonder she is moved. Troilus materialises, as if conjured up by her obsessive thoughts. He is the hero of the hour. This great soldier, her uncle said, was ready to die of love for her. For a second time a compatibility between these two separate people is suggested. In the temple Troilus, disdainful of lovers, is captivated by Criseyde and 'hire chere' / Which somdel deignous was' (I 289–90). Now both blush in successive stanzas, Troilus with modesty (II 645), Criseyde in embarrassment at her own thoughts (652).

At this point the narrator anticipates an objection from his audience:

> Now myghte som envious jangle thus:
> 'This was a sodeyn love: how myght it be
> That she so lightly loved Troilus,
> Right for the first syghte, ye, parde?'
>
> 666–9

He reassures us that she did not love 'sodeynly' (673) but 'gan enclyne / To like hym first' (674–5), that his 'manhod' (676) and suffering caused love to mine her heart and that finally 'by proces and by good servyse, / He gat hire love, and in no sodeyn wyse' (678–9). But the narrator, if not his audience, seems to be the victim of his own preconceptions. He is at pains to defend Criseyde against the charge of being precipitate, when she has seemed cautious and even calculating. The stereotype of the lustful woman scarcely fits this nervous and temporising heroine. The hero did fall in love instantaneously but it did not occur to the narrator that this required defending. The process of falling in love is presented very differently in the two characters and the more psychologically plausible account is the one deemed to need explanation.

Criseyde is stirred by the sight of Troilus but, after he rides from view, she continues to deliberate. She is a worrier and a rationaliser and the narrator powerfully conveys the exhausting obsessiveness of this condition. 'Lord! so she gan in hire thought argue' (694), he exclaims, 'Now was hire herte warm, now was it cold' (698) and catalogues a list of her arguments, first for, then against loving. In favour of Troilus, Criseyde finds, are his noble character and his high position. It might be disadvantageous to alienate him and it sems harsh to despise him. He could have the most eligible woman in Troy, yet he loves her. There is no threat of dishonour: on the worst hypothesis, people might guess his love. How could she be blamed for that? What is the purpose of her loveless existence: 'To what fyn lyve I thus?' (757). Assertions of her independence buttress these considerations. She is her own woman, with no husband to be jealous or dominating, 'unteyd' (752), and Troilus 'shal . . . nevere bynde' (728) her. Unlike Troilus, she believes in her own freedom.

But, after a lengthy rehearsal of the reasons to be sanguine, the opposing case forces itself upon her:

> But right as when the sonne shyneth brighte
> In March, that chaungeth ofte tyme his face,
> And that a cloude is put with wynd to flighte,
> Which oversprat the sonne as for a space,
> A cloudy thought gan thorugh hire soule pace,
> That overspradde hire brighte thoughtes alle,
> So that for feere almost she gan to falle.
>
> 764–70

I quote this transitional stanza in full because the image of clouds conveys the quality of her dismay as suggestively as the conscious 'cloudy thought' (768). On this May morning Criseyde is in a March mood. Where sex is concerned women are conditioned to be less in touch with 'nature' than men. Troilus falls in love instantly and unreflectingly. Criseyde thinks as much as she feels, and her thoughts and feelings are as various as a spring sky. This contrast between hero and heroine is made implicitly through another stanza with the same opening words and a similar natural image. When Pandarus returns to Troilus with the news that he has won Criseyde's friendship for him, the young man's reaction is un-clouded and in harmony with 'kynde':

> But right as floures, thorugh the cold of nyght
> Iclosed, stoupen on hire stalke lowe,
> Redressen hem ayein the sonne bright,
> And spreden on hire kynde cours by rowe,
> Right so gan tho his eighen up to throwe

> This Troilus, and seyde, 'O Venus deere,
> Thi myght, thi grace, yheried be it here!'
>   967–73

A similar passage in Book III, again with the same opening, compares the growing happiness of Troilus to the natural renewal of the spring and emphasises his likeness to others, rather than his differences:

> But right so as thise holtes and thise hayis,
> Than han in wynter dede ben and dreye,
> Revesten hem in grene when that May is,
> Whan every lusty liketh best to pleye;
> Right in that selve wise, soth to seye,
> Wax sodeynliche his herte ful of joie . . .
>   III 351–6

But here, as in the temple scene, Criseyde is isolated and unwilling to abandon herself to the processes of nature and the beauty of the spring. Her cloudy thought raises the vital question of freedom: 'Allas! syn I am free, / Sholde I now love, and put in jupartie / My sikernesse, and thrallen libertee?' (II 771–3). Her vision of love is of uncertain skies: 'love is yet the mooste stormy lyf' (778), always 'som cloude is over that sonne' (781). Women unhappy in love have nothing to do but sit at home, weeping and thinking (a problem to be voiced by later women writers; 782–4). They are vulnerable to scandal and desertion. A brief affair ending in betrayal seems as pointless as her solitary life: 'To what fyn is swich love I kan nat see' (794). Ironically, in view of the outcome, one of the fears voiced most often is that Troilus, not Criseyde, may be unfaithful. Yet this does have its own truth to experience. It reminds us that women risk more in love than men do and is one of the many ways in which the narrative qualifies the narrator's opening statement of his theme of the faithless woman.

Despite Criseyde's ratiocination and faith in her own reason, her dilemma is not to be decided primarily by her conscious mind. She agonises over it at length, 'now hoot, now cold' (811), and then shelves the unresolved problem by going outside. Her garden is large, all its walks are bordered and shady, it has benches and sanded paths, and there Criseyde walks arm in arm with her nieces. This decorous picture of the well-ordered household and the

tranquil companionship of women restores the quiet domestic
setting which Pandarus interrupted with his disturbing news. But
the garden is traditionally the setting for a love poem and Antigone
begins to sing.

The song is a paean to love by a woman who has found it to
bestow blessings of happiness and virtue. She thanks the god for
giving her such a perfect lover. Although she feared to love him at
first, she now knows that there is no danger in it. Wretches speak ill
of love and call it thraldom who know nothing about it. Like the
sun, too bright for humans to behold, love is unaffected by their
lies. It might be an answer to all Criseyde's doubts and fears. When
she asks Antigone who wrote the song, she is told that the author is
'the goodliest mayde / Of gret estat in al the town of Troye' (880–1)
and, as if to authenticate the sincerity of the lyric, that she leads
'hire lif in moste honour and joye' (882). Although female author-
ship was relatively uncommon, this song is written by a woman
and sung by a woman. The name of the singer recalls a classic
instance of female heroism against patriarchal oppression. The
song treats love from a woman's point of view. There is no attempt
to persuade or seduce. The woman is not seen as the prize or object
of desire, as she so often is in the romances. It focuses not on the
excitement of courtship but on a stable relationship between two
virtuous people and confirms that such a love is both joyful and
praiseworthy. It is a minor work in an alternative literary tradition
and, as if anticipating later methods of book production, Criseyde
imprints it in her heart: 'Every word which that she of hire herde, /
She gan to prenten in hire herte faste' (899–900).

Aloud she merely says, 'Ywys, it wol be nyght as faste' (898). The
remarks sounds casual, serving as an excuse for dismissing the
subject of love or concealing her interest in it. But it has another
meaning at another level. Night, darkness, sleep and dreaming
release the mind from the conscious restraints of the daytime world,
freeing it to express the hidden and the intuitive. Alone in bed,
Criseyde thinks and thinks about the disturbing subject until she is
seized by sleep. Outside, in the moonlight a nightingale sings,
perhaps 'in his briddes wise, a lay / Of love' (921–2) and Criseyde's
heart becomes 'fressh and gay' (922) as she listens. Gradually,
Criseyde is gaining some harmony with her nature and its deepest
desires. She has been inadmissibly moved by the words of
Pandarus, the sight of Troilus and the song of Antigone. Now the
woman who will not dress gaily for the spring festival and cannot

respond like a fresh flower to the sun begins to surrender in solitude and moonlight to the music of the nightingale. This Book begins with birdsong interpreted and mythologised, as the swallow Procne disturbs Pandarus with her 'waymentynge' (65), 'cheterynge' (68) of the barbarous injuries done to her sister. Their story of male lust and violence hints at a savage iconographic connection with Pandarus's errand of seduction and verbal oppression of his niece. But now the atmosphere is very different. Here the nightingale is not identified with Philomela. His song, traditionally associated with sex, is left ambiguous: perhaps, in his bird's way, he sings of love. Both the nature of the song and the nature of love remain open. In the lyric sung by Antigone love is described as the traditional exchange of hearts. The idea recurs in Criseyde's dream in a new and haunting form. A white eagle tears out her heart and substitutes his own yet she feels no fear or pain at the exchange. Her anxieties about sexual exploitation, aggression and loss of identity are beginning to be resolved at an unconscious level.[8]

It is characteristic of Criseyde to fear others rather than herself. In Book I she is terrified at her political position and, despite Hector's reassurance, her fears will be justified in Book IV. Her fears of the unscrupulous seducer and her fears of selfhood lost with heart will be realised in her relationship with Diomede. They prove unjust to Troilus but Criseyde will be attacked, exploited and deceived before this becomes clear.

IV

Nought list myn auctour fully to declare
What that she thoughte whan he seyde so,
That Troilus was out of towne yfare,
As if he seyde therof soth or no . . .

III 575–8

This Troilus in armes gan hire streyne,
And seyde, 'O swete, as evere mot I gon,
Now be ye kaught, now is ther but we tweyne!
Now yeldeth yow, for other bote is non!'
To that Criseyde answerde thus anon,
'Ne hadde I er now, my swete herte deere,
Ben yold, ywis, I were now nought heere!'

III 1205–11

Criseyde is the victim of one of the most elaborate seduction plots in English literature. Despite her assertions of freedom and Troilus's abject sense of enthralment, Pandarus views her as the quarry and the two men as the hunters. He uses the metaphor of the chase to Troilus:

> Lo, holde the at thi triste cloos, and I
> Shal wel the deer unto thi bowe dryve.
>   II 1534–5

During Books II and III Pandarus tirelessly goes back and forth between the couple, commissioning and delivering letters, arranging meetings devising fictitious problems for Crisyede. He engineers a meeting for them at the house of Deiphebus by pretending that the litigious Poliphete is plotting against Crisyede and that she needs the help of the prince. At the same time he persuades Troilus to feign an illness and retire to bed in his brother's house so that Criseyde may be prevailed on to visit him. At last in Book III he brings them together to make love in his own house, first telling Criseyde that Troilus is out of town, then insisting that she must stay the night because of the torrential rain, finally leading Troilus to her bed on the pretext that she has given him cause to be jealous of Horaste.

Fortunately for our impression of Troilus, Pandarus's sinister yet ludicrous efforts on his behalf produce a splitting effect. We blame Pandarus for the lies and the double-dealing and the oppression of Criseyde. Troilus seems more seduced than seducing, even comically inept. In this pimp/pawn split Chaucer has effected a masculine counterpart to the whore/virgin polarity of women. And Troilus even manages to authenticate some of Pandarus's deceptions, since he genuinely feels what he is advised to pretend:

> Quod Troilus, 'Iwis, thow nedeles
> Conseilest me that sikliche I me feyne,
> For I am sik in ernest, douteles,
> So that wel neigh I sterve for the peyne.'
>   II 1527–30

But Troilus is compromised by his co-operation with Pandarus. Even when he is finally in bed with Criseyde in Book III and they confide their love to each other, he feels the need to lie to her. She has a shrewd idea that his jealousy of Horaste is a convenient fiction, 'don of malice, hire to fonde' (III 1155). Troilus decides that 'for the lasse harm, he moste feyne' (1158), which he does so feebly, 'as he that nedes most a cause fisshe' (1162), that Criseyde asks 'Wol ye the childissh jalous contrefete?' (1168). Pandarus's tactics presuppose that the lovers are enemies and the sexes at war. Only Criseyde's affectionate realism dispels the smokescreen his lies have created.

Troilus too regards the sexes at war. In recompense for Pandarus's services he offers him

> my faire suster Polixene,
> Cassandre, Eleyne, or any of the frape –
> Be she nevere so fair, or wel yshape,
> Tel me which thow wilt of everychone,
> To han for thyn, and lat me thanne allone.
>
> III 409–13

Like Hector, Troilus might chivalrously protest that it is not the custom in Troy to sell women but he, whose life is to be ruined by the exchange of Criseyde for Antenor, sounds ready to barter the women of his family. He does not even see that this is what he is doing. He proffers his sisters to prove that 'this servise' (408) if given him by Pandarus is an honourable activity, not 'a shame . . . or jape' (408) but 'gentilesse, / Compassioun, and felawship, and trist' (402–3). This kind of procuring is very different from pimping 'for gold or for richesse' (400) and one must make the distinction because 'ther is diversite required / Bitwixen thynges like' (405–6). The argument seems a valid one until Troilus attempts to support it by bargaining with his sisters, as if 'gentilesse, compassioun . . . felawship and trist' (402–3) apply only between men. [9]

Yet Pandarus's support of Troilus is an ambiguous business, seeming both 'bauderye' (397) and 'compassioun' (403). Criseyde herself seems to find it so, from their first conversation on the subject, alternately joking with her uncle and in tears. The reader shares her ambivalence. I both want Criseyde to have an affair with Troilus and feel disgusted with Pandarus for promoting it in the way he does. Troilus neither experiences nor rouses such complex and conflicting feelings. The poem acknowledges that sex is both desirable and dangerous for women and that they are judged more harshly than men whether they engage in or refrain from it. Criseyde worries in advance about gossip and slander, about loss of independence and about the male propensity to begin an affair with enthusiasm and then tire of it as abruptly: 'That erst was nothing, into nought it torneth' (ii 798). 'To what fyn is swich love I kan nat see' (ii 794), she thinks plaintively, echoing the question she has just asked of her single life: 'To what fyn lyve I thus?' (ii 757). Love and loneliness seem equally without meaning. Her fears of love are well-grounded, yet they prove unjust to Troilus, who keeps faith and gives her happiness. Far from preserving her freedom, they are an anxious bondage. When Criseyde first writes to Troilus, urged on by Pandarus, she 'gan hire herte unfettre / Out of desdaynes prison but a lite' (ii 1216–17). Though her uncle's officiousness is distasteful, it introduces her to a relationship which frees her from a self-inflicted prison.

Pandarus himself has doubts and fears after their first meeting at Deiphebus's house. He succeeds Criseyde at the bedside to tell Troilus 'in a sobre wyse' (iii 237) that for his sake he has become 'Bitwixen game and ernest, swich a meene / As maken wommen unto men to comen: / Al sey I nought, thow wost wel what I meene' (254–6). Since Troilus first voiced his love to Pandarus and Pandarus relayed it to Criseyde, all three characters have insisted that no sexual relationship is intended. Yet soon, for all the protestations of the men and the provisos of the woman, all three know at some level that it will occur. Criseyde states her policy firmly in Book ii:

> For pleynly hire entente, as seyde she,
> Was for to love hym unwist, if she myghte,
> And guerdoun hym with nothing but with sighte.
>
> 1293–5

But the go-between knows better:

> But Pandarus thought, 'It shal nought be so,
> Yif that I may; this nyce opynyoun
> Shal nought be holden fully yeres two.'
>
> 1296–8

Through Criseyde Chaucer conveys very delicately the way in which sex and love have a stealthy momentum of their own, working below and perhaps against conscious choice, as well as the process by which love is sown by suggestion and grows by being thought of. Now, in Book III, Pandarus regards the affair as inevitable and wants to avoid its being a scandal. He talks at length to Troilus about the dangers of gossip and about men's tendency to boast of sex, even of sexual encounters that have not actually taken place. Then he turns to the practical question – 'But now to purpos' (III 330) – and vows to Troilus that 'it shal be right as thow wolt devyse' (336).

The seduction is carefully planned, even over-determined. The narrator attributes it to 'Fortune, executrice of wierdes' (617) and exculpates Criseyde: 'execut was al bisyde hire leve' (622). But the 'purveiaunce' (533) is largely that of Pandarus, who works out when an unusual astronomical conjunction will cause a terrific rainstorm and invites Criseyde for that evening. Troilus is ready to take advantage of his friend's ingenuity: he has worked out a standing alibi and let it be known that he is to spend a night alone at a temple where Apollo's oracle will 'telle hym next whan Grekes sholde flee' (544). He exploits his role of pious and responsible citizen as a convenient cover and any amusement or distaste this may arouse is dissolved in the poignancy of the brief dramatic irony: Troilus, preoccupied with his private affair, assumes that Troy will win the war but Troy is doomed and with it Troilus and his love. Criseyde clearly both guesses what is going on and chooses not to know. She appears to accept Pandarus's assurances that Troilus is out of town but the narrator cannot say if she believes him. When she is finally in bed with Troilus and he begins to make love to her, she confides in a beautiful fusion of self-surrender and self-possession: 'Ne hadde I er now, my swete herte deere, / Ben yolde, ywis, I were now nought heere!' (1210–1). She seems both the innocent dupe of her uncle's negotiations and her own diplomatist, as events move in the direction she desires while she remains irresolute, inactive and careful of propriety.

Care for propriety, indeed, plays an almost comically large part in persuading Criseyde to co-operate. When Pandarus says that it is raining too hard for her to leave and she must stay the night, she thinks: 'As good chep may I dwellen here, / And graunte it gladly with a frendes chere, / And have a thonk, as grucche and thanne abide' (641–3). When Pandarus takes her to her room, he tells her where her women are sleeping so that she may call any of them. But when he later reappears through a secret trap-door with Troilus behind him, he quashes Criseyde's nervous 'lat me som wight calle!' by playing on her fears of indiscretion: 'God forbede that it sholde falle . . . that ye swich folye wroughte! / They myghte demen thyng they nevere er thoughte' (761–3). It is an unpleasant moment of bullying, blackmail and competing fears, as Pandarus counters the female horror of an intruder and embarrassment at being surprised in bed or in disarray (the custom at Chaucer's time was to sleep naked) with the dangers for women, which Criseyde feels so acutely, of flouting convention.

From the moment that Pandarus undertook to help Troilus gain Criseyde's love, he has run through a gamut of male seduction techniques on his friend's behalf. His vicarious enthusiasm makes them look doubly comic and doubly squalid. Now all the machinery of his plot – the carefully devised sleeping arrangements, the trapdoor, the concealment of Troilus in the 'stewe' (601), a word both for a small room and for a brothel, the lies told to Criseyde, the intrusive presence and persuasion of Pandarus – is distasteful. It is not only sordid but sadistic. Pandarus does not scruple to cause Criseyde so much distress by his fiction of Troilus's jealousy of Horaste that she questions whether there is any such thing as true happiness. When she is finally pressured into seeing Troilus that night to convince him of her loyalty, she is reduced to tears. At this Troilus realises what he has done, though like Madame Merle ('Have I been so vile all for nothing?'), his remorse is compounded with disappointment. He faints and this strange story of seduction by proxy reaches its astonishing crisis. Pandarus picks him up and puts him into bed with Criseyde.

It is a moment of high comedy and it is amazing that the love scene can survive the risk taken here. Yet Book III continues with Chaucer's most passionate and prolonged account of sexual intimacy. After Pandarus belatedly withdraws from the action with the parting advice, 'If ye be wise, / Swouneth nought now, lest more folk arise!' (1189–90), it no longer trembles on the verge of farce. The hero has been unheroic, weak, *unmanly*, but this does not disable him from becoming Criseyde's lover. Perhaps it makes him a better lover. Most of the conventionally masculine behaviour we have seen in the preliminaries of this affair has been morally very dubious. Pandarus and Criseyde have the same reaction to the swoon, that it is not manly: 'is this a mannes herte?' (1098), 'Is this a mannes game?' (1126). Yet in the earlier bedroom scene when Criseyde visits Troilus, his sensitivity is not criticised as effeminate. He shakes, turns pale and can hardly speak and the narrator describes his emotion as 'manly sorwe' (113). The tremulous courtly lover is, of course, a conventional literary figure. But a suitor who faints away and is picked up and thrown into his lady's bed by her uncle surely violates every code of correct masculine behaviour. Here in this crucial scene Chaucer breaks with convention and initiates the communion of the lovers with an affront to our prejudices about gender role.

This first night of lovemaking is the centre of the poem in several senses. We have heard the first of the double sorrows of Troilus, his agonising love for Criseyde before he wins her. Now the central Book III, which begins and ends with a paean to love, tells of their happiness. It is also the innermost part of the poem. The movement from the public to the private has reached its heart. When Pandarus withdraws, the lovers are at last in a world of their own, safe within the sleeping house, the besieged city and the 'smoky' (628) tempestuous rain. It is also the time of candour and confidences. The affair has been conducted at a distance, by a couple who are nervously aware of the figures they cut and the roles they are expected to play. Now the bliss of sincerity is celebrated as a vital aspect of intimacy. The lies about Horaste are the last Troilus tells to Criseyde.

We regain our sense of the integrity of Troilus, which may have seemed threatened or compromised by Pandarus's devious operations on his behalf. From now on he is, as Shakespeare's Troilus puts it, 'true as truth's simplicity / And simpler than the infancy of truth' (III ii 169–70). For Criseyde things are never so simple. It is now she who seems compromised by her dealings with Pandarus. After the *aubade* in which the lovers lament the coming of day and Troilus's unwilling departure, Pandarus enters the bedroom and asks jokily if the rain has kept her awake. Criseyde is indignant at his role in her seduction, so embarrassed that she blushes and hides her face under the sheet and yet, finally complicit, she 'with here uncle gan to pleye' (1578). By contrast, his next meeting with Troilus is solemn, even sacred. The intervention of the world is a threat to the woman, as it is not to the man, in that it regards her sexuality with more prurience. In public Criseyde has some of the same conflicting feelings after she sleeps with Troilus as she had before. As if to emphasise the continuing privacy of the affair, Chaucer returns to the subject of the *aubade*. Pandarus organises another night together for them, a time of surpassing joy,

which is ended by 'cruel day' (1695), complaint and separation, a
pattern often to be repeated ('many a nyght they wroughte in this
manere' – 1713).

Troilus's relations with the world become more and more
harmonious. He is generous, hospitable, chivalrous, well-dressed
and surrounded by company. Love makes him kinder and more
courageous. Everybody praises him. He perceives love as the power
creating cosmic harmony and celebrates in song its celestial
reconciliation of sun, moon, earth, sea and all discordant elements.
His first song about love in Book ɪ (400–20) is all paradox: how could
such pain be welcomed and such pleasure hurt? Love is a 'quike
deth' (411), a 'swete harm' (411), killing him simultaneously with
heat and cold, pushing him back and forth 'bitwixen wyndes two, /
That in contrarie stonden evere mo' (417–18). Now these contradic-
tions are resolved. But even in the earlier metaphysical torment,
Troilus's anguished questionings have a kind of schematic sim-
plicity. How can two incompatible qualities co-exist, how can
absolute opposites co-inhere? Troilus is an absolutist, Criseyde is a
relativist, and this contrast between the hero and the heroine will
be explored in Book ɪv and Book v when the world finally parts
them.

V

> And now my penne, allas, with which I write,
> Quaketh for drede of that I moste endite.
>
> For how Criseyde Troilus forsook –
> Or at the leeste, how that she was unkynde –
> Moot hennesforth be matere of my book,
> As writen folk thorugh which it is in mynde.
> Allas, that they sholde evere cause fynde
> To speke hire harm! and if they on hire lye,
> Iwis, hemself sholde han the vilanye.
>
> ɪv 13–21

With Book ɪv begins the outward movement into the public world
which will destroy the love affair. This is the second of the double
sorrows of Troilus which the narrator announced at the beginning
of the poem. But since Book ɪ his attitude to Criseyde has changed.

He is now as involved with the heroine as with the hero and he is anxious to excuse her. 'How that she forsook hym er she deyde' (I 56) is adapted into 'How Criseyde Troilus forsook – / Or at the leeste, how that she was unkynde' (IV 15–16). When she is finally unfaithful to Troilus with Diomede, the narrator refuses to report it as other than a rumour: 'Men seyn – I not – that she yaf hym hire herte': v 1050). But a few lines later her infidelity is assumed and the narrator's anxious need not to condemn has been redeployed to the question of how long it took: 'But trewely, how long it was bytwene / That she forsok hym for this Diomede, / Ther is non auctour telleth it, I wene' (v 1086–8). A moment afterwards he is saying that at least she was very sorry about 'hire untrouthe' (v 1098). The excuses sound lame and, ironically, they make Criseyde look worse, not better. The narrator seems to be bending over backwards to defend the indefensible because he likes the heroine. He fusses over the details of his sources as if that will distract attention from their substance.

As in the *General Prologue* to the *Canterbury Tales* we may suspect behind the sympathetic narrator a satirical author. But the two narrators are different versions of Chaucer's naive *persona*. The narrator of the *Tales* is presented as seeing everything and under-standing little. The narrator of *Troilus* emphasises the limitations in his knowledge of the heroine. During the course of the poem we, like him, have grown to know her better. But with her departure for the Greek camp the narrator is usually positioned closer to Troilus and they both speculate about Criseyde. In Book II we shared Criseyde's moving dream, which began to dissolve her resistance to love and sex, of the eagle and the exchange of hearts. In Book v Troilus has a dream symbolising another exchange of hearts: as he walks weeping through a forest, he comes upon a boar 'with tuskes grete' (v 1238) which holds Criseyde closely and on which she lavishes kisses. It might be an image from *A Midsummer Night's Dream*, expressing fear of the disorderly power of sex and perhaps particular terror and disgust at female sexuality. Troilus at once assumes that it is a divine revelation of Criseyde's infidelity. Pandarus, who has already been sceptical about the significance of dreams (v 358–85), suggests a reassuring interpretation. Troilus turns to the prophetess Cassandra to expound the dream and she explains that the boar is an emblem of Diomede and that 'This Diomede hire herte hath, and she his' (v 1517). Troilus angrily refuses to accept this 'and day by day he gan enquere and seche / A

soth of this with al his fulle cure' (v 1538–9). Criseyde is becoming a
problem in hermeneutics. In Book II we watched Criseyde's
confused reception of a letter from Troilus. In Book V Troilus
receives a horribly temporising letter from her and it is her last
word in the poem. She leaves us with indirections. Now the
narrator struggles for facts rather than for understanding. The
question becomes 'Did she do it?' rather than 'Why did she do it?'
Since the answer is yes, she is condemned. The narrator grows
more and more distant, first from his heroine, then from his hero
and finally detaches himself altogether from interest in their
story.

I too want to defend Criseyde, using evidence that the narrator
makes available but does not argue from himself. The case against
her is in some ways a classic example of 'blaming the victim'.
Because she is a woman, Criseyde has no political power and she is
condemned for the consequences of that powerlessness. In Book I
she appealed to Hector for help. But now Hector's opposition to the
exchange is useless. He points out that Criseyde is not a prisoner,
he claims 'We usen here no wommen for to selle' (IV 182) but he is
overruled by public opinion. The people ask angrily: 'what goost
may yow enspyre / This womman thus to shilde and don us leese /
Daun Antenor?' (IV 187–9). Criseyde herself regards women
as belonging to the less important sphere of private life. She
vehemently opposes Troilus's suggestion that they escape together
from Troy: 'God forbede / For any womman that ye sholden so, /
And namely syn Troie hath now swich nede / Of help' (IV 1556–9). It
is easy to separate her from her home and her lover and thus make
her more powerless still. Diomede, with his insistent and correct
predictions of the fall of Troy, presents himself as the protector she
desperately needs. She is manoeuvred away from a man who will
soon be killed and a city which will soon be sacked.

Before leaving Troy Criseyde convinces herself that it will be
quite simple to return in ten days. In the Greek camp the difficulties
and dangers of escape become real to her. She imagines herself
stealing away in the darkness, being apprehended and taken for a
spy or falling into the hands of 'som wrecche' and being raped (v
701–6). It is not so easy to cross this no-man's-land: as he grows
more anxious and distraught, Troilus considers stratagems for
doing so himself and rejects them as too dangerous (v 1576–82).
Criseyde reproaches herself for not having foreseen all the
problems:

Prudence, allas, oon of thyne eyen thre
Me lakked alwey, er that I com here!
On tyme ypassed wel remembred me,
And present tyme ek koud ich wel ise,
But future tyme, er I was in the snare,
Koude I nat sen; that causeth now my care.

v 744–9

But she has spent most of the poem thinking about the future. The fantasy with which she always comforts herself is that she will be in control of it. Troilus is obsessed with the thought of his own helplessness. When he first falls in love with Criseyde he is convinced that he must die and describes his plight in images of bondage and imprisonment. When he despairs in Book IV he lengthily denies the possibility of free will (958–1078). Pandarus sees this hopeless passivity in the face of both sorrows as self-deluding and self-destructive. Criseyde's fantasy of freedom is equally destructive. It lands her in 'the snare' (v 748). While she thinks she is taking responsibility for herself, she is putting off decisions until events make them for her.

Criseyde's terror at the beginning of the poem was compounded by her isolation: she was 'allone / Of any frend to whom she dorste hir mone' (ı 97–8). With her lack of relationships went a lack of roles, a source of strength as well as of weakness. Now in Book v she is alone again: 'And this was yet the werste of al hire peyne: / Ther was no wight to whom she dorste hire pleyne' (727–8). She is forced into a worse isolation, away from Troy, into roles and relationships she did not seek and finally into the stereotype of the faithless woman. First she is depersonalised by being treated as a counter in the exchange of hostages. Then she becomes a medium of other exchanges. The image of the willing exchange of hearts between equal and loving partners is mocked by her circumstances. A traditional movement in comedy is the bestowal of the woman from father to husband or her abduction from father by lover. This pattern is inverted in Criseyde's return to her father in a solemn procession escorted by her lover. In the motif of the love-triangle a woman is ostensibly honoured by the double adoration of two admirers. From another perspective she is mediated between two men, who sometimes seem more interested in their rivalry with each other than their love for her. Troilus fits the first theory, Diomede the second. Diomede is frankly stimulated by the thought

of competition: 'whoso myghte wynnen swich a flour / From hym
for whom she morneth nyght and day, / He myghte seyn he were
a conquerour' (v 792–4).

Both Troilus and Criseyde are constrained by the conventional
gender roles. When the exchange is proposed in the Trojan
parliament, Troilus is stoical and silent: 'Lest men sholde his
affeccioun espye; / With mannes herte he gan his sorwes drye' (iv
153–4). On the morning of her departure when he is to accompany
her, 'He gan his wo ful manly for to hide, / That wel unnethe it sene
was in his cheere' (v 30–1). Criseyde hides her feelings behind a
mask of feminine demureness: when she arrives at the Greek camp
and is greeted by her father, 'She seyde ek she was fayn with hym to
mete, / And stood forth muwet, milde, and mansuete' (v 193–4), the
image of the dutiful daughter. Her politeness allows Diomede to get
some purchase, first on her attention, then on her company, finally
on her affections. Like a Dorigen in far more desperate circum-
stances, Criseyde rebuffs his advances and then qualifies her
rejection:

> Myn herte is now in tribulacioun,
> And ye in armes bisy day by day.
> Herafter, whan ye wonnen han the town,
> Peraventure so it happen may,
> That whan I see that nevere yit I say
> Than wol I werke that I nevere wroughte!
> This word to yow ynough suffisen oughte.
>
> v 988–9

Diomede knows which role to play himself. Although he privately
thinks, as he rides to the Greek camp with her, that a flirtation will
pass the time ('at the werste it may yet shorte oure weye' – v 96), he
employs all the conventional rhetoric of the servant of the God of
Love. He is a travesty of the courtly lover and his wooing is full of
hollow echoes of Troilus. Criseyde's responses to him have an
element of replay. It was, in part, politeness which made her stay in
Pandarus's house on the night of the storm (iii 641–4). In her last
speech in the poem she pathetically tries to substitute the cynical
seducer for the devoted lover and retain some idea of her own
integrity: 'To Diomede algate I wol be trewe' (v 1071).

But this convinces neither the reader nor Criseyde herself. The
affair with Diomede, however understandable, is wrong. It is a

betrayal of a better lover and a better relationship. It seems highly improbable that the philandering Diomede would welcome her permanent fidelity. To him it is surely the kind of casual affair of which Criseyde had a nihilistic vision in Book II: 'That erst was nothing, into nought it torneth' (798). The misplaced fears she had of Troilus will be realised in Diomede. Like oracles, fears are often proved right in unexpected terms. 'Goddes speken in amphibologies' (IV 1406), says Criseyde to Troilus in Book IV, trying to reassure him that, once in the Greek camp, she will be able to argue her father out of his pessimism about the fate of Troy and return. But there she is echoed by Diomede, who insists that Troy will certainly fall, unless 'Calchas lede us with ambages – / That is to seyn, with double wordes slye, / Swiche as men clepen a word with two visages' (V 897–9). It is a curious consonance. Chaucer, poet of ambiguity, is fashioning the word in English. Diomede defines it for Criseyde but she has herself already thus described the 'ambiguous gifts' of the gods. The characters are linked by a sense of the two-facedness of things. To Diomede it justifies exploitation and plausibility. In Criseyde it begins in nervousness and ends in betrayal.

After outlining to Troilus how she will disarm the prophet by revealing that oracles are ambiguous, Criseyde proposes a second line of attack, on religious belief itself: 'Ek "Drede fond first goddes, I suppose –" / Thus shal I seyn' (IV 1408–9). The remark probably does not warrant much theological scrutiny. It is a hypothetical denial of pagan gods and, in context, a rhetorical strategy. But it is characteristic of a kind of scepticism which Criseyde has shown throughout. Like Troilus, she is capable of considering her problems – and tormenting herself – in philosophical terms. 'To what fyn?' (II 757, 794) is her question about both love and lovelessness. She is a pessimist. When Pandarus first tells her of Troilus's love for her, she perceives this vicarious approach as a dark apocalypse: 'of this world the feyth is al agoon . . . This false world – allas! – who may it leve?' (II 410, 420). Here, before the love affair has begun, Criseyde voices for a moment the insight which Troilus will painfully and permanently achieve after it ends. It is potentially a more destructive revelation, of a falsity built into the fabric of the relationships between the sexes rather than their inevitable transience within the beautiful but changing world of time. In the crisis of Book III, when Pandarus blackmails her with the fiction of Troilus's jealousy, her distress takes the form of a Boethian demonstration that earthly happiness is unreal because it is transitory. The last words she speaks in the poem are also a negative variation on the vision Troilus will achieve after her death: 'But al shal passe; and thus take I my leve' (v 1085). But whereas Troilus's final understanding of the vanity of the world in comparison to the felicity of heaven is followed by the narrator's profession of Christian faith, Criseyde fades from the poem with the weary statement that nothing lasts and so nothing matters.

In such a world, no wonder she compromises. Or, since she compromises, no wonder she excuses herself with such a view of the world. In the first half of the poem we saw Criseyde continually at odds with her circumstances – an outsider in her own city, politically threatened, socially isolated, emotionally wary, sexually reluctant. To others she is a number of roles which mean little or nothing to her: her husband's widow, Calchas's daughter, a demi-goddess, the lady of romance. Someone who is always reflected in distorting mirrors is not likely to have much sense of her own integrity. The happiness and candour of the love affair integrates her private life but it remains vulnerably private. It is a personal oasis in a political desert. In Book ɪv the political intervenes. Criseyde becomes a literal outsider in the Greek camp and 'placing' follows displacing. She is regarded as a Trojan, hostage, prize, stereotype. The Proem to Book ɪ acts as a kind of frame to the story, presenting Criseyde merely as the betrayer of Troilus. The poem grows beyond the boundaries of this frame but finally Criseyde is placed within it again and predicts despairingly that she will be viewed thus for ever.

10
The Women in the Books

Thanne thoughte he thus, 'O blisful lord Cupide,
Whan I the proces have in my memorie,
How thow me hast wereyed on every syde,
Men myght a book make of it, like a storie.'

TC v 582–5

'Allas! of me, unto the worldes ende,
Shal neyther ben ywriten nor ysonge
No good word, for thise bokes wol me shende.
O, rolled shal I ben on many a tonge!'

TC v 1058–61

In the last book of *Troilus and Criseyde* the hero draws some bitter comfort from imagining how a book might be written about his suffering in love. But to the heroine the prospect is appalling, a vision of unending obloquy. She is right to fear destruction by books. As long as the poem is read, the story of her infidelity will be repeated, though the poet ensures that her prediction of total condemnation will be inadequate. The contrasting attitudes of the man and the woman might be those of the innocent and guilty parties, envisaging the roles they are to play in the drama summarised by the proem: the suffering of Troilus at the hands of Criseyde.

Throughout the poem Troilus is more assured in his attitude to the outside world, more confident about the integrity of his private and public selves. In Book I he is too lovesick to eat or sleep and his suffering is evident to those around him. By the end of Book I his passion has inspired him to such acts of valour and kindness 'that ecch hym loved that loked on his face' (I 1078) and in Book III his honour and largess are praised from earth to heaven (1723–5). Separated from Criseyde in Book v, he imagines that he is pale and thin and that people are speculating on the cause and sorry for his

189

impending death. His expectation is of sympathy and respect. But
Criseyde is always terrified of what people will say. This fear proves
to be disabling and destructive: it drives her to leave uncomplain-
ingly for the Greek camp and become what she dreads. As Derek
Brewer puts it, Criseyde, 'who is more interested in her own
honour than any other character in Chaucer . . . is represented in
the poem as *the* person in history who has lost her honour. She has
put external social worldly reputation before the internal value of
trouthe to Troilus and has ironically lost the external reputation just
because she preferred it.'[1] There is indeed an irony here but also a
logic. What people most fear has a tendency to come true because
they perceive problems in the present which will have con-
sequences in the future.

Troilus's fantasy of being the hero of a tragic narrative is of
controlling the future from beyond the grave. He sees himself as a
Job-like victim, unjustly tormented by the God of Love, or an epic
figure, whose 'memorie' of his suffering should be faithfully
translated into a monument for posterity. Criseyde fears becoming
a character in a book because it will reduce her to an object 'rolled
. . . on many a tonge' (v 1061): she will become an exemplar of evil
and nothing good will be remembered of her. The visions are very
different but both are of a stable and comprehensible literary
tradition, the view of literature as clear and rational which we find
in the phrase 'read her like a book'. But books are ambiguous and
susceptible to interpretation, as is also acknowledged in the poem.
Troilus sees Criseyde as a book, one which he finds difficult to
understand. When they are first in bed together he kisses her eyes
and says:

> Though ther be mercy writen in youre cheere,
> God woot, the text ful hard is, soth, to fynde!
>   III 1356–7

He is both a worshipper of Criseyde, receiving a direct confirma-
tion of a promise somewhere in scripture, and a reader at once
captivated and confused.

The hero shares the difficulties of the narrator, who continually
emphasises that his knowledge of the heroine is derived from what
he can 'rede' (I 495; v 19), from 'bokes olde' (III 1199), 'clerkes' (III
1199; v 1854), the 'storie' (v 1037, 1044, 1051, 1094), his 'auctour' (II 700;
III 502, 575, 1325, 1817) and that their testimony is patchy. His

problems of transmission range from factual report (how old is Criseyde? – v 826; is she a mother? – i 132–3) to psychological interpretation (what does she think? – iii 575–6, to moral judgement (should he condemn her? – v 1093). He presents the question of whether Criseyde had children as a simple matter of record ('I rede it naught, therfore I late it goon' – i 133). A teasing author, however, lurks behind the apparently trusting narrator, since Boccaccio's poem (the unacknowledged source) states clearly that the heroine did not.[2] Similarly, the ambiguity about Criseyde's awareness of the seduction plot is attributed to the reticence of the source: 'Nought list myn auctour fully to declare / What that she thoughte whan he seyde so, / That Troilus was out of town yfare' (iii 575–7). But Boccaccio's Criseida plans the night of love herself and confides her desire to Pandaro, who grieves her by telling her of Troilo's absence and co-operatively sends a friend to recall him.[3] Chaucer's narrator protests his dependence on an opaque source precisely when his creator is complicating its clarity of action and motive. The narrator finally declares his unwillingness to blame Criseyde 'forther than the storye wol devyse' (v 1094), as if a mere record of events demands credence and will solve problems of interpretation and judgement for him.

The narrator both appeals to the idea of a stable and reliable literary tradition and takes refuge in its gaps and ambiguities. The author pays homage to the great classical poets, imagining their stately progress past his own little book (v 1786–92), but sends his poem forth into his culture of linguistic diversity with a prayer that it be not miswritten, mismetered, misread or misunderstood. Stability, the Epilogue teaches, is to be found only in Christ. Criseyde and her love are an aspect of the transient beauty of this world. Her story is vulnerable to the passing of time and the diversity of tongues. At the end of the poem the author's need to distance himself from their tragedy reduces both Troilus and Criseyde to 'payens' (v 1849), trapped in the mutability of life, the vanity of their beliefs and 'the forme of olde clerkis speche / In poetrie, if ye hire bokes seche' (1854–5). The brief conditional clause has its own pathos, partly inviting reading and scholarship, partly dismissing them as an exercise in futility which will uncover further futility. The poem tries to escape the fate of its characters by its closing acknowledgement of the eternity which, 'uncircumscript' (v 1865), circumscribes all human life and writing.

Before the poem finally loses interest in Criseyde, she occupies several positions in its closing statements. She and Troilus partake in the universal human experience of change and loss. She is also herself what is lost, the object of love, the symbol of earthly beauty, the proof of the world's fickleness. And she is the character closest to the poem's dubieties about its value, its power to communicate, its relativity in a world circumscribed by the absolute of the creator. Can literature convey truth about life and is truth about life worth conveying? For Chaucer, the character who pre-eminently embodies these problems is female. Criseyde is ontologically more complex than Troilus. The mysterious heroine who predicts her survival in the poem as a stereotype becomes a statement about women in books and a question about books and women.

Criseyde's prophecy of her destruction by literature and Troilus's perception of her as an obscure text raise two problems of which Chaucer is continuously aware: the evil images of themselves which women read in literary tradition and the difficulty of literary tradition in reading them. Throughout his poetry women have an uneasy relationship to this tradition. Only the saints can be confident about it. The Virgin Mary, the exception to the female rule, is often depicted in paintings of the Annunciation with a book. Before the appearance of the angel she has been reading the Bible, in particular the prophecies which foretell the coming of the Messiah. Past, present and future accord, prophecy, annunciation and history celebrate her. In Chaucer's early poem the *ABC* every letter of the alphabet serves to honour the Virgin. Those who follow her are correspondingly irradiated by writing, like the initials in illuminated manuscripts: 'Kalenderes enlumyned ben thei / That in this world ben lighted with thi name' (*ABC* 73–4). The Second Nun emphasises that she is translating the story of Cecilia from a book, 'as hir lif seith' (*CT* VIII 120), and the saint's purposes are supported by a vision of God as an old man with a book (*CT* VII 201–16). But fears and perplexity about literature are voiced more often in Chaucer's poems, ranging from Criseyde's nervousness to the Wife of Bath's polemics.

The absent yet vibrantly present heroine of the *Book of the Duchess* has a poise and assurance which owes much to her position as a kind of secular Madonna. She can be confidently placed against the background of biblical and classical tradition:

> To speke of godnesse, trewly she
> Had as moche debonairte

As ever had Hester in the Bible . . .

BD 985–7

She was as good, so have I reste,
As ever was Penelopee of Grece,
Or as the noble wif Lucrece,
That was the beste – he telleth thus,
The Romayn, Tytus Lyvyus . . .

1080–4

Like the Virgin Mary she radiates light. She is teacher and inspiration to her worshipper. He, rather than the woman, is the 'blank page':[4] 'I was', he says,

As a whit wal or a table,
For hit ys redy to cacche and take
Al that men wil theryn make,
Whethir so men wil portreye or peynte . . .

779–83

But framing this central relationship are more anxious attitudes to books and to women which will be further explored in Chaucer's later work. The poem opens with the suffering of the sleepless narrator, presumably for unrequited love. It continues with the story of Alcyone, first of a line of Chaucerian heroines to mourn for a man who does not return. The apparition of her drowned husband tells Alcyone not to grieve but the sorrowful narrator does not compare his case with hers. From the book he takes what suits his immediate need, the discovery that there is a god of sleep who may help his insomnia. Within the dream the Man in Black is equally impervious to the morals which might be drawn from literature. The Dreamer obliquely criticises his obsessive grief by condemning the excesses of those who have died for love – Medea, Phyllis, Dido, Echo and Samson – as mere 'foly' (725–39) but makes no impression on the bereaved lover.

These themes – the power of love, the suffering caused by love, especially to women who are deserted, the questionable value of love, the vexing testimony of literary tradition and the role of the poet in interpreting it – are explored in the later dream-visions. These poems negotiate between the three kinds of knowledge gained from vision, experience and authority.[5] The *House of Fame* opens with a consideration of dreams and then foregrounds the problem of tradition. It suggests that books are quite as problematic a source of information as dreams. After an invocation to the god of sleep (now firmly established in the Chaucerian pantheon), the narrator recounts his dream. He first finds himself in a temple of glass, devoted to Venus, and sees on the walls the story of the *Aeneid*. He summarises this narrative, giving most attention to the events of Book IV, Dido's love for Aeneas, his desertion of her and her suicide. The narrator points to Aeneas as a famous example of the 'untrouthe' of men (*HF* 384) to which both literature and experience bear frequent witness ('As men may ofte in bokes rede, / And al day sen hyt yet in dede' – 385–6). But this interpretation is based on the version in Ovid's *Heroides*, not on Virgil's, in which it is the duty of '*pius Aeneas*' to depart on his divine mission to found Rome. These are two very different readings of the story and Chaucer acknowledges both ('Rede Virgile in Eneydos / Or the Epistle of Ovyde', 378–9) without attempting to reconcile them. Indeed, he points out their discrepancy. After his condemnation of 'such untrouthe' (384) and a catalogue of other women betrayed by false men (some of whom will reappear with Dido as the heroines of the *Legend of Good Women*), he turns 'to excusen Eneas' (427) with the Virgilian interpretation of his destiny. Chaucer may also have known the view that the whole story is a fiction and that Dido and Aeneas never met.[6] The first book of his poem about Fame presents a famous love story about whose truth or meaning there is no consensus.

Questions about the sources of information continue in Book II, when the didactic eagle carries the poet on a journey through the sky towards the House of Fame. Although Geoffrey is a love poet, he has neither experience of love nor 'tydynges / Of Loves folk' (644–5). All his knowledge comes from literature. He is so 'daswed' (658) a bookworm that he does not even hear tidings from his neighbours. The flight corroborates the testimony of some books about celestial voyages, such as the *Dream of Scipio*, the inspiration of the very different dream in the *Parliament of Fowls*. The Dreamer, indeed, firmly prefers the knowledge that comes from literature: he refuses further instruction on the stars from the eagle, since he can read about them with less danger to his sight than gazing on them. In this vision experience and authority concur and the eagle is determined to demonstrate by his lecture on sound waves that the spoken word and tidings of love can equally be regarded as objective. But tidings prove more mysterious than the secrets of the cosmos. As in the *Parliament of Fowls*, the celestial vision fails to explain the problems of the personal life. The eagle proves that the tidings go to the House of Fame, the home and the source of speech, not that the tidings are true. Every speech, indeed, arrives at the House of Fame looking exactly like the man or woman who uttered it (1074–83), which suggests that it shows more about the speaker than about the subject.[7] Geoffrey is going to learn the tidings by experience but all that experience teaches is the unreliability of tidings.

In Book III the capriciousness of renown and ignominy, obscurity and fame is demonstrated. Although her house is attended by the greatest artists, Fame distributes or withholds good or bad reputation without caring for merit or desire.[8] This is shown further in the hubbub of the labyrinthine house where tidings circulate and multiply, lies and truths jostle each other and emerge compounded together. Some of the gossip-mongers are 'pilgrimes, / With scrippes bret-ful of lesinges' (2122–3), casting some proleptic scepticism on the whole enterprise of the *Canterbury Tales*. Finally the poem breaks off unfinished as the dreamer sees a nameless personage who 'semed for to be / A man of gret auctoritee' (2157–8). Surely this ending is a joke. That venerable figure, the man of authority, is introduced as if to solve all the problems that the poem has raised and the poet pointedly disclaims any idea of what he could say. The *House of Fame* opens and closes with two emblems: the seduced and abandoned woman, the wise and powerful man. It begins with one of the most famous and problematic of women in books and ends – or fails to end – with a man who fails to solve the problems or to bring this book to an end.

Chaucer's next dream-vision, the *Parliament of Fowls*, moves in the opposite direction from the *House of Fame*. But it ponders some of the same problems, though its emphasis is on love rather than on fame. The *House of Fame* opens out from a consideration of love to the problem of Fame in general and breaks off with the man of authority. The *Parliament of Fowls* begins with a man with a book, Scipio Africanus and his 'olde bok totorn' (110), which tells of his vision of the universe, but narrows down from the whole cosmos to the heaven-and-hell of earthly love. The stories briefly catalogued in the Temple of Venus are those of tragic lovers, some famous in literature and some – 'many a mayde of which the name I wante' (287) – obscure in anonymity. After his most searching study of

tragic love in *Troilus and Criseyde*, Chaucer will return to some of the
ladies in this catalogue – 'Dido, Thisbe . . . Cleopatre' (289, 291) – to
the mysteries of heaven, hell and theology and the problems of love,
tradition and poetry in the *Legend of Good Women*.

II

> Thow shalt, while that thou lyvest, yer by yere,
> The most partye of thy tyme spende
> In makyng of a glorious legende
> Of goode wymmen, maydenes and wyves,
> That weren trewe in loving all hire lyves;
> And telle of false men that hem bytraien,
> That al hir lyf ne do nat but assayen
> How many women they may doon a shame;
> For in youre world that is now holde a game.
> And thogh the lyke nat a lovere bee,
> Speke well of love; this penance yive I thee.
>
> *LGW* Prologue F 481–91[9]

> And trusteth, as in love, no man but me.
>
> *LGW* 2561

The task of writing the stories of good women betrayed by false
men is imposed on the Dreamer-poet by Alceste in the Prologue to
the *Legend of Good Women*. The *Legend* was undertaken between
Troilus and Criseyde and the *Canterbury Tales*. Its subject is adum-
brated towards the end of *Troilus*, when the narrator begs the ladies
in his audience not to be angry with him for relating Criseyde's
infidelity. He pleads that he inherited the story of her guilt from his
sources and that he himself would rather write of the faithful
Penelope and the good Alcestis. He also expresses the wish for a
change of genre, as well as of subject: in his valediction to his 'litel
. . . tragedye' (*TC* v 1786) he prays for the power to compose a
comedy,[10] a desire which was to be fulfilled in the *Canterbury Tales*.

The *Legend* is a transitional and problematic work. In theme, it
ostensibly atones for *Troilus*. In form, a story collection with an
explanatory Prologue, it anticipates the *Canterbury Tales*. In genre,
the dream-vision Prologue, with its garden setting and its Court of
Love, looks back to Chaucer's earlier work. The Prologue is as

lovely, subtle and suggestive as anything Chaucer wrote but the stories are wooden and vexing. They break off unfinished and it is often assumed that Chaucer found the repetitive nature of the project monotonous and lost interest.[11]

Like the earlier dream-visions, the Prologue mediates between the worlds of vision, experience and authority. Like the *House of Fame* and the *Parliament of Fowls* it modulates from the classic questions of metaphysics to the familiar problems of love and knowledge in this world. It opens with a shimmering account of the limitations of empirical knowledge and the necessity for faith. The narrator, who presents himself as an avid reader, points out that our belief in the joys of heaven and the pains of hell rests on authority. He has never met anyone who has been to either place so we have to trust the authors who tell us of them, to 'yeve credence, in every skylful wise' (20) to 'bokes that we fynde . . . / And to the doctrine of these old wyse' (17, 19). But our lack of first-hand knowledge could equally be used as an argument for scepticism. How are we to define when it is reasonable ('skylful') to give credence? Does the narrator's conclusion, that we should 'honouren and beleve / These bokes, there we han noon other preve' (28–9), present authority as a precious revelation, a last resort or a completely unverifiable source of knowledge? And what is the relationship of this introduction to the project of telling the legends of good women? It has been suggested that it is the first hint of an ironic intention: the goodness of women exists only in fiction and cannot be attested from experience.[12] But this argument (like most others about Chaucer) cuts both ways. Literary and theological tradition is more misogynist than philogynist: perhaps the proverbial badness of women is disproved by experience.

The narrator, at any rate, places complete faith in books. He can be drawn away from them into the open air only by his desire to pay devotion to the daisy on a spring morning. It sounds like a holiday from epistemological problems. The daisy, a wild flower, might seem the epitome of the natural. But for Chaucer's courtly audience it would have evoked a literary tradition of courtly poetry. The flower is celebrated in a genre of its own, the French *marguerite* poem, employed by some of Chaucer's favourite authors, such as Machaut, Froissart and Deschamps, to pay compliments to a lady.[13] The daisy evokes both a morning walk in a spring meadow and a particularly fashionable and sophisticated style of writing about women and romance. This is the *haute couture* of love, the world of the impossibly idealised mistress, the *demandes d'amour*, the elaborate codes and courtesies. Chaucer alludes to this kind of courtly game and dissociates himself from it. He does not join in the coterie dispute and support leaf against flower or flower against leaf. His work draws on the sources of 'olde story' (G 80) long before such controversy. The legends which follow will derive from the classical tradition and will be commissioned by the classical Queen Alcestis. None the less, the meadow is also related to the garden of the *Romance of the Rose* and will soon be entered by the God of Love with his court.

The narrator's fervent celebration of the daisy demands an allegorical reading. He speaks of the flower as 'she' and praises her 'vertu and honour' (54) like a lover his mistress. But we learn later from Alceste that he is no lover ('the lyke nat a lovere bee' – 490) and already it is clear that his concern is as much with love poetry as with love. He asks help from the 'lovers that kan make of sentement' (69), as if his own inspiration does not derive from the felt experience of love and confesses that he is reduced to gleaning in the field of literature. The daisy is his muse, the 'maistresse of my wit' (88), the hand that makes his heart produce music, his 'erthly god' (95). The flower, though Chaucer is careful to define its worship as earthly, looks more and more numinous. The daisy is 'of alle floures flour' (53), like the Virgin Mary in the *ABC* (4). The language of religious devotion was often used in love poetry. But some of the Christian vocabulary applied to the daisy is fresh and striking. Its opening in the morning sunlight is described as a 'resureccioun' (110), as if the narrator's worship resembled the visit of the women to the sepulchre. The daisy, which briefly looked like an escape from the vexing worlds of literature and theology, has its own obscure relationship to the great mysteries of heaven and hell with which the poem opened.

The spring garden is fertile in problems of interpretation. The birds are as amorous and articulate as those in the *Parliament*. They too sing their song to St Valentine, they share in the human experiences of 'Daunger ... Pitee ... Mercy ... innocence and ruled Curtesye' (160–3), they can be held guilty of 'unkyndenesse' (153) and absolved through 'repentynge' (156). But the narrator cannot resist a moment of cynicism at these lovely fictional constructions: the birds also 'diden hire other observaunces / That longeth onto love and to nature; / Construeth that as yow lyst, I do no cure' (150–2). Does the basic sexual instinct need any more 'construing'? Does it need explaining or does it provide an explanatory symbol of other mysteries? The scene is framed in cosmic sexual allegories. The time of year is defined astrologically: the sun is in Taurus, who abducted Europa. The flowers in the meadow bloom through the power of Zephyrus and Flora.

When the daisy closes at sunset, the narrator hurries home and goes to sleep in his garden. He dreams of the meadow and the daisy and another couple of presiding deities. The God of Love appears, accompanied by Queen Alceste. She wears a green robe and a flowered crown of white and gold which 'made hir lyk a daysie for to sene' (224). In this figure the ambiguities of the daisy and of the three kinds of knowledge – vision, authority and experience – are resolved. Alcestis, in classical mythology, chose to die in place of her husband and was restored to life by Hercules. Though there is no metamorphosis in the original story, the God of Love will explain to the Dreamer that she 'turned was into a dayesye' (512). She exemplifies married love rather than romantic passion or, according to the God of Love, reconciles the two: 'she taughte . . . of fyn lovynge, / And namely of wyfhod the lyvynge' (544–5). Like her rescuer Hercules, she acts as a classical symbol of Christ's sacrifice. The application of the term 'resureccioun' (110) to the opening of the daisy was bold but precise. We were misled into suspecting that the daisy was the narrator's mistress and his poem another record of courtly infatuation. Alceste represents a love that the Christian poet can celebrate. She unites the conflicting elements of the Prologue and of Chaucer's earlier poems, classical and Christian, love and death, experience and authority. According to the God of Love, at least, the problems of the polarised images of women dissolve in the light of the example of Alceste, the evidence of books and the narrator's own experience: 'thow knowest here goodnesse / By pref and ek by storyes herebyforn' (G 527–8). The world of vision verifies the testimony of literature ('Hastow nat in a book, lyth in thy cheste, / The grete goodnesse of the queene Alceste?', 510–11) and the narrator's passionate, though puzzling, devotion to the daisy.[14]

Many values meet in Alceste. But the God of Love seems a narrower figure than ever. His artifice is emphasised. In the *Romance of the Rose* he is specifically dressed in flowers rather than silk: 'nought clad in silk was he, / But all in floures and in flourettes' (*RR* 890–1). Here he is 'yclothed . . . / In silk' (226–7), embroidered with green branches. His head-dress is magnificent

but mysterious: 'His gilte heer was corowned with a sonne, /
Instede of gold, for hevynesse and wyghte' (230–1). Presumably he
is wearing a sun-crown of the kind fashionable at the time rather
than a heavier gold crown. But the adjectives 'gilte . . . / Instede
of gold' (230–1), though they qualify different nouns, resonate
together with the suggestion of the superficial and second-best.
The sun is a Christian symbol of divinity. The God of Love is the
sun of his own system. Nineteen ladies, royally dressed, follow the
God, after them comes an innumerable host of women who were
faithful in love and all kneel and do devotion to the daisy. For the
God of Love they are equivalent to the procession of the innocents
who adore the Lamb in *Pearl*. He gives his own blessing to them
and their kind at the end of the Prologue when he assures the
Dreamer 'ne shal no trewe lover come in helle' (553), his solution to
the problems of faith with which the poem opened. Fidelity in love
and marriage is virtuous but to the God it is the *only* virtue.
Alceste's active virtue reaches further, to hell itself. The presenta-
tion of the God raises the problem of whether the Religion of Love is
a blasphemous parody of Christian practice and doctrine. The
example of Alceste suggests that love and religion can be
reconciled. The God reminds the Dreamer that her story occurs in
Plato's *Symposium*: 'No wonder ys thogh Jove hire stellyfye, / As
telleth Agaton, for hir goodnesse!' (525–6). Plato's version does not
include a stellification; like the metamorphosis into the daisy this
may be Chaucer's own invention. (Perhaps Alceste as a genuine
star is to be revered more than the God of Love, a spurious sun?) Its
context in the *Symposium* is suggestive: Alcestis is mentioned in
Diotima's climactic speech, reported by Socrates, which portrays
the experience of love as an ascent from the human to the divine,
from attraction to the beauty of individuals to contemplation of
absolute beauty itself.[15] In her metamorphosis as 'the "dayesye" or
elles the "ye of day" ' (184) she inspires love, a function of the eyes in
neo-Platonic thought, and herself gazes upon the true sun.

The God of Love also has his limitations as a literary critic. He
says that the Dreamer–poet has no right to approach his flower
since he has traduced love and lovers. Chaucer has put 'wise folk'
(331) (a revealing adjective) off love by translating the *Romance of
the Rose*. He has told the story of Criseyde and so made men trust
women less. In G the God also demands to know why Chaucer has
not chosen to write of good women, since there are so many books
which tell their stories. Chaucer himself owns sixty books among

which he could find numerous accounts of virtuous Greek and Roman women. Valerius, Livy, Claudian and Jerome all tell stories of heroines willing to die rather than be unchaste. Ovid writes of faithful women in the *Heroides*. These were heathen, but Christian authors can also supply examples of virtuous women.

This attack on Chaucer is unsubtle in the extreme. The God judges literature merely by its subject-matter and story-line. To him the effect of *Troilus*, since its heroine is unfaithful, will simply be to make men mistrust women. Conversely, he believes that any story of a virtuous woman will promote love and he enlists in defence of his cause St Jerome himself and the very 'book of wikked wyves' (*CT* III 685) with which Jankin tormented Alison. Jerome's examples of good women are those vowed to chastity, hardly a virtue in Cupid's system. But the God is not interested in subtleties and he brushes aside all questions of interpretation. For him it is enough that Chaucer has translated the *Romance of the Rose* 'in pleyn text, withouten nede of glose' (328). (Chaucer himself does feel the need. The Dreamer of the *Book of the Duchess* finds himself in a room whose walls are painted with 'both text and glose' – *BD* 333 – of the poem, a strange but scholarly decor.) In G the God employs the figure of fruit and chaff, which Chaucer uses traditionally, if teasingly, in the *Nun's Priest's Tale* (*CT* VII 3443), to distinguish between meaning and fable, to make a crude case for 'good' and against 'bad' material:

> Let be the chaf, and writ wel of the corn.
> Why noldest thow han written of Alceste,
> And laten Criseide ben aslepe and reste?
>
> G529–31

Alceste comes to the poet's rescue with a wonderfully double-edged defence. Like Hippolyta with Theseus and Prudence with Melibee, she argues for clemency. Chaucer may be falsely accused or he may simply be too stupid to understand what he has translated. Although not a very good poet, he has promoted the God's service among the ignorant with the *House of Fame*, the *Parliament of Fowls*, the *Book of the Duchess*, the story of Palamon and Arcite and many shorter poems. He has also written edifyingly 'of other holynesse' (424): the translations of Boethius and of Origen's work on Mary Magdalen and the life of St Cecilia. She prevails and imposes on him the task of writing the stories of good women betrayed by bad men. She does not engage at all with the problem of whether women are vilified in *Troilus*. As she says, it is no use arguing, 'For Love ne wol nat countrepleted be / In ryght ne wrong' (476–7) and she uses the God's own critical methods to appeal to him. She too judges by subject-matter: she can commend to the God the *Parliament of Fowls* and the story of Palamon and Arcite only because the 'pleyn text' (328) of these poems is about love. A 'glose' (328) would highlight many criticisms, ironies and reservations. The God co-opted Jerome and his tales of chaste Christian women to his side. Alceste similarly appeals to Chaucer's Christian and philosophical work as a generally 'good thing': the *Consolation* is not about love, the story of Magdalen is of a repentant prostitute and the legend of Cecilia extols her celibacy. The only distinction Alceste makes between subject and meaning is a mocking one: Chaucer probably did not understand his sources.

This is a distinction that the Dreamer makes himself. True lovers, he claims, should not be indignant at stories of false lovers, from whom they are quite different, but should support the poet who has written of love in *Troilus* and the *Romance*:

> what so myn auctour mente,
> Algate, God woot, yt was myn entente
> To forthren trouthe in love and yt cheryce,
> And to ben war fro falsnesse and fro vice
> By swich ensample; this was my menynge.
> 470–4

This apologia is brief and modest but it touches on the heart of the matter. Chaucer's own translations and adaptations are not identical to their sources and his intentions cannot be inferred from mere plot summary. Can there be such a thing as the 'pleyn text, withouten nede of glose' (328) which so incenses the God against him? In G the Dreamer seems to agree that there is, when he supports the authority of 'bokes olde' (G 82), at least 'there as there lyth non other assay by preve' (G 84):

> For myn entente is, or I fro yow fare,
> The naked text in English to declare
> Of many a story, or elles of many a geste,
> As autours seyn; leveth hem if yow leste.
> G 85–8

His 'entente' here is theoretically at odds with the 'entente' defended in the passage quoted above. Instead of maintaining his freedom in relation to sources and subject, the narrator promises to transpose the naked ('pleyn'?) text of his sources into English, and perhaps the throwaway what-you-will injunction to believe it if you like suggest scepticism at the stories or at the project.

The project is surely a disastrous one. Alceste prescribes as penance that the poet is to spend most of his time for the rest of his life writing a 'glorious legende' (483) of true women betrayed by false men. The God defines the task more exactly and adds some desiderata of his own. The legends are to include those of the nineteen ladies in attendance who have already been named in the *Balade*: of these Lucretia, Cleopatra, Thisbe, Dido, Phyllis, Hypsipyle, Hypermnestra and Ariadne will appear in the *Legend* as we have it. They are to begin with Cleopatra and to culminate in the story of Alceste, a scheme not fully realised since the poem is unfinished. They are to be brief and rehearse merely the essentials of the narrative according to the ancient sources.

The failure of the Legend can be blamed on these guidelines. The merciful Alceste proposes a life sentence, condemning the poet to the author's nightmare of the book that will never be finished. The God at any rate puts a limit on the work but it seems that Chaucer tired of it before completing the twenty poems he planned. His frequent use of the figures of *abbreviatio* and *occupatio* and his expressions of impatience with the material suggest *ennui*. Robert Payne has queried Chaucer's 'putative boredom with a theme which in fact his poetry never abandons from first to last'[16] but he might well have grown bored not with the theme but with the prescription to approach it always from one point of view. Chaucer is a poet of multiple voices and multiple viewpoints. The form of the story collection in the *Canterbury Tales* functions as a relativity machine. It liberates the poet from any fixed position. The plan for the *Legend* constricts him. He is further cramped by the God's recommendation of brevity. Medieval narrative often suffers from length but here the narrow scope of the legends imposes a narrow outlook: psychological investigation is precluded and the repetitive nature of the scheme is underlined. The view of female virtue is equally reductive: it consists in fidelity to a man and the worse the man, the better the woman. Virtue is equated with victimisation. No wonder the heroines of the Legend look rather stupid. If the men are villains, the women are idiots to believe them. Far from celebrating love, these dreary stories of true women betrayed by false men are as anaphrodisiac as the cautionary tales of wicked wives. The God supposes that the story of a woman unfaithful to a man will put people off love: logically, on his view of literature, these stories would have the same, not the opposite, effect.

It is possible that the entire scheme is ironic, that Chaucer the narrator attempts to follow the God's bidding while Chaucer the poet shows the dire results of his prejudices. If so, the irony may be directed at his taste in literature or at his views of women. Lydgate, who overtly borrowed from the *Legend* in *The Falls of Princes*, seems to find the individual stories of good women panegyric but the total scheme misogynist: he suggests both that Chaucer gave up the poem because he was hard pressed to find as many as nineteen good women and that the nineteen are the absolute maximum and are lent distinction by the contrast with most of their sex. ('ther liff doth shewe / For a clear merour, because ther be so fewe' – 1805–6). H. C. Goddard, perhaps the first modern critic to propose a totally ironic reading, argues that Chaucer takes his revenge on the God's misreading of *Troilus* as a poem against women by producing a truly misogynist work: 'as a penance for an act he never committed, he commits that very act'.[17] A number of recent studies have also presented a *Legend* ironic at the expense of women, the God's romantic code of value or the anti-feminist tradition, arguing from the failure of the poems to produce a tragic effect or an acceptable moral, the treatment of sources, the obscene puns, the moments of humour and the choice of heroines.[18]

The command to begin the stories of good women with Cleopatra certainly suggests irony. Cleopatra is in classical and medieval tradition a notoriously bad woman.[19] But the God's values are his own. Cleopatra risks all for love, finally making the supreme sacrifice of death. She is one of love's martyrs. Chaucer's *Legend* edits out most of the evidence for the other view. It opens 'After the deth of Tholome the kyng' with no hint that Cleopatra married and murdered her brother-king and goes on to the arrival of Antony with no mention of her earlier affair with Julius Caesar. The couple are platitudinously attractive: Cleopatra, 'fayr as is the rose in May' (613), falls in love with 'this knyght, / Thourgh his desert, and for his chyvalrye' (607–8). Their story is presented as a tragedy of love and the war with Rome as mainly caused by Antony's desertion of Octavia. In this version Antony and Cleopatra marry and she is faithful to death. Antony, not she, flees, first from the sea-battle (which is described at disproportionate length as if it were really more interesting than their relationship), he commits suicide and she follows him. To those who know more of the story the statement that Cleopatra 'coude of Cesar have no grace' (663) may recall her attempt to seduce and come to terms with Octavius after Antony's death and her speech before her suicide may open on a slightly comic note: Cleopatra reaffirms the vow of total fidelity made to her love, identifying him in parenthesis, 'I mene yow, Antonius, my knyght' (684), as if to distinguish him from other claimants to this role. Far from presenting a 'naked text' in which the facts speak for themselves, Chaucer has produced a story which reads one way if you know the sources and another if you do not. In isolation it appears to celebrate a loyal, though not very interesting, wife who commits a kind of suttee by serpents. But if we recognize it as a new version of an ancient tale we are aware of strange gaps – incest, murder, adultery and treachery are politely not mentioned – and may suspect that the only way of constructing a 'good woman' is to leave out all the evidence to the contrary.

This seems like an ironic start to an ironic project. A similar strategy occurs in the story of Medea, whose murder of her children is pointedly or conveniently omitted. But I do not find that any effect is clear or sustained in the *Legends*. This is partly because the tone seems so uncertain, partly because the poems fail to hold my attention. They are neither brilliantly satirical nor profoundly tragic. They oscillate between perfunctory narrative, inflated rhetoric, comic subversion and genuine pathos. In Chaucer's other poems the sudden changes of tone and register produce dazzling and complex syntheses. Here I become bemused and bored. I also find the world of the Legends depressing. Even if it is read straight, the Legend of Cleopatra paints a dismal picture of female virtue. The powerful and magnificent queen of history has dwindled into an appendage, introduced as a woman waiting 'after the deth' (580) of one husband 'tyl' (583) the arrival of the next. The action of the poem belongs to Antony. The emotional dependence of the women on the men is reflected in the narrative focus of the Legends. The most striking example is the double Legend of Hypsipyle and Medea, heroines yoked together by common bond of betrayal by Jason. The role of the women is merely to be destroyed by their dealings with men. The naked body of the dying Cleopatra is emblem of this 'naked text' (G 86). The Legends purport to celebrate such immolations but the narrator of the *Book of the Duchess* had cited some of these heroines – Medea, Phyllis and Dido – as examples of the damnable folly of dying for love. Although the

Legends are ostensibly poems with a message, there seems a dreary
pointlessness about the desertions and deaths in which they
culminate. They break off towards the end of the tale of
Hypermnestra with the provoking line 'This tale is seyd for this
conclusion –' (2723). Was Chaucer unable to draw any conclusion
from the Legends. Does he suggest that the reasonable conclusion
might not be what the God of Love ordered? Did he ever mean to
come back and conclude the project?

V. A. Kolve suggests that the story of Alceste would have
provided a conclusion and a solution to the problems first raised by
the Legend of Cleopatra.[20] He argues that the morbid atmosphere of
the Legends and the meaningless loves and deaths of their heroines
are characteristic of the unredeemed suffering of the pagan world
which they inhabit. The G Prologue makes the specific point that
the good women were pre-Christian: 'And yit they were hethene, al
the pak' (G 299). The story of Cleopatra, like all other stories, leads to
the grave and her Legend ends in a 'worm'-infested pit. Alceste
figurally brings to death a Christian interpretation and its faith in
resurrection. In this reading the absent Alceste would have retro-
spectively cast light upon these gloomy stories and, as in the
Prologue, reconciled the worlds of classical and Christian, love and
religion, literature, experience and revelation. It would rescue the
Legends from the charge of misogyny, since the problems would be
seen to come not so much from the heroines as from their world and
would be resolved by the Legend of Alceste.

The ironic readings transform the negative qualities of the
legends into satiric positives or transpose their positive statements
into debunking negatives. Kolve proposes that the Legends are
made up of a series of negations which would be redeemed by a
symbolic affirmation. Though very different in direction, both
interpretations begin from a position of unease and dissatisfaction
with the 'naked text'. Throughout the Legends the inadequacies of
the 'naked text' view of narrative are glaring. These stories were
never neutral records of fact but, as far back as we can trace them,
fraught with values, design and polemic. At the opening of the
Legend of Philomela, the narrator attests the power and the poison
of the story:

> And, as to me, so grisely was his dede
> That, whan that I his foule storye rede,
> Myne eyen wexe foule and sore also.

Yit last the venym of so longe ago,
That it enfecteth hym that wol beholde
The storye of Tereus . . .

2238–43

Tereus, who raped his sister-in-law and cut out her tongue, will find few defenders. But Cleopatra, the heroine of the opening Legend, can easily be made to look as venomous as the serpents who poison her. The subject of the second Legend, Pyramus and Thisbe, is for post-Shakespearian readers a notorious example of the power of presentation. Is their burlesque in *A Midsummer Night's Dream* merely the last accident to befall this accident-prone couple? Or did Shakespeare recognise in the Legends tragedies with irresistibly comic potential, stories which could all too easily go another way? Dido is the subject of the third Legend. Chaucer makes clear in the first book of the *House of Fame* that there are two conflicting interpretations of her story. He names the versions again at the opening of the Legend and suggests that he will extract the 'naked text' of both to support his argument: 'In thyn Eneyde and Naso wol I take / The tenor, and the grete effectes make' (928–9). But the earlier dream-visions demonstrate that the same 'tenor' may yield very different 'effectes'. The narrator of the *House of Fame* draws from Dido's tragedy the ostensible moral of the Legend, that it demonstrates the 'untrouthe' (*HF* 384) of men to women in literature and experience, past and present, 'As men may ofte in bokes rede, / And al day sen hyt yet in dede' (*HF* 385–6); he points to other examples of women betrayed who will be the heroines of the later poem, Phyllis, Medea and Ariadne. But the narrator of the *Book of the Duchess* uses Phyllis, Medea and Dido as examples of culpable stupidity. The poet of the Legend knows of both 'effectes'.

I am inclined to think that the ironies of the Legend are less at the expense of men or of women than at the blinkered view of literary tradition as unambiguously supporting one side or the other.[21] Any narrative is open to other interpretations. The God of Love reveals his prejudice in reading *Troilus* as a poem against love and women. Alceste defends the poet by citing his poems in praise of the God, such as 'the love of Palamon and Arcite' (420). But the *Knight's Tale* is no more simply 'for' love than *Troilus* is 'against' it. The God's command is to 'reverse the *Troilus*'[22] and, at an equally simplistic and questionable level, the Legend does just that. But it also reverses the *Knight's Tale* or shows the underside of the chivalric

and romantic world of Palamon and Arcite. Their story could go
another way. Chaucer also wrote an unfinished poem, *Anelida and
Arcite*, which begins similarly to the *Knight's Tale*, with the same
epigraph from Statius and the same episode of Theseus's
triumphant return to Athens with Hippolyta and Emily. But then
the story diverges to Thebes and to a very different Arcite who
betrays the devoted Anelida as soon as he is attracted by the novelty
of a new lady. From his perfidy the narrator draws the Legend-like
moral, 'gret wonder was hit noon / Thogh he were fals, for hit is
kynde of man' (*AA* 148–9) and he warns women to take this story as
'ensample' (*AA* 197): 'The kynde of mannes herte is to delyte / In
thing that straunge is, also God me save! / For what he may not gete,
that wolde he have' (*AA* 201–3). In her contrasting 'stidfastnesse'
(*AA* 81) and plaintive suffering Anelida 'passed hath Penelope and
Lucresse' (*AA* 82) and could easily qualify for inclusion in the
Legend. This Arcite is a disconcerting *alter ego* to his namesake in
the *Knight's Tale*. The Legend of Ariadne also reverses the tale of
Palamon and Arcite. There Theseus was the wise and stable ruler:
here he betrays Ariadne, who has rescued him from the Minotaur,
because he prefers her sister. He sails away with Phedra, leaving
Ariadne marooned on a desert island, one of the few unambigu-
ously poignant scenes of the Legend. In the *Knight's Tale* Theseus
and Pirothous have journeyed to Hell and returned but in the
Legend this role, with its potentiality for Christian symbolism,
belongs to Alceste. The scene in which the sisters become aware of
the imprisoned Theseus reads like a gross and ironic replay of the
scene in which the blood-brothers fall in love with Emily. Like
Palamon and Arcite, Theseus is incarcerated in a tower. Theirs is
'even-joynant' to a garden, his 'was joynynge in the wal to a
foreyne' (1962) or privy. This is the passage which carries his
complaint to Ariadne and Phedra so that they plan to 'make . . .
balles' (2003) for him to find his way safely through the 'queynte
weyes' (2013) of the 'krynkeled' (2012) house. The situation is
analogous to the *Knight's Tale* but every term is reversed. Two
women replace the two men as rivals in love, the privy replaces the
garden, the prisoner is re-placed at the bottom of the tower,
obscenity replaces idealism and treachery replaces faith. The
opening of the next Legend replaces the *Knight's Tale's* exposition of
an orderly cosmos bound in a chain of love by the First Mover and
descending from the incorruptible to the corruptible. Instead, the
narrator asks why the 'yevere of the formes' (2228) should create or

allow the creation of Tereus who 'fro this world up to the firste hevene / Corrumpeth' (2236–7). Like the imprisoned Theseus, the vantage-point of the *Legends* is lower than in the *Knight's Tale* or in *Troilus*. Instead of soaring above human perplexity, the narrator looks up and sees our pollution rising. Whereas the lovers of the *Knight's Tale* escape from their prison, the *Legend of Good Women* breaks off with Hypermnestra – whose husband has jumped out of the window, run away and forgotten her! – 'caught and fetered in prysoun' (2722). It is an apt image for the world of the *Legend*.

The legend of Phyllis opens with the familiar terms 'preve' and 'autorite' (2394). Both will demonstrate that evil is inherited, that 'wiked fruit cometh of a wiked tre' (2395) and Demophon, the son of Theseus, is as false in love as his father. It ends with one of the most back-handed lines in the *Legend*:

> Be war, ye wemen, of youre subtyl fo,
> Syn yit this day men may ensaumple se:
> And trusteth, as in love, no man but me.
>
> 2559–61

This closing advice undermines the whole project of the poem. We are reminded that the narrator is a man and the assurance that he is exceptional raises the doubt that he is not. Is his indictment of his own sex a manoeuvre to eliminate male rivals and draw female readers into his confidence? The literature of satire against women reinforces and draws support from a Christian tradition of celibacy. Is literature in praise of women merely a more complex kind of seduction? Can any other kind of fruit come from this tree?

We are aware throughout the *Legend* of the presence of the narrator. Although it purports to be his restitution and homage to the female sex, the poem belongs to him and not to the 'good women' it celebrates. Even the expressions of boredom confess that the narrator is controlling and refusing to be controlled by his subject. He leaves his ladies stranded – Ariadne literally on a desert island, the final heroine in prison as a victim of male absent-mindedness – and voiceless. Although the women have plenty – pathetic and bathetic – to say for themselves, the final image of each poem is a silenced heroine and a sententious narrator. Philomela is literally made dumb and reduced to telling her own story in a woman's way by weaving it. When her sister Procne receives the terrible news in the woven cloth, she is equally dumbfounded: 'No

word she spak, for sorwe and ek for rage' – (2374). More of the
heroines are silenced by death, leaving the narrator to point – or
search for – a moral in the story. After relating the suicide of Dido,
he remembers that she left a letter but he wearies of transmitting it:
'But who wol al this letter have in mynde, / Rede Ovyde, and in hym
he shal it fynde' (1366–7). The Legend of Medea ends similarly,
breaking off her Ovidian letter to Jason, 'which were as now to long
for me to wryte' (1679). The deserted Ariadne's lament is similarly
truncated: 'What shulde I more telle hire compleynying? / It is so
long, it were an hevy thyng. / In hire Epistel Naso telleth al' (2218–
20). Leaving aside the question of whether the narrator is bored, we
are aware of the presence of a narrator. Whether the Legends praise
or satirise women, we are aware that their stories are being
interpreted. The accounts of women are mediated to us through a
tradition which is mainly masculine. Chaucer draws our attention
to this fact in the *Legend*. The *Canterbury Tales*, though ultimately
open to the same objection, attempts to free women's voices far
more than the *Legend* does, one of many reasons why it has more
interesting things to say. And it is through the voice of a female
character, the Wife of Bath, that Chaucer raises the issue of
mediation.

III

Experience, though noon auctoritee
Were in this world, is right ynogh for me
To speke of wo that is in mariage . . .

CT iii 1–3

Biside a welle, Jhesus, God and man,
Spak in repreeve of the Samaritan:
'Thou hast yhad fyve housbondes,' quod he,
'And that ilke man that now hath thee
Is noght thyn housbonde' . . .

CT iii 15–19

The first part of the Wife of Bath's Prologue is a parody sermon in
which she inverts some of the most familiar medieval hierarchies.
She vindicates experience against authority and sex against
virginity. Both positions imply a defence of the laity against the

clergy and so of women against men. They raise immediate questions about the status of literary and theological tradition. The Wife opens her Prologue with a statement of faith in experience and turns almost at once to Scripture, the supreme written authority. The Prologue will culminate in Alison's physical attack on her man and his book. It begins with an example of a woman in *the* book and an enquiry into the use made of her by the clerks.

Alison's first parade of the experience which qualifies her to speak brings her into an apparent clash with authority:

> For, lordynges, sith I twelve yeer was of age,
> Thonked be God that is eterne on lyve,
> Housbondes at chirche door I have had fyve –
> If I so ofte myghte have ywedded bee. . . .
>
> III 4–7

She has had five husbands – but is she allowed to marry five times? She has heard the the Lord's single reported attendance at a wedding teaches symbolically that only one marriage is permissible. 'Me was toold' (9) suggests her dependence, as a woman and therefore a lay person, on the authority of others. To her this seems a strained interpretation but perhaps it is supported by another passage of Scripture which has been held specifically to condemn *five* marriages, the conversation of Jesus with the woman of Samaria:

> 'Thou hast yhad fyve housbondes,' quod he,
> 'And that ilke man that now hath thee
> Is noght thyn housbonde . . .'
>
> 17–19

What is the objection to husband number five? asks the Wife, understandably puzzled at this apparently arbitrary ceiling of four marriages:

> What that he mente therby, I kan nat seyn;
> But that I axe, why that the fifthe man
> Was noon housbonde to the Samaritan?
> How many myghte she have in mariage?
>
> 20–3

The Wife of Bath has been criticised for turning Scripture to her own purposes. But in this passage she senses a gap between the meaning of Christ's words, which she always takes as binding, and the interpretation she has been taught. She has, in fact, put her finger on a very weak link in the chain of clerical exegesis. The condemnation of more than one marriage was made not by Jesus to the Samaritan but by Jerome in his polemic against Jovinian, who had contended that a virgin was not inherently better than a wife. Jerome's attack on this position, *Adversus Jovinianum*, is not named here but will recur and be identified in Jankin's book of wicked wives. It is mediated to the Wife of Bath by her fifth husband, one of the many ironies which play about the transmission of authority in her Prologue. Jerome adduces the passage in which 'the Samaritan woman in St John's Gospel who said that she had her sixth husband was reproved by the Lord because he was not her husband' and seems to make it do double duty as evidence against a love affair and against a sixth marriage. He uses it as proof of his assertion in the preceding sentence: 'For it is better to know a single husband, though he be a second or third, than to have many paramours: that is, it is more tolerable for a woman to prostitute herself to one man than to many.' Marriage although a form of prostitution, is preferable to the relationship with the sixth 'husband' to whom the Samaritan was not really married. But in the following sentence Jerome suggests that the couple were indeed married and that Jesus reproved her because he would recognise only a first marriage: 'For where there are more husbands than one the proper idea of a husband, who is a single person, is destroyed.'[23] Perhaps, since Jerome sees little difference between one marriage, serial monogamy and prostitution, it is gratuitous to point out the illogicality of his distinctions. It is more important to recognise his general garbling of authority, which will be clear if we return to the passage in St John's Gospel.[24]

In the original story the Samaritan makes no claim to have a sixth husband:

> Jesus replied, 'Go home, call your husband and come back.' She answered, 'I have no husband.' 'You are right,' said Jesus, 'in saying that you have no husband, for, although you have had five husbands, the man with whom you are now living is not your husband; you told me the truth there.' 'Sir,' she replied, 'I can see that you are a prophet.'
>
> *John* 4: 16–18[25]

Jerome himself has introduced the sixth husband, the emphasis on reproof and the slanting of the story towards female sexuality. His two readings of the passage, though contradictory, agree in finding the Samaritan woman guilty: if the couple are married, Jesus is condemning multiple marriages; if they are not, the Lord is reproving her falsehood and her fornication. In fact, the falsehood is entirely Jerome's. The Samaritan says that she has no husband and Jesus comments that she speaks truly. She does not take his statement that she is living with a man to whom she is not married as a reproof but as a sign that he is a prophet. The point of the story is the revelation of the Messiah, not the unmasking of the Samaritan. The Wife of Bath quotes Jesus more accurately than Jerome did but repeats one of his two conflicting interpretations of the story, that it condemns the latest marriage, so that the question logically becomes the status of the *fifth* marriage. Like Chaunticleer's authenticating of '*Mulier est hominis confusio*' by juxtaposing it with the biblical '*In principio*', Jerome's partisan, peculiar and misogynist gloss has become part of the 'meaning' of the sacred text.

If we return to the actual passage of St John's Gospel, we find that Jesus' conversation with the woman of Samaria has other resonances than this specific misuse of it as an argument against fifth (or sixth) marriages. It is one of many examples in the Gospels of Christ's lack of exclusiveness, his willingness to consort with publicans, sinners, Samaritans and women. It takes place at Jacob's well. Jesus asks the woman to draw water for him and she is surprised at a Jew willing to drink from a Samaritan well. This wellside encounter reminds us of other solemn meetings between men and women, of Jacob and Rachel, of Isaac and Rebecca, to whom Chaucer alludes when Griselda sets down her waterpot before Walter. The Samaritan, similarly, leaves her waterpot and returns to her city to announce that she has met the Christ. In later Christian tradition the Annunciation was said to have taken place by a well; in this story the coming of the Messiah is revealed to the Samaritan and she announces it to her people. The Wife of Bath locates the story 'biside a welle' (III 15) and later returns to the words of 'Crist, that of perfeccion is welle' (107), as if Chaucer were encouraging us to look beyond Jerome's narrow and niggling distortion to the source and the larger perspectives offered by the Gospel.

Another aspect of the story is characteristic of Jesus' teaching, though one might not guess it from Jerome's version: his rejection of religious legalism. When the woman points out that Samaritans worship at their holy mountain rather than at the temple in Jerusalem, Jesus replies that the time is at hand when God will be worshipped in neither sacred place but 'in spirit and in truth' (*John* 4: 19–25). His fourteenth-century followers are as infected with literalism as his fourth-century exegetes: the Wife of Bath has made three pilgrimages to Jerusalem and, like Jerome, cites Scripture for her purpose. She struggles to speak against a patristic misogynist tradition whose method she has inherited along with its material. But her respect for the living water of Scripture and her alertness to the problems of filtering and adulteration make her return – with salutary as well as satirical effect – to the source.

Jesus contrasts the temporary with the eternal, the water drawn from the Samaritan's well, which will slake thirst only for the moment, with his own waters of everlasting life. The Wife of Bath's reaction to the Pardoner's interruption provides a neat parody: the much-married woman offers the false preacher not the pure, if transitory, refreshment of spring water but a bitter story of marital tribulation: 'thou shalt drynken of another tonne . . . shal savoure wors than ale' (III 170–1). Throughout her Prologue she locates herself and the kind of knowledge she possesses in the realm of the temporal. She has experience for 'sith I *twelve yeer was of age*, / Thonked be God that is *eterne on lyve*' (4–5; my italics), she has been married five times. Might she be married 'so ofte' (7)? She was told otherwise 'nat longe agoon is' (9). Yet she has never heard 'in myn age' (24) a definition of the number of husbands permissible. The wise King Solomon had plenty of wives and she would like 'to be refresshed half so ofte as he!' (38) No man 'that in this world alyve is' (40) has had such a gift from God. Where can it be proved that God forbade marriage 'in any manere age' (59)? She is 'expert in al myn age' (174) in the tribulation of marriage and she means to wed again 'whan myn housbonde is fro the world ygon' (47). Sexual experience, like the water from Jacob's well, satisfies desire only temporarily: on the death of one husband, another is soon needed. Wisdom consists in acknowledging the desire, along with the tribulation, accepting the end of youth ('age, allas! that al wole envenyme, / Hath me biraft my beautee and my pith' – 474–5) and being thankful for the memory of what one has experienced ('I have had my world as in my tyme' – 473).

The Wife's 'experience' is rooted in temporality. God is 'eterne on lyve' (5). 'Authority' relates to both dimensions. 'Jhesus, God and man' (15) dispenses the living waters of everlasting life. Theological writings, such as Jerome's, claim to transmit the eternal teaching of the Lord to the passing generations. Written authority can survive the lifetime of the individual writer; books are sometimes described as conferring 'immortality' on their authors. Yet authorship is not divinely authoritative. The authorities derive from particular times, places, societies, personalities and experiences. They are neither eternal nor perfectly objective. Nor are the subsequent interpretations which in their turn derive from particular circumstances. The curious effect of treating all authorities as if they had precisely similar status is felt in the catalogue of Jankin's miscellany of wicked wives, 'Valerie and Theofraste / . . . Seint Jerome / . . . Tertulan, / Crisippus, Trotula and Helowys / . . . and eek the Parables of Salomon, / Ovides Art, and bookes many on, / And alle thise were bounden in o volume' (III 671–81). Part of the comedy of the Wife's use of authority – her citation of the polygamy of Solomon, Abraham and Isaac to justify her five marriages – stems from the recognition that she is getting it 'wrong'. But it is also a parody – and a valid criticism – of the people who get it 'right', the theologians adept as 'glosing' the text to produce an interpretation consistent with their special interests.[26] Authority – the painting of the lion, the misogynist writing of the old and impotent clerk, Jankin's lectures to his wife – has its own bias.

Authority is mediated. The teaching of Jesus may be considered a well or pure source but it is mediated by Jerome and Jankin's teachers and Jankin and the Wife of Bath. The Wife does not have the conventional qualifications but this gives her some freedom from the conventional prejudices. The margin is, after all, traditionally a place for interpretation. The other text for her parody sermon actually writes into itself the awareness of its own mediation. It is the seventh chapter of the Epistle to the Corinthians, in which St Paul gives the Church at Corinth his advice on marriage. The Wife's summary is much fairer than some Chaucerian scholars suggest:[27] she stays closer to Paul than Jerome does to Jesus. Paul teaches that virginity and widowhood are preferable to marriage, because chastity allows more singleminded service of the Lord. Nevertheless, God has given different gifts to different people. Marriage is not sinful in itself and it is better to marry than to fornicate or burn with lust. Paul makes it clear that he mediates the teaching of Jesus and is careful to distinguish when he is quoting and when he is interpreting: 'To the married I give this ruling, which is not mine

but the Lord's . . . To the rest I say this, as my own word, not as the
Lord's . . . On the question of celibacy, I have no instructions from
the Lord, but I give my judgement as one who by God's mercy is fit
to be trusted' (I *Corinthians* 7: 10, 12, 25). The Wife of Bath reports
this accurately – 'Th'apostel, whan he speketh of maydenhede, / He
seyde that precept therof hadde he noon' (III 64–5) – and asks the
obvious question: 'Wher can ye seye . . . That hye God defended
mariage / By expres word? . . . Or where comanded he virginitee?'
(59–62). She is distinguishing, as does the Epistle itself, between the
different levels of authority. St Paul has directed her back to the
source of his teaching rather than forward to the increasing
preference shown by Christian 'authority' for celibacy. As an
apologist for marriage the Wife is finding what she looks for in the
Bible but so do the advocates of virginity. Alison neatly suggests
Paul's own bias without misrepresenting him 'But natheless, thogh
that he wroot and sayde / He wolde that every wight were swich as
he / Al nys but conseil to virginitee' (80–2). Paul stresses that he
recommends but does not enjoin celibacy; 'All this I say by way of
concession, not command. I should like you all to be as I am myself'
and he continues with another idea taken up enthusiastically by the
Wife of Bath: 'but everyone has the gift God has granted him' (I
Corinthians 7: 6–7). Perhaps Paul, like the Wife, did not practise
what he preached so much as preach what he preferred and he has
the grace in this instance to be aware of the personal factors which
contribute to the Christian tradition in the making.

The Wife's treatment of authority is much less outrageous than
one might expect from a Lady of Misrule preaching a parody
sermon in a deliberately provocative tone. Her position is, in fact, a
moderate one. (Recent feminist accounts have indeed regretted its
conservatism.) She honours the word of God as revealed in the
Bible, though her quotation from it is selective (as any work shorter
than the Bible itself must be) and she is aware that it can be 'glossed'
in many ways. She is reasonably baffled by some of Jerome's
glossing and underlines the distinction which St Paul made himself
between the teaching of Jesus and his own. Her own distinction
between authority and experience is not an absolute antithesis. She
does not oppose experience to authority but uses it as additional
evidence: even if there were no authorities to teach us, she can
speak from experience on the woe of marriage. She holds the same
view of the woefulness of the condition as the clerks were meant to
form from reading Jankin's book of wicked wives, though her

response is not renunciation but a generous acceptance of ordinary human life with its pleasures and pains. She does not reject the authority of the Bible but is justifiably puzzled by some patristic interpretation of it. She does not exalt marriage over virginity. She agrees that virginity is the perfect state but the Bible does not enjoin it upon everybody and she herself has not been called to be perfect.

St Paul admits that God has bestowed different gifts on different people. The Wife of Bath echoes him when she uses the metaphor of the different vessels in the Lord's household, identifying herself as useful wood rather than fine gold, and when she quotes 'everich hath of God a propre yifte – / Som this, som that' (103–4). The closing words of this couplet, 'as hym liketh shifte' (104), are not mere ballast to provide the rhyme but a tribute to the divine creativity manifested in the variety of the cosmos and its creatures. Her other way of putting it, 'God clepeth folk to hym in sondry wyse' (102), reminds us of another creator, the author of the book she inhabits, the tales of the 'sondry folk'. Chaucer's own pleasure in human diversity embodies itself in the characters of the Canterbury pilgrimage and in the worlds and characters which they themselves generate in their stories.

The Wife of Bath shares his delight in fictional and narrative diversity. She is fictionally the most wide-ranging of the pilgrim narrators and – like pilgrim Chaucer's own performance in the *Tales* – her contributions extend from one literary extreme to the other – from the romance, that most fictive of fictional genres, to versions of the most earnest and didactic forms, the sermon and the moral treatise. Her Prologue even contains a short *mise-en-abîme* of the *Canterbury Tales*: 'I loved ... / ... for to walk in March, Averill, and May, / Fro hous to hous, to heere sondry talys' (545–7) Of the pilgrims she is closest to Chaucer. Like her creator, she criticises through comedy, she weighs authority against experience and experience against authority, she is aware of the sexuality in textuality and she jokily subverts the conventions of male authorship. She represents aspects of his creativity which, sadly, Chaucer seems finally to renounce.

11

Sex, Discourse and Silence

In felaweshipe wel koude she laughe and carpe
CT I 474

In the *General Prologue* we are told that the Wife of Bath laughs and
talks well in company, whereas the first attribute in the portrait of
the Prioress is her 'coy', or quiet, smile. This is one of the most
significant contrasts between these very different women. One is
quiet, one is voluble throughout the *Canterbury Tales*. The Prioress
never speaks during the Links between the stories. Harry Bailly
goes into uncharacteristic contortions of politeness when he invites
her to tell her tale, as if he were broaching a matter of the utmost
delicacy. At the other extreme, the Wife is the most talkative of the
pilgrims. She arrogates to herself a 'long preamble' (III 831) of an
autobiographical prologue as well as a tale and her skill in speaking
is remarked by some of the professional speakers in her audience.
Assertive and expansive, she spreads herself and dilates, spilling
into other *Canterbury Tales* and out of the *Tales* altogether.[1] She
receives an ironic bow at the end of the *Clerk's Tale*, she breaches
literary decorum by irrupting into the *Merchant's Tale* and she
reappears in a quite separate poem, 'Lenvoy de Chaucer a Bukton'.
This contrast between the women is reflected in their stories.
Prioress celebrates the piety of the child who learns a holy song by
rote and sweetly reproduces the words of others. The Wife
describes her verbal violence to her husbands, questions what she
has been told, argues with authority and tells a tale in which victory
is won by a woman's power of discourse.

This is one of the most important respects in which the Prioress is
very feminine by the standards of her age, the Wife unfeminine or
even an example of female vice. The Prioress is consciously refined,
aping the manners of the court. The Wife is 'wandrynge by the
weye' (I 467) and breaking the rules. Modern feminist discussion
has emphasised that language privileges the male, that the female
subject has particular problems in entering its symbolic order. In

218

Chaucer's Europe different linguistic behaviour was prescribed for men and women. Medieval books of advice for women recommended them not to speak much and not to laugh or joke.[2] Women are meant to be quiet. Loquacious women are a favourite target of medieval satire and types of discourse that are considered womanish but not feminine – 'labbyng', nagging, scolding, gossip – come in for heavy criticism. Alison exemplifies all these habits of speech. She expatiates on how she would abuse her husbands and betray all their secrets. When she relates the anecdote of Midas's ears, she substitutes for the indiscreet barber of the sources an indiscreet wife. But while speaking ill is unattractive in a woman, speaking well is far more subversive. Alison competes with the most articulate men in her society, the clerks, and invades such masculine territories of discourse as preaching and interpretation of Scripture. Perhaps her laughing and joking are also subversive, the comedy of the satirist, the dreaded female 'tee hee' at male pretension.[3]

The archetypes of Eve and Mary also lend themselves to this contrast between improper and proper female behaviour. The Original Sin has been variously interpreted: as pride, disobedience, gluttony, lust and *speech*. The Nun's Priest blames it on Eve's words – 'Wommannes conseil broght us first to wo, / And made Adam fro paradys to go' (vii 3257–8) – making woman the cause and man the victim of the Fall, supporting Chaunticleer's *'Mulier est hominis confusio'* and defining Pertelote's rationalist persuasion as potential death to her husband. The Madonna-like Constance also attributes the Fall to 'wommanes eggement' (ii 842) and is strengthened to bear and belittle her own suffering, caused ultimately by Eve and surpassed infinitely by Mary. In contrast with Eve, who counsels disobedience to God, the Virgin accepts her divinely appointed role, saying at the Annunciation 'Be it unto me according to thy word'. Eve usurps words and power, Mary resigns herself to God's will and God's word.

'Good' and 'bad' wives differ sharply in their discourse. This is underlined in the *Clerk's Tale*. Griselda's absolute submission to Walter's trials is manifested in her lack of verbal resistance. Walter wonders if 'by his wyves cheere he myghte se, / Or by hire word apercyve, that she / Were chaunged' (iv 598–600) and 'waiteth if by word or contenaunce / That she to hym was changed of corage' (708–9). But 'she was ay oon' (711), as 'sad', 'sobre' and loyal in her words as her actions. Her vow to Walter is almost her last exercise and expression of individual will. The Envoy to the Tale ironically advises wives to be the opposite of Griselda and make their husbands thoroughly wretched: 'Folweth Ekko, that holdeth no silence . . . Ay clappeth as a mille . . . The arwes of thy crabbed eloquence / Shal perce his brest' (1189, 1200, 1203–4). The talkative woman is the examplar of bad wives and her words are weapons, the more piercing if she is eloquent. At this the Merchant pours out his misery at his recent marriage to a shrew and tells his bitter story of January and May. This provokes the Host to some rueful comments on his own wife, who sounds more like the Merchant's than like May: she is 'as trewe as any stel' (IV 2426) but also 'a labbying shrew' (2428). He returns to the subject after the *Tale of Melibee*. Harry's scolding wife is quite different from patient Prudence: violent and a counsellor of violence, she wants to exchange gender roles, take his knife and give him her distaff (VII 1889–1922). Interestingly, the 'real' wives in the pilgrimage frame of the *Tales* – the Wife of Bath, Harry's Goodelief and the Merchant's bride – are all at odds with the ideal of quietness. In the *Merchant's Tale* Justinus advises caution against wedding a woman who may be, among other bad things, a 'shrewe / A chidestere' (IV 1534–5), implies that it is wiser not to marry and refers back to the Wife's Prologue for corroboration: 'The Wyf of Bathe, if ye han understonde, / Of mariage, which we have on honde, / Declared hath ful wel in litel space' (1685–7). Ironically, the Wife is condemned by her own eloquence. Her ability to speak 'ful wel' becomes evidence against her and against all women. Similarly in 'Lenvoy de Chaucer a Bukton', Bukton is advised to read the Wife of Bath before being trapped in marriage: her example will presumably serve as an awful warning and her forthrightness is contrasted both with the guarded ironies and *occupationes* of the poet and the silence of Christ before Pilate.

The *Merchant's Tale* suggests (but no one seems to notice) that silence too has its drawbacks. The young wife is quiet throughout the Tale but 'God woot what that May thoughte in hir herte' (IV 1851). Like silent Emily, she has unvoiced desires of her own, though they are very different. There are many voices in the *Canterbury Tales*. There are also various kinds of silence, ranging from Emily's political helplessness to May's sneaky opportunism, from the charming reticence of the Prioress to the pious self-effacement of the Clerk, who never speaks a word more than is necessary (I 304). When they are particularly powerless some of

Chaucer's heroines turn a well-bred silence to advantage and shelter behind an impassive façade: on her arrival at the Greek camp Criseyde 'stood forth muwet, milde and mansuete' (TC v 194); May is 'broght abedde as stille as stoon' (iv 1818). Characters have different reasons for silence and are silent in different ways. In *The History of Sexuality* Michel Foucault discusses the relationships between sex, power, discourse and silence and dissolves the absolute opposition between silence and speaking:

> Silence itself – the things one declines to say or is forbidden to name, the discretion that is required between different speakers – is less the absolute limit of discourse, the other side from which it is separated by a strict boundary, than an element that functions alongside the things said, with them and in relation to them within over-all strategies. There is no binary division to be made between what one says and what one does not say; we must try to determine the different ways of not saying such things, how those who can and those who cannot speak of them are distributed, which type of discourse is authorized, or which form of discretion is required in either case. There is not one but many silences, and they are an integral part of the strategies that underlie and permeate discourse.[4]

Foucault is right to deny any absolute binary division between the spoken and the unspoken. But the usual binary division by gender is at its vicious work again in authorising less and fewer types of discourse and demanding more and more types of discretion in women. The Wife of Bath's appeal to experience as well as authority points to her lack of authorisation. The inequity, with its consequences for both behaviour and perception, seems to continue: modern studies of conversation and gender suggest that women tend to say less than men but are perceived as saying more.[5]

May exemplifies first strategic silence, then strategic speech. When she is exposed in adultery, Proserpina comes to her aid and supplies her and all future women with the capacity to excuse themselves, no matter how guilty they are. They will always have the last word: 'For lak of answere noon of hem shal dyen' (iv 2271). The goddess shares the garrulity attributed to her sex – 'I am a womman, nedes moot I speke (2305) – but sees her own aggressive speech as an apt response to male verbal aggression against women: 'For sithen he [Solomon] seyde that we been jangleresses

... I shal nat spare, for no curteisye, / To speke hym harm that
wolde us vileynye' (2307–10). Her juxtaposition of 'curteisye' and
'vileynye' provides more than a rhyme. It suggests the doubly
double standard that is applied to male and female discourse:
women are not only *wrong* to speak but *indecorous*. It is unmannerly,
unattractive, unbecoming to their sex. This is unjust yet, since we
value courtesy, it also suggests some of the further complexities of
the distribution of gender roles. Like many modern feminists,
Proserpina could be accused of being 'unfeminine' in her indif-
ference to courtesy and might well reply that there are more
important things. But courtesy is important in that it can be
expressive and symbolic of consideration in personal relationships.
It is a problem for feminism that some genuine virtues are
particularly expected of women: this encourages women to behave
better in some areas than men but it is also unjust in exposing them
to more censure and inhibiting them from behaviour incompatible
with their role. The same moral standards should be applied to both
sexes, as Chaucer implies when he describes the courtesy of his
heroic Knight, a veteran of many campaigns, who is 'of his port as
meeke as is a mayde. / He nevere yet no vileynye ne sayde / In al his
lyf unto no maner wight' (i 69–71). It is morally inadequate to
confine gentleness and delicacy to one sex, strength and candour to
the other.

One consequence is that articulacy and initiative are blamed
in women, gentleness and unassertiveness suspected in men.
Qualities praised in one sex are feared or despised in the other. The
narrator of the *Canterbury Tales* commends the Knight for bearing
himself as meekly as a maid but the Host finds the quietness of the
Clerk effeminate and tries to spur him into the manly self-assertion
of telling a story:

> Ye ryde as coy and stille as dooth a mayde
> Were newe spoused, sittynge at the bord;
> This day ne herde I of youre tonge a word.
>   iv 2–4

The comparison is revealing. The silent Clerk is not only like a
young woman but like a bride. The parallels here between sex,
gender and discourse are obvious: on the one hand, coy, still, shy,
silent, virginal, feminine; on the other, confident, active, articulate,
experienced, sexual, masculine. The bride is expected to be quiet

because she is a woman, probably a young woman and deemed to be a virgin. She faces sexual initiation and is assumed to be less eager for it than her partner: if the Virgin Mary is the ideal of womanhood, marriage represents defilement and diminution to the bride. Blushing, bashfulness, shyness and silence are proper responses. The female eagle in the *Parliament of Fowls* somehow manages to blush as red as a fresh rose in sunlight when her suitor expresses his love for her (*PF* 442–5). That paragon of maidenhood, Virginia in the *Physician's Tale* is 'Discreet . . . in answeryng alwey' (VI 48), modest verbally and sexually, and, when her virginity is threatened, her father chooses for her the ultimate silence of death. Though a man, the Clerk, like the bride, is presumed to be a virgin. He blurs the binary division by combining maleness with chastity and silence. This double position – more than a man? less than a man? – excites both admiration and unease. The sexuality of the clergy is a potent source of comedy in the *Canterbury Tales*: even with the more austere of them, such as the Clerk and the Nun's Priest, Harry Bailly cannot resist the subject. His suspicions would be justified of some of Chaucer's seducers, whose amorous adventures are furthered by a modest and maidenly demeanour: Nicholas, in the *Miller's Tale* is 'sleigh and ful privee / And lyk a mayden meke for to see' (I 3201–2); Jason in the *Legend* is 'as coy as is a mayde' (*LGW* 1548) and when he meets Hypsipyle, his first victim, he 'answerde mekely and stylle' (*LGW* 1491). The 'feminine' behaviour of these men should be a danger signal. The Wife of Bath conversely snipes at the binary division, a female whose forthright speech argues (in both senses) her frank sexuality. No wonder she has such a love/hate relationship with clerks.

The other pilgrim whom Harry twits for his silence is Chaucer himself. The Host notices that he rides with his eyes on the ground, talking to nobody, and challenges his author with the question 'What man artow?' (VII 695). He speaks for all of us who find it impossible to tell what Chaucer thinks. The author has disguised himself as the pilgrim and the pilgrim is silent. Does the Host also imply that manliness should be more verbally assertive? Does he express and assuage his nervousness about gender with an instant jokey reference to the man's sexuality? This is Harry's reaction when he compares the quiet Clerk to a bride, a verbal nudge, and insists that the celibate Nun's Priest would have made a 'trede-foul aright' (VII 3451), a verbal slap on the back. Similarly, the poet-pilgrim would be 'a popet in an arm t'enbrace / For any womman, smal and fair of face' (VII 701–2), reassuringly masculine in his orientation but oddly feminine in his smallness, fairness and passivity. For the Host the suggestion of androgyny is comically incongruous but Harry, the first critic of the *Tales*, is one of the least subtle. Six hundred years later Donald Howard seriously proposes that Chaucer in his understanding of both sexes transcends gender boundaries and is an androgynous poet.[6] I agree and would want to add this. Chaucer lived in a society which tended to polarise the genders. He writes of some qualities as 'womanly' and others as 'manly'. The Shavian distaste for a 'womanly woman' or a 'manly man' would be foreign to him. But he certainly implies that some virtues particularly associated with women, such as pity, should be common to both sexes and he shows men learning from women. His *persona* in the *Canterbury Tales* tells a story in which a man learns pity from a woman and which demonstrates that he is right to do so.

'Chaucer' is the only Canterbury pilgrim who tells two stories, though this is because his first attempt is not successful. When the Host calls on him, he says modestly that he knows no stories but 'a rym I lerned long agon' (VII 709). This is the *Tale of Sir Thopas*, at one level a tedious example, at another a sophisticated parody of a vapid late medieval romance. The Host characteristically sees only the obvious and interrupts to stop this feeble performance. The pilgrim weakly protests that this is unfair, since it is the best he can do, but Harry is adamant that he can bear no more of this 'drasty rymyng' (VII 930). So Chaucer obliges him with the prose *Tale of Melibee*. It is the most beautiful of the many jokes the poet plays with his literary *personae*. Chaucer, the author of the *Canterbury Tales*, the creator of the pilgrims and their stories, has only one party piece and is told that it is 'not woorth a toord!' (vii 930). The lengthily edifying *Tale of Melibee* could be seen as his revenge on his obstreperous creation. The two tales told by the pilgrim-poet himself are at fictional extremes. Harry originally proposed a prize for the 'Tales of best sentence and moost solaas' (I 798); after *Sir Thopas* he despairs of receiving improvement *and* entertainment from Chaucer and merely demands 'som murthe *or* some doctryne' (VII 935; my italics). *Sir Thopas* is (if you see the joke) all mirth, *Melibee* all doctrine. *Sir Thopas* presents a fizzy travesty of the knightly ethic, *Melibee* a grave debate on violence and revenge which concludes in the forgiveness of enemies. Opposite in every way, the two Tales propose opposite ideals of the relationship between the sexes.

Many maidens suffer vain and improbable agonies of unrequited love for Sir Thopas 'whan hem were bet to slepe' (VII 744); he decides that no real woman is worthy of him and that he will love an elf-queen. In the *Tale of Melibee* the wife, Prudence, and the daughter, Sophie, derive from the venerable tradition of allegorical female figures of wisdom, such as the Boethian Philosophy. Prudence converts Melibee from the plan of vengeance to the practice of mercy, disposing first of his objections that he should not heed her counsel because all women are wicked and he would be giving her mastery over him. In the bathetic mock-romance Sir Thopas sets his heart on an imaginary, invisible and impossible ideal. In the earnestly didactic allegory Prudence does represent an ideal and in her wisdom solves at the theoretical level some of the problems which bedevil other couples in the *Canterbury Tales*.

Sir Thopas is forcibly left unfinished, as impotent as its hero to reach its destination. The *Tale of Melibee* is a closed structure: in a clear and orderly progression the correct counsel of Prudence prevails over the other competing voices and brings the story not only to a happy ending but to the promise of 'the blisse that never hath ende' (VII 1887–8). These are formal extremes which we may find elsewhere in Chaucer's poetry but between which most of his poems operate. His two earliest surviving poems end in perfect closure and attempted closure. The *ABC* concludes at the letter Z with the prayer for heaven. The narrator of the *Book of the Duchess* takes his leave with the blunt 'This was my sweven; now hit ys doon' (*BD* 1334): the dream has ended, the poem has been written. But we do not know what has been concluded by this double conclusion, whether the Man in Black has learnt from the Dreamer or the Dreamer has learnt from the dream. The *Parliament of Fowls* ends with a frank statement of the Dreamer's disappointment. Other poems – the *House of Fame, Anelida and Arcite*, the *Legend of Good Women* – are unfinished. Within the *Canterbury Tales* the stories of the Cook, Monk and Squire are abandoned or truncated by their audience. The *Canterbury Tales* as a whole is both incomplete and decisively closed. The plan proposed by Harry Bailly that each pilgrim shall tell two tales on the way to Canterbury and two on the way back to the Tabard is not realised. No pilgrim except Chaucer tells two stories, some tell none, the tales are grouped in fragments whose order is disputed and the poem leaves the pilgrimage at an anonymous 'thropes ende' (X 12), probably but not certainly on the outward journey. But its closure is emphatic.

Night is falling, the Host calls upon the Parson to 'knytte up wel a gret mateere' (x 28) with a final tale, the Parson refuses to utter fiction or poetry and preaches his 'myrie tale in prose' (x 46) on sin and repentance. This is followed by the words 'Heere taketh the makere of this book his leve' and Chaucer's Retractions.

In the *Canterbury Tales*, as we have them, it seems that the *Manciple's Tale* is intended to come immediately before the Parson's. The two fragments are linked by the line 'By that the Maunciple hadde his tale al ended' (x 1). If so, the stern attitudes expressed in the *Parson's Tale* and the Retractions are prepared for by a narrowing of sympathy in the *Manciple's Tale*. Both the Tale and its Prologue echo and contrast with the generous scope of the First Fragment. In a sense the last movement of the *Tales* begins where the first left off, with an abortive attempt to extract a Tale from the Cook and some sparring and suggestion of professional antagonism between the Cook and another pilgrim. But the Cook is too drunk to speak, the Manciple comments scornfully on his condition and offers to take his place, the Host remarks that the Cook could probably expose some of the Manciple's dishonest reckonings, the Manciple agrees but reconciles the Cook with an offer of a drink. The Host apostrophises Bacchus, the god who can turn 'ernest into game' (IX 100), but the drink seems no more than a parody of friendship. The taste of carnival is growing sour.

The First Fragment celebrates plenitude. It descends, socially and morally, in its progression from Knight's Tale to Cook's, but the narrator declares the obligation to record the stories of all pilgrims faithfully, 'be they bettre or werse' (I 3174). His language should reflect theirs, even if this obliges him to speak 'rudeliche and large' (I 734): such accuracy is sanctioned by the example of Christ and the opinion of Plato that 'the wordes moot be cosyn to the dede' (I 742). The Manciple cites the same passage of Plato in the interest not of presenting every point of view as authentically as possible but of levelling all concepts down to the lowest common denominator. Women significantly provide the example of treacherous signifiers: a woman with a lover is called 'lady' if she is of high birth, 'wenche or . . . lemman', if she is poor (IX 207–22). Yet 'myn owene deere brother, / Men leyn that oon as lowe as lith that oother' (IX 221–2). The argument seems to have a certain rough egalitarian justice until one considers the way it is expressed. The speaker draws his implied audience into an implied group of men betrayed but not bemused by women. If the 'owene deere brother' implies a friend rather than a sibling, it emphasises male bonding at the expense of trust and love between the sexes. After this address the general term 'men' suggests 'men' rather than 'one' and the wordplay of the next line confirms this interpretation. The lay/low/lie pun identifies discourse with intercourse: it equates male lovemaking with defamation and degradation of women and approves the equation. Women are devalued by their sex and by their sexuality.

Like the first Tale, the last opens in the world of classical mythology but it signally lacks the splendour and dignity of the *Knight's Tale*. It introduces 'Phebus', the god Apollo, when he 'dwelled heere in this erthe adoun' (ix 105), but he is in this version very ungodlike, created in the image of that stock medieval comic character, the cuckolded husband. When his musical white crow reveals his wife's infidelity, he precipitately murders her and promptly regrets it. His one exercise of his divine power is to turn the crow black and spoil his voice, a sad miracle from the god of sun and music. This is the only metamorphosis in the *Canterbury Tales* and it disfigures. It also silences. The unfaithful wife is totally silent. She is not even named and her murder is hurried over in two lines. Her introduction is almost identical to the crow's, though he takes precedence over her: 'Now hadde this Phebus in his hous an crowe / Which in a cage he fostred many a day' (ix 130–1); 'Now hadde this Phebus in his hous a wyf / Which that he lovede moore than his lyf' (139–40). The similarity of the first line of each couplet suggests a metaphorical similarity in the second: Phebus, like John the carpenter, the first jealous husband of the *Canterbury Tales*, tries to keep his wife 'narwe in cage' (1 3224). The notion of the cage recurs a moment later, when the narrator demonstrates by analogy the futility of trying to constrain a wife: a pet bird will escape a golden cage and a luxurious diet to eat worms in the forest; the well-fed cat prefers to chase a mouse; a she-wolf will evince her 'vileyns kynde' (ix 183) by choosing to mate with 'the lewedeste wolf that she may fynde, / Or leest of reputacioun' (1 184–5). 'Alle thise ensamples speke I by thise men / That been untrewe, and nothyng by wommen' (ix 187–8), explains the narrator disingenuously, adding that men lecherously want to satisfy their appetites on lower things than their wives, that the flesh is 'newe-fangel' and that we have pleasure in nothing 'that sowneth into vertu any while'. The grossness of the evasion reflects back on the speaker: perhaps it is another example of the way the Manciple cooks the books; perhaps his moral shabbiness is reflected in this all-purpose cynicism. But he raises issues that have been explored more subtly in earlier Tales. The Franklin's 'Wommen, of kynde, desiren libertee, / And nat to been constreyned as a thral; / And so doon men' (v 768–70) is both more generous and more glancingly ironic, suggesting that the sexes are morally and emotionally alike and implying that their common ground may therefore be an area for conflict.

The Franklin uses a different analogy from the Manciple, one that points to the social basis of sexual politics. It is natural to want freedom rather than slavery. The conjunction of nature and liberty here oddly anticipates Romantic thought. Perhaps not so oddly, since the Franklin is presented as a 'new man' with an interest in levelling up and blurring traditional hierarchy: his Tale ends with the implication that *gentillesse* is innate and can be found in any class. The Franklin's generosity may finally seem rather bland: the woman question is no longer asked, the *gentillesse* of the men is not questioned. His Tale presents a comfortable optimism, egalitarian-ism and tolerance. The Manciple's bitter conservatism, mis-anthropy and misogyny are based on a blinkered pessimism. He uses animal analogies to explain and debase human behaviour. And the debasement goes both ways. Within the animal analogy he uses human analogies, so that humans look brutish and animals ignoble. The she-wolf is not only wolfish but has the 'vileyns kynde' of a noble lady who lacks *gentillesse*: she prefers the 'lewedeste wolf that she may fynde, / Or leest of reputacioun', as if there were honour among wolves for her to misprize. The language makes the woman-as-beast message seem ludicrous. But it also achieves a confused sort of generality, a sour condemnation of every kind of creature. The Manciple does not mislead me into anachronisms about Romantic thought: he despairs of nature, despises animals and uses the symbol of the bird in flight to prove that we are hopelessly earthbound. His disclaimer – that the satire is directed at men, not at women – may be meant to creak so badly that it reinforces the misogyny. But it works in that the Manciple dislikes men as thoroughly as women and his impartial cynicism also extends to animals and gods. His creed is that we needs must love the lowest when we see it and the events of his story bear him out. The god behaves like a man, a foolish and vindictive man: he displays the very emotions – anger, jealousy, vengefulness and regret – that theologians carefully defined as 'accommodated language' when they were attributed to the Christian God. The woman behaves like a she-wolf of the poorest character. The crow loses his beauty, his song and 'eek his speche' (ix 306), the attribute which he shared with humanity.

The god's final vengeance is on the crow. The wife and the crow seem linked as objects of Phebus's love. But the crow also seems like an image of the poet. Like the narrator of the *Canterbury Tales*, he can 'countrefete the speche of every man / . . . whan he sholde telle a tale' (ix 134–5). His tale-telling is condemned, first by Phebus and finally by the Manciple. The moral of the story proves to be not 'Thou shalt not commit adultery' nor 'Thou shalt not kill' but 'Kepe wel thy tonge' (ix 362). It concludes with a long speech to this effect, the counsel the mother gave her son. 'Thus taughte me my dame' (ix 317) was a proverbial expression, approving an idea as obviously sensible: here it is both literalised as the advice of the Manciple's mother and generates a host of proverbs on the folly of speaking. She passes on the lessons that women were given. Her culminating advice to her child is 'My sone, be war, and be noon auctour newe / Of tidynges, wheither thei been false or trewe' (ix 359–60). This is a counsel of silence and, for the poet, of despair. In his biography of Chaucer, Donald Howard claims that the passage directly expresses the poet's 'disillusionment': 'the end of the last story told on the pilgrimage is an overlong speech commending silence. And its last image is a wagging tongue making meaningless noise. With this Chaucer brings the tale-telling game to a close'.[7]

It is a depressing conclusion. I am reluctant to identify Chaucer's point of view so absolutely with the Manciple's. The faults of the teller are reflected in the limitations of the Tale. But the Tale and its closure do lead into the closure of the Tales. Perhaps the Manciple figures *in malo* what the Parson intends *in bono*. The Manciple certainly anticipates the Parson's suspicion of fiction and twice dissociates himself from literature in the same words as the Parson: 'I am noght textueel' (ix 235, 316; x 57). Perhaps his sour statement of human depravity – 'we ne kanne in nothyng han plesaunce / That sowneth into vertu any while' (ix 194–5) – modulates into the fear expressed in the Retractions that some of the Tales 'sownen into synne'. In the last two fragments speech and sin, poetry and sexuality are connected and suspected as the 'wrecchednesse' (ix 171; x 34) which fallen nature prefers.

Chaucer's delight in human diversity is manifested in the scheme of the *Canterbury Tales*. 'Diverse folk diversely they seyde' (i 3857) could be a summary of the project. We hear from all the estates, the voices of rich and poor, good and bad, *lerned* and *lewed*, men and women. Chaucer's creative sympathy expresses itself in plurality and androgyny. But it seems to narrow as we move towards the emphatic closure of the *Tales*. Some readers have sensed that Chaucer became depressed as he grew older.[8] The Retractions convey the anxiety of one near death. Chaucer's poetic achievement is now a source more of concern than consolation to him. He revokes and asks forgiveness for his 'translacions and enditynges of worldly vanitees' (x 1083–4), including 'the book of Troilus; the book also of Fame; the book of the xxv. Ladies; the book of the Duchesse; the book of Seint Valentynes day of the Parlement of Briddes; the tales of Caunterbury, thilke that sownen into synne' (x 1085–91). He is comforted only by the memory of the translation of Boethius and 'othere bookes of legendes of seintes, and omelies and moralitee, and devocioun' and thanks 'Lord Jhesu Crist and his blisful Mooder, and alle the seintes of hevene' for them. Although Chaucer does not specify which of the *Canterbury Tales* promote sin, it seems clear that his conscience finally dictates an absolute separation between secular and religious literature. It is a melancholy farewell to a poetic career of such imaginative range and courageous experiment.

The career began, as far as is visible to us, with a prayer to the Virgin Mary. The *ABC* concludes in penitence and the hopes of paradise: 'Now, ladi bryghte, sith thou canst and wilt / Ben to the seed of Adam merciable, / Bring us to that palais that is bilt / To penitentes that ben to merci able. Amen' (181–4). The last work, the *Canterbury Tales* ends similarly with the prayer to Christ, his mother and the saints, the expression of repentance and the hope of salvation. But between these two utterances Chaucer has often carefully defined his arena as neither heaven nor hell. Like the Wife of Bath he has been quizzical in balancing the teaching of authority and the claims of experience. His creativity and sexuality, sympathy and criticism interfuse. At the beginning of the *Canterbury Tales* he presents it as his obligation to report the discourse of all his pilgrims and justifies 'brode' speaking by the example of Christ himself (i 739). The similar defence in the first link, between the Tales of the 'gentil' Knight and the 'cherl' Miller (i 3167–86), suggests that the range of the poetry imitates the plenitude of the divine Author. Now faith and focus narrow. Experience submits to authority and the many voices to silence.

Notes

Notes to the Introduction

1. Daniel M. Murtaugh, 'Women and Geoffrey Chaucer', *ELH*, 38 (1971) pp. 473–92; Hope P. Weissman, 'Antifeminism and Chaucer's Characterization of Women', in *Geoffrey Chaucer*, ed. George D. Economou (New York, 1975) pp. 93–110; A. Diamond, 'Chaucer's Women and Women's Chaucer', in *The Authority of Experience*, ed. A. Diamond and L. R. Edwards (Amherst, Mass., 1977) pp. 66–88 and 45–59; Ann Haskell, 'The Portrayal of Women by Chaucer and his Age', in *What Manner of Woman?*, Ed. Marlene Springer (New York, 1977) pp. 1–14; David Aers, *Chaucer, Langland and the Creative Imagination* (London, 1980); Sheila Delany, *Writing Woman: Women Writers and Women in Literature Medieval to Modern* (New York, 1983); Ruth M. Ames, *God's Plenty: Chaucer's Christian Humanism* (Chicago, 1984) ch. 5: 'Faith and Feminism', pp. 145–78; David Aers, *Chaucer* (Brighton, 1986); David Aers, *Community, Gender, and Individual Identity: English Writing, 1360–1430* (London, and New York, 1988).
2. G. L. Kittredge, *Chaucer and his Poetry* (Cambridge, Mass, 1915) p. 13.
3. D. W. Robertson Jr, *A Preface to Chaucer* (Princeton, NJ, 1962) pp. 321, 265.
4. On obsolescence and the *Canterbury Tales*, see Donald Howard, *The Idea of the Canterbury Tales* (Berkeley, Cal. 1976) pp. 89–108.
5. Stephen Knight, *Geoffrey Chaucer* (Oxford, 1986): 'her independence is constructed primarily from a patriarchal viewpoint: her mobility is implicitly sexual . . . she is both the most complex and most marginal of the figures, as is suggested by her lack of a professional title and by the way in which social and sexual matters interweave, both here and in her prologue and tale' (p. 79).

Notes to Chapter 1   The Man with the Book, or 'Who Painted the Lion?'

1. Quotations from Chaucer are from *The Riverside Chaucer*, general editor, Larry D. Benson (Boston, 1987).
2. W. C. Curry, *Chaucer and the Mediaeval Sciences* (New York, 1926, 2nd edn. 1960) has chapters on 'Medieval Dream Lore' (195–218) and on 'Chaunticleer and Pertelote' (219–40). The contrast between their interpretations of dreams is usefully discussed by Peter Elbow, *Oppositions in Chaucer* (Middletown, Conn., 1973) pp. 95–113, who argues: 'Behind everything else, of course, is an opposition of gender, especially with respect to language' (p. 101), and by Sheila Delany, in ' "Mulier est hominis confusio": Chaucer's Anti-Popular Nun's Priest's Tale', *Mosaic*, 17 (1984) pp. 1–8, who considers that

Chaucer's treatment of his sources indicates an antifeminist pur-
pose. Charles A. Owen, Jr analyses the speech in 'Crucial Passages in
Five of *The Canterbury Tales*: A Study in Irony and Symbol', *JEGP*, LII
(1953) pp. 294–311, reprinted in *Chaucer: Modern Essays in Criticism*,
ed. E. Wagenknecht (New York, 1959) pp. 251–70, and argues that
Chaunticleer expresses the Nun's Priest's misogyny.

3.   On Latin as a male preserve see Walter J. Ong, *Orality and Literacy:
The Technologizing of the Word* (New York, 1982) pp. 112–15.

4.   Discussions of the Paradise motif in the *Nun's Priest's Tale* include J.
Burke Severs, 'Chaucer's Originality in the *Nun's Priest's Tale*', *SP*, 43
(1946) pp. 22–41; David Holbrook, 'The Nonne Preestes Tale' in *The
Age of Chaucer*, ed. Boris Ford (London, 1954) pp. 118–28; John
Speirs, *Chaucer the Maker*, 2nd edn (London, 1960) pp. 185–93; B. F.
Huppé, *A Reading of the Canterbury Tales* (New York, 1964) pp. 174–
84; Bernard S. Levy and George R. Adams, 'Chaunticleer's Paradise
Lost and Regained', *Medieval Studies*, 29 (1967) pp. 178–92.

5.   On Chaucer's continuous awareness of hermeneutical problems see
Judith Ferster, *Chaucer on Interpretation* (Cambridge, London and
New York, 1985).

6.   On Chaucer and the 'counter-culture' see Derek Brewer, 'Gothic
Chaucer', in *Writers and their Background: Geoffrey Chaucer*, ed. Derek
Brewer (London 1974) pp. 1–32.

7.   The scene is usefully discussed by David Aers, *Chaucer, Langland and
the Creative Imagination* (London, 1980), and by Paula Neuss, 'Images
of Writing and the Book in Chaucer's Poetry', *RES*, n.s., 32 (1981)
pp. 385–97, who emphasises the resentment of the illiterate wife
against the book, though in my view she underestimates the Wife's
critical capacities.

8.   Sandra M. Gilbert and Susan Gubar, *The Madwoman in the Attic* (New
Haven, Conn. 1979) p. 11.

9.   Robert A. Pratt, 'Jankyn's Book of Wikked Wyves: Antimatrimonial
Propaganda in the Universities', *AnM*, 3 (1962) pp. 5–27.

10.   On the Wife's horoscope, see Curry, *Chaucer and the Medieval
Sciences*, pp. 91–118, a less deterministic interpretation by Chauncey
Wood, *Chaucer and the Country of the Stars*, (Princeton, NJ, 1970)
pp. 172–80, and an interesting recent article by H. Marshall Leicester,
Jr, 'The Wife of Bath as Chaucerian Subject', in *Studies in the Age of
Chaucer*, Proceedings no. 1 (1984) pp. 201–10, who proposes the
Wife's various applications of astrology as a 'shifting activity of self-
construction' (p. 210).

11.   Much of the material is derived from Jerome, *Adversus Jovinianum*.

12.   Especially from D. W. Robertson Jr, *A Preface to Chaucer* (Princeton,
NJ, 1962) and his followers.

13.   Dolores Palomo thinks that the Wife's 'revulsion [at the story of
Pasiphae] may seem curiously inconsistent since she has earlier
made her own infatuation with a boy of twenty seem almost a virtue'
(*ChR*, 9 (1975) p. 311) as though the fifth marriage were equivalent to
bestiality.

14.   Christine de Pizan, *The City of Ladies*, tr. Earl Jeffrey Richards
(London, 1983) pp. 3–5.

15.   After I had written this chapter I found that the two passages were also juxtaposed in an interesting essay on female reader-response by Susan Schibanoff, 'Taking the Gold out of Egypt: The Art of Reading as a Woman', in *Gender and Reading*, ed. Elizabeth A. Flynn and Patrocinio P. Schweickart (Baltimore, Md, 1986) pp. 83–106.

16.   E.g. Robin Lakoff, *Language and Women's Place* (New York, 1975); Dale Spender, *Man-Made Language* (London, 1980); Deborah Cameron, *Feminism and Linguistic Theory* (London, 1985).

Notes to Chapter 2   Two Ideals: the *Dame* and the *Duchess*

1.   Quoted in *The Riverside Chaucer*, p. 1076.
2.   *The Works of Geoffrey Chaucer*, ed. F. N. Robinson (Boston, Mass., and London, 1957) p. 520.
3.   For a brilliant critical and historical account of images of the Virgin see Marina Warner, *Alone of All Her Sex: The Myth and the Cult of the Virgin Mary* (London, 1976).
4.   Ibid., p. 142.
5.   For various interpretations of the poem see Wolfgang Clemen, *Chaucer's Early Poetry* (London, 1963) ch. 1; Helen Storm Corsa, *Chaucer: Poet of Mirth and Morality* (Notre Dame, Ind., 1964), ch. 1; B. F. Huppé and D. W. Robertson, Jr, *Fruyt and Chaf: Studies in Chaucer's Allegories* (Princeton, NJ, 1963); Stephen Knight, *Geoffrey Chaucer* (Oxford, 1986) pp. 8–15; A. C. Spearing, *Medieval Dream-Poetry* (Cambridge, 1976) pp. 49–73.
6.   For an account of the Boethian aspect of the poem, see Michael D. Cherniss, 'The Boethian Dialogue in Chaucer's *Book of the Duchess*', *JEGP*, 68 (1969) pp. 655–65.
7.   On the ideal of moderation in the poem, see John Norton-Smith, *Geoffrey Chaucer* (London, 1974) pp. 14–15. On White as a kind of Chaucerian 'New Woman', see David Aers, *Chaucer* (Brighton, 1986) p. 93.

Notes to Chapter 3   Two Misfits: The Nun and the Wife

1.   See Ruth Mohl, *The Three Estates in Medieval and Renaissance Literature* (New York, 1933) especially pp. 20–1, and Shulamith Shahar, *The Fourth Estate: A History of Women in the Middle Ages* (London and New York, 1983) especially pp. 1–8.
2.   Studies of the portraits include Muriel Bowden, *A Commentary on the General Prologue to the Canterbury Tales* (London, 1948) pp. 92–104, 214–29; R. M. Lumiansky, *Of Sondry Folk: The Dramatic Principle in The Canterbury Tales* (Austin, Tx, 1955) pp. 79–83, 117–29; H. F. Brooks, *Chaucer's Pilgrims* (London, 1962) pp. 15–19, 31–3.
3.   A distinction first made by E. T. Donaldson in 'Chaucer the Pilgrim', *PMLA*, LXIX (1954) pp. 77–96, and reprinted in *Chaucer Criticism*, ed. R. Schoeck and J. Taylor (Notre Dame, Ind., 1960) vol. 2, pp. 1–134.
4.   The 'femininity' of the Prioress has often been remarked; e.g.

Bowden, *Commentary on the General Prologue*, describes her as the 'eternal feminine' (p. 98); Brooks, *Chaucer's Pilgrims*, as 'ultra-feminine' (p. 15).

5. J. L. Lowes, 'Simple and Coy: A Note on Fourteenth-Century Poetic Diction', *Anglia*, 33 (1910) pp. 440–51.

6. *RR* 13408–32.

7. Hope P. Weissman, 'Antifeminism and Chaucer's Characterization of Women', in *Geoffrey Chaucer*, ed. George D. Economou (New York, 1975) pp. 93–110.

8. Jill Mann, *Chaucer and Medieval Estates Satire: The Literature of Social Classes and the General Prologue of the Canterbury Tales* (Cambridge 1973) pp. 134–7, discusses 'spiritual courtesy . . . the ladylike aspect of the spiritual life' (p. 134).

9. In 'Sense and Sensibility in the *Prioress's Tale*', *ChR*, 15 (1980) pp. 138–82, Carolyn B. Collette places the Prioress's taste and temperament in the mainstream of late medieval spirituality. See also Johan Huizinga, *The Waning of the Middle Ages* (London, 1924) especially ch. xiv.

10. In an unpublished paper, 'Monks and Tears', Brian Patrick McGuire argues that under Cistercian influence tears of grief at bereavement became more acceptable in Christians in the later Middle Ages. If weeping over even the death of a relation or close friend needed theological defence, tears for pets were presumably indefensible. Margery Kempe was moved to tears by the sight of animals being struck but because it reminded her of the suffering of Christ: 'yf sche sey a man had a wownde er a best whethyr it wer, er yyf a man bett a childe before hir er smet an hors er an-other best wyth a whipp, yyf sche myth sen it er heryn it, hir thowt sche saw owyr Lord be betyn er wowndyd lyk as sche saw in the man er in the best' (*The Book of Margery Kempe*, ed. S. B. Meech and H. E. Allen, *EETS* (London, 1940) p. 69).

11. A characteristically harsh appraisal of the Prioress as 'a particularly striking exemplar of false courtesy' is made by D. W. Robertson, Jr, *A Preface to Chaucer* (Princeton, NJ, 1963) p. 246. A similar judgement is made on the basis of a detailed examination of the semiology of the portrait by Chauncey Wood, 'Chaucer's Use of Signs in the Portrait of the Prioress', in *Signs and Symbols in Chaucer's Poetry*, ed. John P. Hermann and John J. Burke Jr (University of Alabama, 1977) pp. 81–101.

12. In a learned and influential article, 'Chaucer's Prioress: Mercy and Tender Heart', reprinted in *Chaucer Criticism*, ed. R. J. Schoeck and J. Taylor (Notre Dame, Ind. 1961) vol. ii, pp. 245–58, R. J. Schoeck argues that the 'ritual murder legend is held up for implicit condemnation as vicious and hypocritical' (p. 246). This view is not accepted by Florence Ridley, *The Prioress and the Critics* (Berkeley, Cal. 1965); G. H. Russell, 'Chaucer: The Prioress's Tale', in *Medieval Literature and Civilisation*, ed. D. A. Pearsall and R. W. Waldron (London, 1969); J. R. Hirsh, 'Reopening the Prioress's Tale', *ChR*, 10 (1975) pp. 30–45.

13. See David Lawton, *Chaucer's Narrators* (Cambridge, 1985) and C

Benson, *Chaucer's Drama of Style: Poetic Variety and Contrast in The Canterbury Tales* (Chapel Hill, NC and London, 1986) and 'The *Canterbury Tales*: Personal Drama or Experiments in Poetic Variety?', in *The Cambridge Chaucer Companion*, ed. Piero Boitani and Jill Mann (Cambridge, 1986).

14.   '[The Jews] are symbols of pure evil, and they belong to a large class of fairy-tale villains. . . . The tale is certainly appropriate for the Prioress because it brings out the childlike qualities that are evident in her portrait and in her Prologue'. Alfred David, *The Strumpet Muse* (Bloomington, Ind. and London, 1976) pp. 208–9.

15.   Roger Ellis, *Patterns of Religious Narrative in the Canterbury Tales* (London and Sydney, 1986), believes that the 'childlike' attitude of the Prioress to her story is implicitly criticised (pp. 78–9) and suggests that the punishment of the Jews in an 'incongruous development' (p. 80) in contrast to the fourteenth- and fifteenth-century English analogues of the story (pp. 79–81).

16.   See W. C. Curry, *Chaucer and the Medieval Sciences* (New York, 1926, 2nd edn 1960) and Wood, *Chaucer and the Country of the Stars*.

17.   *Proverbs* VII 10–12. See G. R. Owst, *Literature and Pulpit in Medieval England* (Cambridge, 1933) pp. 385–404; Bowden, *Commentary on the General Prologue*, p. 219; and Weissman, 'Antifeminism'.

18.   A particularly stern view of the Wife of Bath is argued by Robertson, in *Preface to Chaucer*, pp. 317–31. Maintaining that 'Alisoun of Bath is not a "character" in the modern sense at all, but an elaborate iconographic figure', Robertson argues that, properly understood in the light of scriptural tradition, the Wife is revealed as 'hopelessly carnal and literal' (p. 317).

Notes to Chapter 4   The Amazon and the Wise Woman, or 'God Knows What She Thought'

1.   *Iliad* XXIV 804, tr. E. V. Rieu (Harmondsworth, Middx, 1950) p. 459.

2.   See Rieu, *Iliad*, p. 460.

3.   *Iliad* XIX 301–2.

4.   For a general account of the hostility to Amazons in European literature, see Abby Wettan Kleinbaum, *The War against the Amazons* (New York, 1983), especially ch. 2: 'The Sword of Vengeance: Amazons in the Middle Ages'.

5.   Quotations from Boccaccio are from Nicholas Havely, *Chaucer's Boccaccio* (Woodbridge, Suffolk, 1980).

6.   Ibid., p. 112.

7.   Ibid., p. 112.

8.   Ibid., p. 113.

9.   My response to this passage was clarified for me by V. A. Kolve's fine account in *Chaucer and the Imagery of Narrative* (London, 1984) of the prison/garden motif, pp. 85–105: 'The two young knights fall in love with Emelye for her beauty, unmistakably, but for the beauty of her freedom most of all . . . we are made to see this gratuitous decision to

love – this act of pure will – as their only available expression of something within them still free, not limited by prison walls, leg-irons or exile' (p. 90). Kolve (Fig. 37, p. 89) reproduces an illustration to the *Teseida* from Vienna National Library MS 2617, fol. 53, showing Emilia in the garden but does not comment on how the scene has been domesticated. Instead of roaming and picking flowers, Emilia is seated and weaving them in a garland, an icon of the correct courtly lady at her needlework.

10.   For brief accounts of the philosophical concerns of the *Knight's Tale*, see R. M. Lumiansky, 'Chaucer's Philosophical Knight', *TSE*, 3 (1952) pp. 47–58 and P. G. Ruggiers, 'Some Philosophical Aspects of *The Knight's Tale*', *CE*, 19 (1958) pp. 298–302.

11.   E.g. E. T. Donaldson, *Speaking of Chaucer* (London, 1970): '[Emily is] one of the least interesting of Chaucer's heroines. . . . She has no mind or character of her own, desiring only what most desires her' (pp. 48, 50); to Norman E. Eliason, 'Chaucer the Love Poet', in *Chaucer the Love Poet*, ed. J. Mitchell and W. Provost (Athens, Ga, 1973), Emily is 'possibly the most mindless heroine in all literature' (p. 14); Elizabeth Salter, *Chaucer: The Knight's Tale and the Clerk's Tale* (London, 1962): 'Chaucer's Emelye exists only to provide the immediate cause of the lovers' rivalry' (p.11).

12.   The subject of women's silence is a central issue for feminist criticism. E.g. 'The sense of women's marginality to culture was palpable. Absence and partial presence were not philosophical ideas, not fashionable analytic categories but descriptions of female experience. Silence, invisibility, poverty and enclosure were not just words but markers and marks of the female condition' C. R. Stimpson, 'On Feminist Criticism', in *What is Criticism?*, ed. P. Hernadi (Bloomington, Ind., 1981) p. 232.

13.   Havely, *Chaucer's Boccaccio*, p. 134.

14.   Ibid., p. 134.

15.   B. F. Huppé, *A Reading of The Canterbury Tales* (New York 1964) finds Emily's prayer 'comic' and argues that 'Sende me hym that most desireth me' veils a desire for 'sovereyntee': 'The man who loves her most will surely be the most manageable' (p. 70). I see no comedy in the revelation that Emily is to be married against her will and take the second part of her prayer as evidence of her 'pitee'.

16.   By, e.g., A. C. Spearing (ed.), *The Knight's Tale* (Cambridge, 1966) p. 31.

17.   Several critics strangely (to me) argue that the Wife enjoys the idea of the rape: T. L. Burton, 'The Wife of Bath's Fourth and Fifth Husbands and her Ideal of a Sixth: The Growth of a Marital Philosophy', *CR*, (1978) pp. 34–50; 'One's impression is that she *envies* the girl this encounter with a man so sexually powerful' (p. 45); Robert P. Miller, 'The *Wife of Bath's Tale* and Medieval Exempla', *ELH*, 32 (1965) pp. 442–56: 'This rape of the maiden . . . does not otherwise seem specially outrageous in the moral scheme of Alice' (p. 452). Tony Slade, 'Irony in the *Wife of Bath's Tale*', *MLR*, 64 (1969) pp. 241–7, reprinted in *The Canterbury Tales: A Casebook*, ed. J. R. Anderson

(London, 1974) pp. 161–71: 'one gets the impression that she is not worried by the fact of rape in the sense that we might be' (p. 165). Huppé, *A Reading of The Canterbury Tales*, appears to think that the opening shows female supremacy: 'The reality of the knight's courtly world, as the wife reveals it, is the power of women. Guinevere rides rough-shod, not only over her husband Arthur, but also over the "cours of lawe" which had condemned "this knyght for to be deed" ' (pp. 132–3).

18. Interesting and opposite accounts of this version of the Midas story are offered by D. W. Robertson, Jr, 'The Wife of Bath and Midas', *SAC*, 6 (1984) pp. 1–20, whose interpretation turns on the evil 'figurative connotations of "wife" or "woman" ' (p. 5) as fleshly and sensual, and by Lee Patterson, ' "For the Wyves love of Bathe": Feminine Rhetoric and Poetic Resolution in the *Roman de la Rose* and the *Canterbury Tales*', *Speculum*, 58 (1983) pp. 656–95, who analyses the narrative in terms of deferral and proposes that the Wife's 'telling argues that men, their listening obstructed by the carnality symbolized by their ass's ears, will naturally prefer the immediate self-gratifications of anti-feminism to the severer pleasures of self-knowledge' (p. 658).

19. E.g. Susan Schibanoff, 'The Crooked Rib: Women in Medieval Literature', *Approaches to Teaching The Canterbury Tales*, ed. Joseph Grimaldi (New York, 1980) pp. 121–8: 'while the Wife is impressive for her complex, often contradictory, nature, the protagonist of her tale is disappointing in her willingness to assume a one-dimensional role, that of "beautiful young thing", so typical of romance women ... the extent of the Wife's achievements in her Prologue is underscored by her later failure to create anything other than a conventional ending to her Tale'; and Mary Carruthers, 'The Wife of Bath and the Painting of Lions', *PMLA*, 94 (1979) pp. 209–22.

20. Tony Slade, 'Irony in the *Wife of Bath's Tale*, *MLR*, 64 (1969) pp. 241–7, reprinted in *The Canterbury Tales: A Casebook*, ed. J. R. Anderson (London, 1974) p. 168, and Ian Bishop, 'Chaucer and the Rhetoric of Consolation', *MA*, 52 (1983) pp. 38–49.

21. Sandra M. Gilbert and Susan Gubar, *The Madwoman in the Attic* (New Haven, Conn., 1979): 'Feminist criticism began as a disruptive attack against cultures that had often cast women as the angelic upholders of the civilised or as monsters and breeders beyond its bounds'; Stimpson, 'On Feminist Criticism', p. 238.

22. Several critics have discussed Alison's ambivalence about 'maistrye', e.g. Charles A. Owen, Jr, 'Crucial Passages in Five of *The Canterbury Tales*: A Study in Irony and Symbol, *JEGP*, LII (1953) pp. 294–311; Burton, 'The Wife of Bath's Fourth and Fifth Husbands'.

23. On 'counter-culture' see Derek Brewer, 'Gothic Chaucer', in *Writers and Their Background: Geoffrey Chaucer*, ed. Derek Brewer (London, 1974).

Notes to Chapter 5   The Merchandise of Love: Winners and Wasters

1. A point made by Stephen Knight, *Geoffrey Chaucer* (Oxford, 1986), who sees the relation between the two tales as 'in classic Marxist terms dialectic; they are in historical contradiction to each other' (p. 92).
2. Knight, ibid., comments on this line: 'The Reeve . . . is finally revealed as working for his private interests, not the common good' (p. 81) and sees him as symptomatic of changes in society: 'Mobility, personal and social, was shaping people into behaviour that, from an old-fashioned point of view seemed . . . selfish and . . . revolutionary' (p. 82). He does not investigate the sexual and theological connotations of 'pryvetee'.
3. John Dryden, Preface to the *Fables* in *Works*, ed. James Kinsley (Oxford, 1958) vol. IV, p. 1455.
4. John Leyerle, 'The Heart and the Chain', *The Learned and the Lewed: Harvard English Studies, 14 5 (1974)* pp. 113–45, reprinted in *Chaucer's Troilus: Essays in Criticism*, ed. Stephen Barney (London, 1980) pp. 181–209.
5. There are perceptive accounts by E. T. Donaldson, 'The Idiom of Popular Poetry in the *Miller's Tale'*, *EIE* (1950) pp. 116–40, Charles Muscatine, *Chaucer and the French Tradition: A Study in Style and Meaning* (Berkeley, Cal., 1957), and Helen Cooper, *The Structure of the Canterbury Tales* (London, 1983) pp. 111–13.
6. This remark seems to travel by oral transmission. I have often heard it quoted but do not know its source.
7. 'His golden hair . . . recalls that of his namesake, King David's comely son, whose luxuriant hair brought about his death and made him in medieval Scriptural exegesis an example of the effeminacy of sin' V. A. Kolve, *Chaucer and the Imagery of Narrative* (London, 1984) p. 164.
8. W. H. Auden, 'Letter to Lord Byron', *Collected Longer Poems* (London, 1968) p. 41.
9. See M. Copland, 'The Reeve's Tale: Harlotrie or Sermonyng?' *MA*, 31 (1962) pp. 14–32.
10. Kolve, *Chaucer and the Imagery of Narrative*, pp. 237–52, discusses the motif of the unbridled horse in terms of 'the tradition in which the horse stands for all that is not rational or spiritual in man's nature' (p. 239).
11. The *Cook's Tale* would repay more critical attention than it has received. There are two excellent accounts: E. G. Stanley, 'Of this Cokes Tale maked Chaucer na moore', *Poetica*, 5 (1976) pp. 36–59 and Kolve, *Chaucer and the Imagery of Narrative*, pp. 279–85. Kolve considers, partly on the basis of scribal presentation, that the Tale is genuinely unfinished. He cautions that the Tale as it stands may be anachronistically satisfying to modern taste: 'We are at ease with fragments and amid ruins. We are indeed suspicious of closure, preferring open-ended forms on the ground that they bear a stricter mimetic relationship to current ideas of truth'. (p. 280); 'This is not how tales end and certainly not how medieval tales end' (p. 469).

12. Aristotle, *Nichomachean Ethics and History of Animals*, ed. R. McKeon (New York, 1941) p. 637, and *The Generation of Animals*, tr. A. L. Peck (London, 1943) pp. 335–9.
13. Guido delle Colonne, *Historia Destructionis Troiae*.
14. Kolve analyses the two voices of the Tale in terms similar to mine: 'Only 24 lines – the first 24 – celebrate what is attractive in Perkyn, while 34 lines . . . are spoken from out of a prudential, mercantile ethic, severely distanced from any pleasure in youth and carelessness and folly' (*Chaucer and the Imagery of Narrative*) p. 269.
15. W. W. Skeat, *The Works of Geoffrey Chaucer* (Oxford, 1894) vol. iv, p. 130.
16. Northrop Frye, *The Anatomy of Criticism* (Princeton, NJ, 1957) p. 42.

Notes to Chapter 6   The Merchandise of Love: Wives and Merchants

1. See Gardiner Stillwell, 'Chaucer's "Sad" Merchant', *RES*, 20 (1944) pp. 1–18 and Janette Richardson, *Blameth Nat Me: A Study of Imagery in Chaucer's Fabliaux* (The Hague, 1970) pp. 100–22.
2. However, the *Riverside Chaucer* points out that the sense of 'cheat' for 'cozen' is not recorded before 1453.
3. See Albert H. Silverman, 'Sex and Money in Chaucer's *Shipman's Tale*', *PQ*, 32 (1953) pp. 329–36.
4. See Richardson, *Blameth Nat Me*.
5. Nevill Coghill, 'Chaucer's Narrative Art in *The Canterbury Tales*', *Chaucer and Chaucerians*, ed. D. S. Brewer (London, 1966) p. 126.
6. This theory was first presented by Vernon Hall, Jr in the form of a parody in the *Baker Street Journal*, iii (1948) pp. 84–93, and was perhaps intended only as a spoof. It was revived by Beryl Rowland in 'On the Timely Death of the Wife of Bath's Fourth Husband', *Archiv*, 209 (1973) pp. 273–82, and argued anew by Dolores Palomo, 'The Fate of the Wife of Bath's "Bad Husbands"', *ChR*, 9 (1975) pp. 303–19.
7. E.g. Stephen Knight, *Geoffrey Chaucer* (Oxford, 1986) p. 79.
8. For a summary of the central doctrines on procreation see J. J. Noonan, *Contraception: A History of its Treatment by the Catholic Theologians and Canonists* (Cambridge, Mass., 1966) pp. 193–9.
9. An aspect briefly but suggestively discussed by Paul G. Ruggiers, *The Art of the Canterbury Tales* (Madison and Milwaukee, 1965) pp. 196–200.
10. C. S. Margulies, 'The Marriages and the Wealth of the Wife of Bath', *Medieval Studies*, 24 (1962) pp. 210–16.
11. See W. C. Curry, *Chaucer and the Mediaeval Sciences* (New York, 1926, 2nd edn 1960).
12. See Mary Carruthers, 'The Wife of Bath and the Painting of Lions', *PMLA*, 94 (1979) pp. 209–220.
13. E. T. Donaldson, 'The Effect of the Merchant's Tale', *Speaking of Chaucer* (New York, 1970) pp. 30–45, offers one of the first feminist readings of the Tale. See also Paul Olson, 'Chaucer's Merchant and January's "Hevene on erthe heere"', *ELH*, 28 (1961) pp. 203–14, on the mercantile values of the Tale.

Notes to Chapter 7   Real Women in Imaginary Gardens

1. V. A. Kolve, *Chaucer and the Imagery of Narrative* (London, 1984): 'The garden, in short, is finally seen as prison; the "evene joynant" wall falls away, revealing the garden as merely a part of a larger structure' (p. 104).

2. See J. J. Noonan, *Contraception: A History of its Treatment by the Catholic Theologians and Canonists* (Cambridge, Mass., 1966) pp. 193–9.

3. Jacques de Vitry, *Vita B. Mariae Ogniacensis*, quoted in *Not in God's Image*, ed. Julia O'Faolain and Lauro Martines (New York, 1973) pp. 140–1.

4. For an account of the garden in classical and European tradition see Ernst Curtius, *European Literature and the Latin Middle Ages* (Bern, 1948) tr. W. R. Trask (London, 1953) ch. 10: 'The Ideal Landscape', pp. 183–202; on the symbolism of the garden in Old and Middle English poetry, see D. W. Robertson, Jr, 'The Doctrine of Charity in English Literary Gardens: A Topical Approach through Symbolism and Allegory', *Speculum*, 26 (1951) pp. 24–49; on Chaucer's use of the *Song of Songs* see James I. Wimsatt, 'Chaucer and the Canticle of Canticles', *Chaucer the Love Poet*, ed. J. Mitchell and W. Provost (Athens, Ga, 1973) pp. 66–90.

5. Important accounts in English of *The Romance of the Rose* are Alan M. F. Gunn, *The Mirror of Love* (Lubbock, Tx, 1952) and John V. Fleming, *The Roman de la Rose: Study in Allegory and Iconography* (Princeton, NJ, 1969); see especially ch. 2: 'The *Hortus Deliciarum*', pp. 54–103.

6. See Louis Vinge, *The Narcissus Theme in Western European Literature up to the Early Nineteenth Century* (Lund, 1967).

7. Valuable accounts of the poem are provided by J. A. W. Bennett, *The Parlement of Foules: An Interpretation* (Oxford, 1957); A. C. Spearing, *Medieval Dream-Poetry* (Cambridge, 1976) and James Winny, *Chaucer's Dream-Poems* (London, 1973).

8. See 'The Goddess Natura', in Curtius, *European Literature*, pp. 106–27.

9. My discussion of the garden scene in the *Merchant's Tale* is deeply indebted to an impressive study of its relationships with its sources and analogues by Elizabeth Simmons-O'Neill in ' "Sires, by Youre Leve, that am nat I": Romance and Pilgrimage in the Works of Chaucer and the Gawain/Morgne-Poet', Ph.D. diss., University of Washington, Seattle, 1988. Other helpful accounts are by John Burrow, 'Irony in The Merchant's Tale', *Anglia*, 75 (1957) pp. 199–208; Charles A. Owen, Jr, 'Crucial Passages in Five of *The Canterbury Tales*: A Study in Irony and Symbol', *JEGP*, LII (1953) pp. 294–311; and Emerson Brown, Jr, 'Chaucer, the Merchant and their Tale: Getting Beyond Old Controversies', *ChR*, (1978–9) pp. 141–51 and 247–62.

10. A seminal analysis of the mixed style of the Tale was made by Charles Muscatine, *Chaucer and the French Tradition: A Study in Style and Meaning* (Berkeley, Cal., 1957) pp. 230–6.

11. By G. L. Kittredge, 'Chaucer's Discussion of Marriage', *MP*, IX

(911–12) pp. 435–67, reprinted in *Chaucer Criticism*, ed. Richard J. Schoeck and Jerome Taylor (Notre Dame, Ind., 1961) pp. 130–59.

12. Ibid.

13. Ibid.

14. Vinge, *The Narcissus Theme*, thinks that 'Chaucer has brought in the comparison [with the story of Narcissus] in a manner which suggests that it is already a poetic cliché '(p. 110).

15. Robert B. Burlin, 'The Art of Chaucer's Franklin', in *The Canterbury Tales: A Casebook*, ed. J. R. Anderson (London, 1974), seems to consider Aurelius the victim of Dorigen: 'Our sympathy has turned to the badly treated squire . . . his woe has driven him to raving and we are fully prepared to enjoy the spectacle of this haughty woman writhing in turn through her *exempla*-ridden complaint . . . it is not until we observe her treatment of the squire Aurelius that we fully appreciate the scope of her irrational, almost giddy femininity' (pp. 196–7).

16. See Alan T. Gaylord, 'The Promises in *The Franklin's Tale*', *ELH*, 31 (1964) pp. 331–65.

17. For an account of the controversy, see Ian Donaldson, *The Rapes of Lucretia* (Oxford, 1982).

18. For a discussion of the term 'honour' in relation to both sexes and a consideration of how it operates in this Tale, see Derek Brewer, 'Honour in Chaucer', *Tradition and Innovation in Chaucer* (London, 1982) pp. 89–109.

19. On this aspect of the Tale, see the fine discussion, 'The Bourgeois Sentimentalist', in Alfred David, *The Strumpet Muse* (Bloomington, Ind. and London 1976) pp. 182–92.

Notes to Chapter 8   The Saints

1. V. A. Kolve, *Chaucer and the Imagery of Narrative* (London, 1984) pp. 285–93, argues persuasively that the *Man of Law's Tale* is told on the first morning of the pilgrimage and should be considered part of the first fragment.

2. Sheila Delany, 'Womanliness in the Man of Law's Tale', *Writing Woman: Women Writers and Women in Literature Medieval to Modern* (New York, 1983) pp. 36–46, makes a similar contrast between the two women and, like me, finds the class/gender analogies of the Tale distasteful. She suggests: 'To Chaucer's courtly pilgrims, employers and friends, the tale of Constance must have been a welcome reaffirmation of the hierarchical values which had so recently been attacked' (p. 63).

3. See Kolve, *Chaucer and the Imagery of Narrative*, pp. 302–56, for a detailed discussion of the symbolism of the rudderless boat.

4. Lee Patterson, ' "For the Wyves Love of Bath": Feminine Rhetoric and Poetic Resolution in the *Roman de la Rose* and the *Canterbury Tales*', *Speculum*, 58 (1983) pp. 656–95, interestingly connects the authority of men with the authority of literature as problematic for

Chaucer (though he mistakenly suggests that Alla exiles Constance): 'we are not allowed to forget that her suffering, however edifying it may be to us, is to her both very real and a function of the sexual authority of men, just as, at the level of narrative form, her exemplary role is a function of the generic authority of hagiography' (p. 692).

5. Essays which engage with the central problems of the Tale include James Sledd, '*The Clerk's Tale*: the Monsters and the Critics', *MP*, LI (1953) pp. 73–82, reprinted in *Chaucer: Modern Essays in Criticism*, ed. E. Wagenknecht (New York, 1959) pp. 226–39, and *Chaucer Criticism*, ed. R. J. Schoeck and J. Taylor (Notre Dame, Ind., 1961) vol. II, pp. 160–74; Anne Middleton, 'The Clerk and his Tale: Some Literary Contexts', *SAC*, 2 (1980) pp. 121–50; Jill Mann, 'Satisfaction and Payment in Middle English Literature', *SAC*, 5 (1983) pp. 31–45; Charlotte C. Morse, 'The Exemplary Griselda', *SAC*, 7 (1985) pp. 51–86.

6. Michael Wilks, *Chaucer and the Mystical Marriage in Medieval Political Thought* (Manchester, 1962) investigates this analogy with particular reference to the *Wife of Bath's Tale* and points out: 'During the course of the thirteenth and fourteenth centuries it came to represent a double tradition. On the one hand the analogy, particularly as used by the medieval papacy, stood for the principle of absolutism. . . . Against this there came to stand a tradition of limited rulership. . . . Aristotle, in his comparison of marriage and government, had declared that whilst the wife should uphold the forms of obedience to her husband, there was nonetheless a basic equality between them – and had added that governor and governed might change places. . . . The ruler's *imitatio Christi* comes to involve the acceptance of limitations: his authority ceases at the point at which it would become harmful' (pp. 520–1, 529).

7. Lawrence L. Besserman, *The Legend of Job in the Middle Ages* (Cambridge, Mass., 1979) points out that Chaucer redistributes Job's patient and impatient utterances to a woman and a man respectively: 'By attributing Job's patient words to Griselde and Job's impatient curse to her father [901–3], Chaucer in a sense splits the biblical figure. Griselde becomes a new, more perfect Job' (p. 113).

8. Roger Ellis, *Patterns of Religious Narrative in The Canterbury Tales* (London and Sydney, 1986), proposes a 'double reading' (p. 65) of the *Clerk's Tale*: 'By the end of the work Petrarch's authority has been so undermined that it is necessary to recall it in order to support an interpretation in which the narrator seems to have lost confidence. . . . At first, it affected to ignore the claims of the audience in favour of the tradition. Increasingly, as it proceeds, it shifts the balance in favour of the audience' (p. 64); Elizabeth Salter, *Chaucer: The Knight's Tale and the Clerk's Tale* (London, 1962) pp. 61–2, similarly argues on the basis of style that the tale presents a double world.

9. Sheila Delany, ' "Mulier est hominis confusio": Chaucer's Anti-Popular *Nun's Priest's Tale*', *Mosaic*, 17 (1984) pp. 1–8.

10. Ellis (*Patterns of Religious Narrative*, pp. 93–7) emphasises the importance Chaucer placed on translation and remarks that for the

Second Nun 'literature is not pastime, as it is for most of the other pilgrims, but business' (p. 101). Ruth M. Ames, *God's Plenty: Chaucer's Christian Humanism* (Chicago, 1984) pp. 48–9, also emphasises her active virtue.

11. John Fisher (ed.), *The Complete Poetry and Prose of Geoffrey Chaucer* (New York, 1977) p. 309.

12. C. David Benson, *Chaucer's Dream of Style: Poetic Variety and Contrast in 'The Canterbury Tales'* (Chapel Hill, NC. and London, 1986) p. 141.

Notes to Chapter 9   Criseyde

1. Ian Bishop, *Chaucer's Troilus and Criseyde: A Critical Study* (Bristol, 1981) pp. 19–31, gives a perceptive analysis of the 'epiphanies' of Criseyde.

2. John Fowles, *The French Lieutenant's Woman* (London, 1967) p. 68.

3. I owe this point to David Aers, *Chaucer, Langland and the Creative Imagination* (London, 1980) p. 120.

4. Charles Muscatine, *Chaucer and the French Tradition: A Study in Style and Meaning* (Berkeley, Cal., 1957) notices consideration of role and stereotype (though he does not use the terms) as part of the cynicism of Pandarus's approach to her: 'As Troilus appeals to her highest and most intangible standards of value, Pandarus addresses himself to the widow, the niece, the traitor's daughter, and the lonely female' (p. 155).

5. Stephen Knight, *Geoffrey Chaucer* (Oxford, 1986) ch.2, pp. 32–65, analyses the poem as a dialectic between public and private forces: 'Criseyde is . . . not only a step towards feminism. She is a figure of a new self-consciousness for both men and women; it is because women were in so many ways excluded from the authority of a patriarchal public order that Chaucer is able to exploit them as a terrain for the exploration of privacy' (p. 36).

6. On the question of determinism in *Troilus* see Howard R. Patch, 'Troilus on Determinism', *Speculum*, 6 (1931) pp. 225–43; M. W. Bloomfield, 'Distance and Predestination in *Troilus and Criseyde*', *PMLA*, 72 (1957) pp. 14–26; W. C. Curry, 'Destiny and *Troilus and Criseyde*' in *Chaucer and the Mediaeval Sciences* (New York, 1926, 2nd edn 1960). All three are reprinted in *Chaucer Criticism*, ed. R. J. Schoeck and J. Taylor (Notre Dame, Ind., 1961) vol. ii. See also Jill Mann, 'Chance and Destiny in *Troilus and Criseyde* and the *Knight's Tale*', *The Cambridge Chaucer Companion*, ed. Piero Boitani and Jill Mann (Cambridge, 1986) pp. 75–92. Alastair Minnis, *Chaucer and Pagan Antiquity* (Cambridge, 1982), makes this distinction: 'The pagans regard their supposed destinies as necessary facts; the Christian historian regards them as conditional facts. By being so utterly convinced that their actions are fated, the pagans determine their actions' (p. 70).

7. Marvin Mudrick discusses the bird symbolism of Book ii in 'Chaucer's Nightingales', *On Culture and Literature* (New York, 1970)

pp. 88–95, reprinted in *Chaucer's Troilus: Essays in Criticism*, ed. Stephen Barney (London, 1980) pp. 91–9. See also Beryl Rowland, *Birds with Human Souls: A Guide to Bird Symbolism* (Knoxville, Tn, 1978).

8.   There are fine accounts of the garden and nightingale scene by A. C. Spearing, *Criticism and Medieval Poetry* (London, 1964) pp. 100–8 and Donald R. Howard, 'Experience, Language and Consciousness: "Troilus and Criseyde"', ii, 596–931, in Barney, *Chaucer's Troilus*, (London, 1980), pp. 159–80.

9.   A phenomenon discussed with relation to *LGW* by Richard Firth Green, in 'Chaucer's Victimized Women', *SAC*, 10 (1988) pp. 3–21.

Notes to Chapter 10   The Women in the Books

1.   Derek Brewer, *Tradition and Innovation in Chaucer* (London, 1982) p. 106.

2.   *Filostrato* i 15.

3.   Ibid. iii 21, 22.

4.   For the significance of this image in feminist criticism, see Susan Gubar, ' "The Blank Page" and the Issues of Female Creativity', in *Writing and Sexual Difference*, ed. Elizabeth Abel (Chicago, 1980) pp. 73–94 and Xavière Gautier, tr. Marilyn A. August, 'Is there Such a Thing as Women's Writing?', *New French Feminisms*, ed. E. Marks and I. de Courtrivon (Amherst, Mass., 1979) p. 164, who argues that female communication is characteristically 'blank pages, gaps, borders, spaces and silence, holes in discourse'.

5.   On the relationships between dreams, books and experience in the dream-visions see Robert O. Payne, *The Key of Remembrance: A Study of Chaucer's Poetics* (New Haven, Conn., 1963) chs 3 and 4, pp. 91–146, and Piero Boitani, 'Old Books brought to Life in Dreams', in *The Cambridge Chaucer Companion*, ed. Piero Boitani and Jill Mann (Cambridge, 1986) pp. 39–58.

6.   On the historicity of Dido and the centrality of the problem, see George Kane, *Geoffrey Chaucer* (Oxford and New York, 1984) pp. 40–1, Sheila Delany, *Chaucer's House of Fame: The Poetics of Skeptical Fideism* (Chicago and London, 1972) pp. 48–57 and John M. Fyler, *Chaucer and Ovid* (New Haven, Conn., 1979) pp. 30–41.

7.   Pointed out by Elizabeth Simmons-O'Neill in ' "Sires, by Youre Leve, that am nat I": Romance and Pilgrimage in the Works of Chaucer and the Gawain/Morgne-Poet', Ph.D. diss., University of Washington, Seattle, 1988.

8.   A fine unpublished paper by Leroy Perkins on the sexual allusiveness of the poem added a new dimension to my understanding of the meretricious nature of Fame.

9.   All future references will be to the F Prologue unless G is indicated.

10. For a perceptive discussion of the generic complexity of *TC* see Monica McAlpine, *The Genre of Troilus and Criseyde* (Ithaca, NY, 1978).

11. The most detailed defence of the *Legend*'s literary merit is by R. W. Frank, Jr, *Chaucer and The Legend of Good Women* (Cambridge, Mass., 1972). Frank demonstrates the interest of the stories as experiments in narrative but does not for me clarify their meaning.

12. First by H. C. Goddard, 'Chaucer's Legend of Good Women', *JEGP*, 7 (1908) pp. 87–129.

13. See James I. Wimsatt, *The Marguerite Poetry of Guillaume de Machaut* (Chapel Hill, NC, 1970).

14. For a clear analysis of the role of Alceste see Michael D. Cherniss, 'Chaucer's Last Dream Vision: the *Prologue* to the *Legend of Good Women*', *ChR*, 20 (1985–6) pp. 183–99.

15. *Symposium* 208d. See Russell Peck on the Platonism of the scene in *Chaucer in the Eighties*, ed. Julian N. Wasserman and Robert N. Blanch (Syracuse, NY, 1986) pp. 39–55.

16. Payne, *Key of Remembrance*, p. 148.

17. H. C. Goddard, 'Chaucer's Legend of Good Women', *JEGP*, 7 (1908) pp. 87–129 and 8 (1909) pp. 47–111.

18. Elaine Tuttle Hansen, 'Irony and the Anti-Feminist Narrator in Chaucer's *Legend of Good Women*', *JEGP*, 82 (1983) pp. 11–31, finds the irony against the narrator, the God of Love and the anti-feminist tradition rather than against women; Fyler, *Chaucer and Ovid*, finds the *Legend* 'a wonderfully comic exercise in censorship' (p. 99); Sheila Delany, 'The Logic of Obscenity in Chaucer's *Legend of Good Women*', *Florilegium*, 7 (1985) pp. 189–205, detects obscene puns and argues for an ironic reading but one that produces a more natural view of women; Janet M. Cowen, 'Chaucer's *Legend of Good Women*: Structure and Tone', *SP*, LXXXII (Fall 1985) pp. 416–36, offers a sensitive and balanced account of the poems and concludes: 'To read *The Legend of Good Women* as some critics have done, as a work which functions neatly by doing the opposite of what it professed to do, and which under the guise of eulogy propounds an antifeminist thesis, is itself too neat, exaggerating the formulaic quality of the legends. But there can be no mistaking the suppressed antifeminist joke that runs through the work' (p. 433).

19. Beverley Taylor, 'The Medieval Cleopatra: The Classical and Medieval Tradition of Chaucer's *Legend of Cleopatra*', *JMRS*, 7 (1977) 249–69.

20. V. A. Kolve, 'From Cleopatra to Alceste: An Iconographic Study of *The Legend of Good Women*', in *Signs and Symbols in Chaucer's Poetry*, ed. John P. Hermann and John J. Burke Jr (U of Alabama, 1977) pp. 130–78.

21. Lisa J. Kiser, *Telling Classical Tales: Chaucer and the Legend of Good Women* (Ithaca, NY, 1983) argues persuasively that the *Legend* is primarily a poem about literature. Similar views are briefly proposed in the articles cited by Hansen and Delany.

22. Donald C. Baker, 'Dreamer and Critic: The Poet in the *Legend of Good Women*', *University of Colorado Studies: Series in Language and Literature*, 9 (1963) pp. 4–18, argues that the command to reverse the *Troilus* is inept and yet does raise the problem of the value of earthly love for the Christian poet.

23. Jerome, *Adversus Jovinianum, Patrologia Latina,* ed. J. P. Migne (Paris, 1845) vol 23. I quote from W. H. Fremantle's translation, used by Robert P. Miller, *Chaucer: Sources and Backgrounds* (New York, 1977) pp. 415–36. Ralph Hanna III in '*Compilatio* and the Wife of Bath: Latin Backgrounds, Ricardian Texts', *Latin and Vernacular: Studies in Late Medieval Texts and Manuscripts,* ed. A. J. Minnis (Cambridge, 1989) pp. 1–11, points out the deficiencies of the manuscript used by *PL*. He gives this version of the passage as it appears in the oldest manuscript, Verona, Biblioteca capitolare 17: 'Paul prefers marriage for virgins, rather than the danger of lechery, and thus makes excusable what in itself should not be desired; he likewise prefers for widows second marriages rather than that same lechery. Nonetheless, it is better to know a single man, even though he may be the second or the third, than to sleep with many: that is, it is more tolerable to be the whore of one man than of many. This is so, in as much as the Lord rebuked the Samaritan woman in the gospel, the one who said that she had a sixth husband; the Lord said he was not her husband. Indeed, where there is a number of husbands, there the man, who is properly single, ceases to be.'

24. I was stimulated to return to the source myself by a vigorous unpublished paper on the Wife of Bath's Prologue by Carla Copenhaven, who notes that the point of the story in the Gospel is the revelation to the Samaritan that Jesus is a prophet. E. T. Donaldson, in *The Swan at the Well* (New Haven, Conn. and London, 1985) pp. 135–6, and in a fuller discussion in 'Designing a Camel: or Generalizing the Middle Ages', *TSL*, 22 (1977) pp. 1–15, points out that Jerome distorts the passage in inventing a sixth husband but does not note the saint's further distortions and perversions of Scripture. B. F. Huppé, *A Reading of the Canterbury Tales* (New York, 1964) writes as if Alison alone 'gloses' Scripture. He seems unaware that Jerome has already 'glosed' this text and assumes that its interpretation is quite straightforward before Alison questions it: 'Her experience with her five husbands qualifies her as an expert, but though she flaunts the authorities, she exhibits an uneasiness about the number of her marriages. . . . She begins with the greatest of authorities, Christ, who seems to state flatly that a fifth husband is not a husband. If she can gloss this text to make it come out on her side, she should have little difficulty with others. She suggests first that Christ's statement is anything but as clear as it flatly seems to be' (p. 111).

25. Quotations are from the *New English Bible*.

26. See David Aers, *Chaucer, Langland and the Creative Imagination* (London, 1980) pp. 83–4, 147–51. For manuscript glosses on the Wife herself, see Susan Schibanoff, 'The New Reader and Female Textuality in Two Early Commentaries on Chaucer', *SAC*, 10 (1988) pp. 71–108.

27. E.g. D. W. Robertson, Jr, *A Preface to Chaucer* (Princeton, NJ, 1963): 'The support for her position that Alisoun is able to derive from St Paul is obtained only by quoting him out of context or by

disregarding the obvious implications of what he says'. (p. 324). But several recent critics have argued for her orthodoxy: e.g. Kenneth J. Overempt, 'Chaucer's Anti-Misogynist Wife of Bath', *ChR*, 10 (1975–6) pp. 287–302, demonstrates her 'underlying moderateness and orthodoxy'; Donald Howard, *The Idea of The Canterbury Tales* (Berkeley, Cal., 1976): 'Her ideas are in keeping with orthodox thought . . . it is hard to fault her theology.' See also the witty and scholarly account by Anne Kernan, 'The Arch-Wife and the Eunuch', *ELH*, 41 (Spring, 1974) pp. 1–25.

Notes to Chapter 11   Sex, Discourse and Silence

1. On the Wife of Bath's rhetoric and 'dilation', see Lee Patterson, ' "For the Wyves love of Bath": Feminine Rhetoric and Poetic Resolution in the *Roman de la Rose* and the *Canterbury Tales*', *Speculum*, 58 (1983) pp. 656–95. Also Ellen Schauber and Ellen Spolsky, 'The Consolation of Alison: The Speech Acts of the Wife of Bath', *Centrum*, 5 (1977) pp. 20–34: 'Major credit for our perception of her separateness goes to the force with which she constantly sets herself and her opinions in opposition to the opinions of others – she defines herself as apart by these patterns of speech' (p. 26).

2. Diane Bornstein, 'As Meek as a Maid: A Historical Perspective on the Language for Women in Courtesy Books from the Middle Ages to *Seventeen Magazine*', *Women's Language and Style: Studies in Contemporary Language* (Akron, Ohio, 1978) I, 136–7.

3   A phenomenon from which Angela Carter wittily draws far-reaching conclusions in 'Alison's Giggle', *The Left and the Erotic*, ed. Eileen Phillips (London, 1983).

4. Michel Foucault, *The History of Sexuality: An Introduction*, tr. Robert Hurley (London, 1979) p. 27.

5. See Dale Spender, *Man-Made Language* (London, 1980) pp. 41–50.

6. Donald R. Howard, *Chaucer and the Medieval World* (London, 1987) p. 97.

7. Ibid., pp. 494–5.

8. Ibid., pp. 482–3, 486–8.

Index

Also by Priscilla Martin and published by Macmillan

PIERS PLOWMAN: The Field and the Tower
SHAKESPEARE: *TROILUS AND CRESSIDA* (Casebook) (*editor*)

POPULAR LOAN

This book is likely to be in heavy demand. Please RETURN or RENEW it no later than the last date stamped below